SOCIAL SCIENCES DIVISION
CHICAGO PUBLIC LIBRARY
400 SOUTH STATE STREET
CHICAGO IL 60605

D0916559

A Theologian's Journey

Also by Thomas F. O'Meara, O.P.
Published by Paulist Press—

Theology of Ministry
(Completely Revised Edition)

THOMAS F. O'MEARA, O.P.

• • • • • • • • • •

A Theologian's Journey

BX 4705 .O4883 A3 2002
O'Meara, Thomas F., 1935–
A theologian's journey

 PAULIST PRESS   New York/Mahwah, N.J.

Cover design by Valerie Petro · Interior design by Joseph E. Petta

Copyright © 2002 by Dominicans, Province of St. Albert the Great (USA)

All rights reserved. No part of this book may be reproduced or transmitted in any form or by any means, electronic or mechanical, including photo-copying, recording or by any information storage and retrieval system with-out permission in writing from the Publisher.

LIBRARY OF CONGRESS CATALOGING-IN-PUBLICATION DATA

O'Meara, Thomas F., 1935-
   A theologian's journey / Thomas F. O'Meara.
     p. cm.
   Includes bibliographical references and index.
   ISBN 0-8091-4078-0
   1. O'Meara, Thomas F., 1935-   2. Vatican Council (2nd : 1962-1965)
3. Catholic Church—History—20th century. I. Title.
BX4705.O4883 A3 2002
230'.2'092—dc21

                                    2002006695

Published by Paulist Press
997 Macarthur Boulevard
Mahwah, New Jersey 07430

www.paulistpress.com

Printed and bound in the
United States of America

R03037 42696

SOCIAL SCIENCES DIVISION
CHICAGO PUBLIC LIBRARY
400 SOUTH STATE STREET
CHICAGO, IL 60605

Contents

Introduction

● ● ● ● ● ● ● ● ● ●

This book is not an autobiography, although the narrative tells something about its author's life. The chapters tell mainly of a time the writer witnessed as a young man—only a few years but years coinciding with epochal change. Are these pages memoir, recollection, history? Regardless of what they are, they describe changes so deep that they altered the course of history and touched hundreds of millions of people. They tell of momentous events and unseen shifts occurring within society itself, shifts that the author observed at their inception and during the turbulent years that followed.

Whatever drama there is in this story lies not with battles fought or with millions of dollars earned, but with changes in ideas and institutions, even in church and religion. The social and religious shifts in the 1960s and in the years following have marked my life since my twenty-fifth year. Amid them, however, I was a student, an observer of their direction.

The thought of recording something about these cultural and religious changes has long hovered at the edge of my consciousness. Could I write about ideas as well as about people and events? What my experience and memory recall of a time in the Catholic Church during and after the 1960s makes the following a narrative about history as a force, about ideas and thinkers and events, about the force of the new coming from nowhere and never going back.

1

●

Does change arrive like an unexpected visitor at the door or like an airplane at its gate? Can you see change? Who could define the day, the year in which the Renaissance or the Enlightenment began? It would be foolish to try to do so. Still, cultures do come and go, and around 1220 or 1520, 1910 or 1960 the world changed.

Today I see society and church still marked, not infrequently marked for good by the alterations of the 1960s. There is in society an expectation of peace and a hope of ending endemic poverty, a presumption that justice should come to all citizens and that institutions and cliques should not exploit people. There is considerable energy seeking new directions although in recent decades people have become withdrawn, uncertain about political and religious leadership, and fatigued by a self-aggrandizement of the few. National politics is the preserve of the superrich while religion is directed too often by the ambitious, the anxious, and the ignorant. There is no lack of publicized prophets celebrating their control of the miraculous and no lack of others desirous of cutting away all religion from life and society.

My experiences serve only to contrast one church ending after a period of four centuries from 1550 to 1950 with one beginning in the 1960s and to appreciate how Vatican II liberated Christian thought and praxis to draw freely from its many traditions. American Catholics live now amid an expansion of theological knowledge, spirituality, and ministry: They face a future of opportunities and growth, but also a distraction of defeatism and ecclesiastical attraction to the trivial and theatrical.

●

The end of my seminary education coincided with the beginning of the Second Vatican Council. That worldwide assembly of bishops and their advisers was only the third ecumenical council held by the Roman Catholic Church since the Middle Ages. By the year of its opening, 1962, I had lived for seven years in a religious community under the vows of poverty, celibacy, and obedience; I was a member of the Dominican Order, as I am today, a religious community that was, as the Order's superiors never tired of repeating to us young recruits, more than seven centuries old. Its recent period, a time of expansion (as it was for many religious groups in the church), began in the 1830s after the French Revolution and the Napoleonic secularization had violently repressed most orders and congregations of monks, priests, and nuns. That subsequent time of growth was reaching its climax during my years in Dominican houses of formation, that is, in the communities educating men for the priesthood. After 1955, I was living passively and anonymously in a quasi-medieval world situated in the middle of America, in the cloisters and chapels of the novitiate and *studia* (as we called our seminaries) of the Midwestern Dominican province located in Minnesota, Illinois, and Iowa. In those enclaves, Latin in the classroom and the chapel might be heard more often than English in the recreation room. The years of my 20s—during which I spent few days outside of the priories—unfolded happily, if slowly, in buildings whose well-kept grounds served as a buffer between the Order and modern society.

Entry into a monastery, into a religious order begins with a year of reflection called the novitiate. Our novitiate was situated in Minnesota on high bluffs not far from the Mississippi River. That summer, on the feast of the Sacred Heart of Jesus whose symbol of a human heart radiating fires of love was mirrored in the red vestments of the liturgy, I was walking in the fields behind the priory as the day was coming to an end. That evening—the novitiate would end in two months—after a particularly hot June day the sun was setting in a fiery red. I was thinking of great men and women (as the novitiate encouraged), people fortunate to be caught up in the opportunities and conflicts of history, martyrs, dramatic preachers, nurses to slave ships, missionaries on the Amazon or the Congo, saints of all kinds. Those lives and worlds seemed in 1956 to have gone forever, to have disappeared into nothingness or into eternity beyond the flaming sun. I could look forward to no such drama, expect not the slightest challenge or innovation. The American Catholic Church would continue on with its anonymous crowds, its routines, its separation from wherever the poor and the unbelieving had hidden themselves. History itself existed no more. The four seasons and the cycles of a long and dull Latin liturgy spoke not of time but of repetition, the opposite of time.

The sun sank and I walked back through the humid summer evening filled with the frantic activity of birds. The monotonous span of my life stretched ahead of me indifferently. At 21, I had no future.

●

In fact, a new time, an epochal shift in history lay only a few years ahead. Society would pass through the 1960s, while the 4 years of meetings in Rome called Vatican II would change the Catholic Church forever, and the following years would be shaped by social and religious alterations. My generation would inevitably see everything marked by before and after the 1960s, before and after the 4 years of Vatican II.

Just before the second session of Vatican II began in September 1963, I was sent to Europe to study. The boy who had seen little beyond Iowa and Wisconsin would live in medieval and Baroque monasteries, would meet ecumenism in Protestant seminaries and at the institutes of the World Council of Churches, and would hear professors lecture on contemporary philosophy and theology at German and French universities. This book describes the eve of the Council, my years of study in Europe during Vatican II, the turbulent time of my return represented by the year 1968, and, briefly, the course of the postconciliar years up to its recent curtailment.

If the reader has expectations that in the following chapters I assist at some political cataclysm or reach a high level of ecclesiastical power, he or she will be disappointed. My contacts with significant people were rare, for the famous were busy, and I, a student in the world of the 1960s, was distinguished only by being at a dramatic intersection of history. Without much money and pressed to learn new languages and cultures, I was an apprentice.

In Italy, Germany, and France I would learn not only ideas, the philosophies and theologies of Christianity past and present, but also come to see that buildings and statues can depict a time and that the arts express the message of Christ in various styles of color and line. In Europe, I experienced the diversity of ages and cultures. I enjoyed experiencing. As a Catholic I had been taught that faith is a way of seeing, and that in the last analysis we are not alone on earth: The supernatural is the real.

●

My introduction has begun to grow tedious. It is time to hear the sound of jet engines, to smell the sunny Roman morning and feel the cold Bavarian night. Memory, time's child, is taking us into a past that was once present. In fact, we are already there—but not yet in Munich or Rome or Paris, not yet in the turbulent 1960s but close to them. First, we need to revisit the 1950s as they unfold placidly along the banks of the Mississippi. There, hills above the great river look out to farms and towns set on the plains under the gray sky of winter or the blue one of summer, look out on the present and toward the future.

• • • • • • • • • • •

CHAPTER ONE

Under the Sun of Being

A church council, the Ecumenical Council Vatican II, began in October 1962 and divided history. Catholics were thrown onto a moving surface of changes, while the rest of the world saw the ancient church seeking to serve a society it no longer dismissed.

Vatican II was one event in a decade of change, the 1960s. The figures of Pope John XXIII, John Fitzgerald Kennedy, and Martin Luther King, Jr., of student protesters and priest activists would become influential, and the surrounding forces of secularism and modernity, Puritanism and fundamentalism, capitalism and Communism would decline or reconfigure their presence.

I was ordained a priest in June 1962. The ordination ritual had elements from the fourth and thirteenth centuries, although the priesthood was understood within ecclesiastical traditions from the sixteenth and the nineteenth centuries. The Dominican Order, one of the numerous communities of men and women in the Catholic Church but one of the few that had lasted many centuries, had established its own liturgy within Western Christianity in the mid-thirteenth century and that fixed form of worship lasted in the Order through subsequent centuries. Consequently, when I said Mass the first time at my home parish in Madison, Wisconsin, the day after my ordination, the liturgy I used was much the same ritual as that used by Thomas Aquinas seven centuries earlier. America then seemed a tranquil place and the Catholic Church appeared content to live out of its past (a new enterprise in parish life was rare: Suggestions of change in a high school or in a poor parish were quickly suppressed). But only a few months ahead of that static time, like an unexpected avalanche approaching unaware villagers and skiers, lay the 1960s with its changes in art and movies, politics and religion, freedom and temporality.

Vatican II would change Roman Catholicism so much so that the year 1962 would have more in common with 1262 or 962 in terms of many of the forms of the church than it would have with 1982 or 2002. The upheaval of the Council at first appeared as a mild renewal, but its impetuses, surfacing with irresistible vigor 10, 20, 30 years after the conciliar texts had been published, led to change after change. No ecclesiastical plan, no charismatic movement, no pope, no prophet could have produced the upheavals and expansion of the decades after 1965. There was evidently some powerful but unseen force at work, a force with its own intentions.

Ritual Time

My story begins, however, in a tranquil, almost timeless set of years, in the 1950s. My classmates and I began our journey into Dominican life at a monastic building in the bluffs above the Mississippi. There, where the river expands into a vast lake between Wisconsin and Minnesota, we novices left for some years in 1955 the ordinary experience of time, withdrawing from days and months as the newspapers recorded and described them. Here and in other locations, for seven years, we would rarely leave the monastic buildings of our formation and would have little contact with the world outside. The buildings of the novitiate were constructed out of local sandstone and set out in the shape of a cross; inside, the tables of the refectory's dining area and the choir stalls of the chapel were of blond wood. At the center of the architectural cross where living quarters met chapel and refectory, the walls were of travertine marble and the floor held a brightly colored mosaic in marble of St. Dominic. The house held about 60 people. Finished only seven years before I arrived, it was well designed; doors opened out onto a huge sky above hills or plains holding farm after farm. Behind the novitiate grounds, woods of birch trees and rocky slopes led down to streams. Summers in the Midwest bring storms arriving on their journey from the Rocky Mountains across the plains, storms occasionally spawning violent winds, lightning, hail, and even tornadoes. Several times I was caught in such a summer storm in the valley behind the novitiate.

We novices accepted the tradition that we must leave the world and immerse our individuality in the Order. Our uniforms of white T-shirts and tan wash pants under identical white monastic habits symbolized a renunciation of identity and diversity. What a mix of feelings accompanied entering at 20 a world partly of the past. To step out of one's own time and place, to live in a monastic tunic and hood, to pray and learn in Latin, to live according to rules, customs, and rituals from a distant time whose origins and meaning were often not explained—this brought a wrenching, an alteration, an exhilaration. Still, for youth solitude and asceticism can be adventures. One of my neighbors during high school had put it this way: Some people enter the Marines for a few years, and others go to a seminary. Going off to the priesthood was simply what some guys did. Later they would find that it was not quite the same as joining the police or going to law school. Worshiping in liturgical rites and memorizing texts in Latin from the thirteenth century were my "brothers," young men who had grown up in Chicago, Albuquerque, Cedar Rapids, or Minneapolis during and after World War II. Educated in Catholic schools of varying quality, owning the generosity and hope of youth, we felt called by God to the priesthood (of which we had no experience), had high ideals, and waited through a long preparation for what we thought would be a liberation into the service of the church.

For the next seven years each day would be much the same, although the novitiate year replaced classes with prayer. The 365 days of that first year began early, at 5:10 A.M. By 5:30, we were in line in the corridor to recite the psalm *De Profundis* and enter the chapel for the early liturgy of Prime, Pretiosa, and Terce, which were followed by High Mass, a few minutes of meditation, and breakfast. The morning was then made up of work, classes in Dominican history and constitutional rules, a half hour of meditation, and the rosary. The first half of the day ended with the liturgies of Sext, None, and Vespers. Before Vatican II, the times of the liturgical hours of the divine office, mainly chanted on a single tone and not sung, were skewed; Matins, whose texts referred to night or dawn was anticipated by 5 to 12 hours at the previous twilight, and Vespers of the evening was at noon. Lunch was the main meal that we ate in silence while listening to reading. This was followed immediately by sung Compline, which was supposed to be the liturgy of the night, a procession in honor of the Blessed Virgin and St. Dominic, and part of the office of the dead. Then in the afternoon we could relax, talk with one another, go for walks, play handball, volleyball, or hockey. Some who had not sat through four to six years of conjugations and paraphrastics had a class in Latin. Later in the afternoon came again meditation and the rosary, and the recital of a smaller parallel liturgical office just for the novices, "The Little Office of the Blessed Virgin Mary." Matins and Lauds for the next day, since we did not rise at midnight or 4:00 A.M., were again anticipated at 5:00 P.M. and followed by dinner. After dinner, there was a third half hour of meditation preceded by the third part of the rosary. After brief recreation we went to our rooms, and I, at least,

St. Peter Martyr Priory, the Dominican novitiate in Winona, Minnesota, as it appeared in 1956, when the author was a novice

was asleep long before 10 o'clock. In the novitiate we were in church more than five hours a day, and the duplication of the hours of the divine office was tedious: On days when Dominicans said the entire office of the dead together, the novices would have said Matins and Lauds three times. So much time was spent in reciting prayers that there was little time to pray.

Our life in the novitiate was very much like the routine of a contemplative order, and so the activities of a Dominican novice had little to do with being a priest or a teacher but were more like the Trappist's routine of work and liturgical prayer. I spent not a few days in the hills and woods of Minnesota imagining myself to be a Carthusian. The novice master soon noticed my proclivity to read about the contemplative monastic orders and mandated the substitution of a history of Dominican missionaries evangelizing Ohio, an antidote to the romance of cloistered monks. The novitiate routine could be mystical and liberating, and it could also be compulsive and exhausting. Despite drawbacks, it was a powerful, beautiful experience: a year in a monastery set on bluffs learning how the Bible and the liturgy permeated the cycle of life. I was adrift in symbols.

My early years in the Dominican Order could not, of course, be really and totally medieval: What were presented as ancient forms had frequently been modified by devotions and academic theories of the nineteenth century. A neomedieval revival of the nineteenth century was evident in church architecture, Gregorian chant, and scholastic philosophy. A Romantic view of the Middle Ages gave the thirteenth century a Technicolor glory it had never possessed (G. K. Chesterton said that the world around 1900 tended to see the Middle Ages by moonlight). Furthermore, some religious attitudes were handed on to us midwesterners by Dominican superiors from the large urban Catholic areas in the East whose political world and neighborhood parishes were close to immigrant Catholicism and different from ours. The multilayered world that I entered in the Dominicans in the 1950s—a collage of philosophy from the thirteenth century, moral theology from the seventeenth century, ascetic practices from the nineteenth century, and American organization from the twentieth century—was somewhat alien, but how much so was understood only later.

To enter the Dominican novitiate was to enter several circles of time. There was the calendar's weeks and months, and there were the periods of the biblical history of salvation; there was solar-seasonal time and there was liturgical time. Each year, liturgical time played out a dual cycle: one of seasons and one of feasts. In late November, as a new liturgical year began, the shortest days beginning winter were adorned with Advent's purple vestments. Advent alone narrated three different times: history leading up to the birth of Jesus; the weeks leading up to Christmas; history pointing to the return of Christ at the end of all time. The feasts of Christmas, St. Stephen, New Year, and Epiphany led to Lent, dark and abstemious, when winter was at its worst. Nature arose with Easter in spring—in Minnesota, paschal April did not coincide well with the vernal season, for snowstorms arrived during Holy Week. Timeless summer illumined the fields, and then the bare trees of late autumn waited for Advent to return.

A second course of time was composed of feast days of the saints: Teresa of Avila in October, November for Albert the Great and Bruno of the Carthusians, Thomas Aquinas and the Annunciation during bleak March countering Lent's austerities, and the apostles in May. Summer's heat accompanied the procession of Corpus Christi with fragrances of flowers.

I loved those cycles with their words and symbols, a succession of saintly visitors, and recalled biblical events. Intent on being active on earth, God entered into historical and liturgical time.

Although the days of those years of religious initiation and journey were not filed away in the paper, ink, and film of Wall Street and Hollywood, were they not important? The absence of news, of people, of the sound of traffic could lead to an inner silence. I remember standing one morning at the edge of a field, a half mile west of the novitiate, during a cold week in January and watching a horse's white breath against the blue sky in the morning sunlight. Time stood still.

How did I come to this monastic priestly life? My adult life was just beginning. At this point, it might be expected that I would describe in detail my previous years. They, however, hold no drama. Since this is a story of places and their spirits, I should mention that Des Moines, Iowa, in the 1940s where I lived until we moved to Madison, Wisconsin, as I was beginning high school, was for me a place of exploration and mystery. There were parks with outdoor theaters for plays and dances, golf courses and softball diamonds, the woods around the water works, the heights of the buildings downtown. The center of the city was not far from the woods and the river behind my house. The unvoiced permission of my mother and father let me roam where I wanted during years whose climaxes were afternoon movies in winter and hot summer days spent at swimming pools. I felt that the parks and the city, in short, the world, were inviting me and were inhabited by friendly spirits.

Meanwhile, the Catholic Church and Catholic school intimated some transcendent realm. Three experiences from grade school days remain in my memory, perhaps because they jostled my prosaic boyhood and forecast a little what of lay ahead.

My parish church in Des Moines, St. Augustine's, was built in a beautiful English Gothic style. Fr. O'Connell, whose youth in Ireland had been one of destitution, lavished research and money on his church. Set on grounds in the affluent part of the city, built out of muted red brick and carved stone, it stood proudly next to the more Puritan churches of wealthy Protestants set along Grand Avenue. Inside tile, floors and dark carved wooden beams set off golden Byzantine symbols glowing on rich wallpaper. Light poured into the quiet church and side chapel through windows dominated by blue glass. Fr. O'Connell delighted in bringing the church to life with elaborate processions, and those ceremonies of a Baroque sensibility altered a little by Irish and American taste made a great impression on me. On the feasts of Christ the King and Holy Thursday, at Christmas Midnight Mass and at the May Crowning of the statue of the Blessed Virgin, candle-bearers, thurifers, banners, and priests entered into the church followed by the entire grade school, boys dressed in cassocks, collars, and cravats, and girls in suits and berets. Those liturgies had to be practiced at length—mistakes were unacceptable to the pastor—and the maneuvering of hundreds of little kids (many of whom like myself had fun and disruption on their minds) was not easy.

The most dramatic and curious of these Baroque-Hiberno-American liturgies was the beginning of Midnight Mass. That Christmas Eve liturgy began at 6:30 A.M., since Mass was not celebrated outside of the morning at that time. A huge procession of grade school children followed banners and cross, and they were in turn followed by altar boys, carriers of candles enclosed in red lanterns, incense bearers, with thurible and boat, and the three priests needed for the solemn High Mass in the rite of the Council of Trent. Between the acolytes and the priests came six boys from the seventh or eighth grades who were, curiously, dressed like cardinals of the Roman church. Once I was privileged to be among this group. Before the Christmas Mass began, with the ministers standing on the side, these six boys (three sopranos and three altos), having handed their broad red cardinals' hats to lowly acolytes, and their leader having sounded on a pitch pipe two tones, turned to the congregation and sang "Silent Night" in harmony. Then, careful not to stumble over the vestments of high office, they moved to the side, and Fr. O'Connell's brogue intoned: *"Introibo ad altare Dei."*

Why did those liturgies affect me? The candles and music, the lights playing on gold and red brought forth a kind of mysticism of the divine presence in people and images. A confluence of strong emotions in spite of the boredom of Latin prayers and repetitive litanies drew faith into a kind of ecstasy, a passing out to something or someone. Faith expanded seeing; the supernatural was the real.

Another experience, a few years later, was born not only of grace but of puberty. During two summers and one cold fall I delivered the Des Moines newspapers, the *Register* and the *Tribune*. In the morning the paper had to be on people's porches before 7:00 A.M., and so I had to be out of the house by 5:30. What seemed to be at first an impossible challenge, to get up that early, was fun in the summer. The first sunshine was warming Iowa as the neighborhood slept. It was an era without air conditioning when people slept on porches or on apartment floors trying to get a few hours rest after a desperately hot and humid night in August. My paper route (always mispronounced to rhyme with "out") wound among old large homes where there were still servants living above garages, and then turned down into streets where backyards sloped down into brush leading to the Raccoon River. One of the houses had behind it an extraordinary addition, a private swimming pool. In people's gardens you could fill up on strawberries or black raspberries (I already had an intimation of the moral axiom, "The law does not concern itself with small things"). One morning in August, when I was about 13, after I had delivered my 60 or so papers, I was sitting on a hill and noticed the red sun beginning to rise above the steamy woods along the river. I had a feeling I had never experienced before, a feeling that was to return and whose inner conviction had, I thought, a source outside of me. Seeing how good the world and life were, I felt that there was some force moving through that beautiful August morning that wanted to communicate with me. For some reason, that someone did not or could not speak to me in words—but that did not mean it did not exist or was absent. There was something more within the woods, the homes, and the sky—and it was friendly toward me. Was this presence not as real as the sun? As close to me as my beating heart? Then it was time to get up, walk past the growing vegetable gardens in the backyards, and think of spending the day at the swimming pool or the golf course, or of cutting the grass or painting the garage.

A third experience gave me a positive image of a priest. The brother of my mother's mother, my great-uncle, lived in Des Moines: Monsignor Hanson had been born the year the Civil War ended and had been ordained to the priesthood by the first American Cardinal, Gibbons. He had been a rural pastor in eastern Iowa before 1900 and in the 1920s had become pastor of one of the larger parishes on the east side of Des Moines. In his mid-seventies he had married my parents; around the same time he had been hit by a car on the street but survived. Nothing brought more unhappiness to me and my brother and sister than the announcement that it was time for a visit to the rectory in which Monsignor Hanson and two of his sisters lived in a state of voluntary poverty. Meals consisted of soup, crackers, raisins, and prunes. The pastor had contact but not interplay with money; the income from the collections went into old cigar boxes marked for different bills, and the rest was given to needy people. Monsignor had no interest in his personal life or entertainment and spent each day in some form of ministry; he had no bank account, no insurance, and no retirement plan. I could not understand him because he was old and spoke in an Irish accent, although he had been born in Iowa. Raised on stories of the English persecution of the Irish from the great famine at the time of his parents to the recent atrocities of the Black and Tans, he did not like the English or churches connected to them.

Shortly after coming to Visitation parish, at the age of 70, Monsignor Hanson started a mission church a dozen or so miles outside of Des Moines for a community of Irish-Americans who had no place to practice their faith. His eightieth birthday and the fiftieth anniversary of his ordination more or less coincided in 1944, and my family and relatives attended the celebration. Monsignor took the several thousand dollars given to him and purchased a store in the section of Des Moines where Mexican immigrants had just begun to settle and rehabilitated it into a church for them, Our Lady of Guadeloupe. My father took me to see how this new missionary outpost was taking shape, and we found Monsignor on the roof tearing off shingles. Of course, he and his new flock could not really communicate; he did not speak Spanish, and his English was not easily understandable to them. So at 80, "the bishop of the east side" had three parishes. It was said that when the bishop sent a young priest to be an assistant at Visitation, taking into account the cuisine, the finances, and the work under Monsignor's brusque direction, he only asked him to do it for a year or two. Busy and eccentric, Monsignor Hanson, nonetheless, projected an image of a priest who believed in hard work and energetically sought out new challenges, an attitude not uncommon before World War II, but afterward a little neglected amid the proliferation of church institutions, buildings, and clergy.

I grew up in an atmosphere critical of the church. In my recollections of listening to adults, when they talked about their parishes they had little good to say about autocratic pastors and about the boredom of Sunday mornings. The lazy rigidity of some who represented the church was constantly driving people out of the church.

To come close to the church in the 1950s was to sense that American Catholicism had slowed, was coming to a halt. The liturgical year could still flourish in rural monasteries but was absent from most people's lives. The drama of Catholic Christianity, visible in the movies *Going My Way* and *The Song of Bernadette,* haunted us, for irrelevancy was much more prominent. The magazine *Jubilee* wrote about how a few lay people in Manhattan read the liturgical breviary in the subway on their way to work, but those examples of deeper Catholic life were rare and unrealistic. American Catholicism, once poor and oppressed, was now full of churches and schools and elaborate episcopal residences. The personal Christian life and the moral issues it pondered and untangled were mentioned only in the dark confessional. And yet, the movies everyone saw told different stories, existential lives caught between virtue and sin, stories of men and women whose inner agonies occurred without the gospel or theology offering light or solace. Each Catholic was asked to live a life of good choices assisted by a grace dispensed by a strict God, Vatican dispensations received, meatless Fridays circumvented by travel, and a Mass visited before it was 40 percent finished. The believer, passing out of the immigrant neighborhood and now somewhat alone in an America moving from being Protestant to being secular, awoke each morning relatively on his own, needing to reestablish contacts with the apparatus of divine forces, while at death the texts of the Requiem Mass spoke of human failure and divine punishment.

Between 1945 and 1960, the priesthood in the United States drew thousands of young men to monastic life. They had a confidence in God's call and an insouciance concerning their future lives. Many were bright; some had been leading athletes or valedictorians of their classes; most were idealistic, although a few were fearful and uncertain and looked not for activity but for regimentation and certitude. The institutions they entered, however, were not really prepared for them. Novitiates in an increasing number after 1950 had buildings and chapels constructed unwisely on too grand a scale in isolated areas; they did not have directors with a knowledge of psychology or spirituality. Surely, to dedicate a life to God through the church was not complicated, and God's will and grace would take care of things. Some might have read the novel *The Cardinal* about an honest and dedicated young priest whose life is rewarded by the patronage of a prince of the church and who also eventually reaches that same summit by becoming a cardinal. Or they might have been inspired by the autobiography and monastic journals of Thomas Merton where the austere cloistered life of Trappists found drama and beauty; or by the life of Charles de Foucauld, soldier, ascetic, and evangelist of presence among the Touaregs in Algeria. One of the cruelties of the decades before Vatican II was that much of this youthful energy and talent met in the church inactivity and frustration. Just as its teaching was limited to a catechism and its activities to rapid Masses, the church offered little beyond its routine of communions, confessions, and anointings or beyond the needs of its many schools. The laity were urged to have a deeper faith (about what?) and charity (to whom?) and to avoid materialism (to what degree?). Thousands of candles burned in churches before saints who had been heroic activist Christians, but the church discouraged in practice, if not in rhetoric, the style and activity of these saints. The priest who wanted to work with the poor was removed; the nun who wished to move from teaching third grade to working with the blind or deaf found that suggestion rejected as unnecessary. When, after 1955, the first hints of new ways to think about Christianity began, a constant *No* resounded: no meetings with Protestants, no seeking out the needy, no purchasing European theology books, no improving religion classes.

A rejection of the new is the wrong spirituality for young people intent upon service. In the 1950s, without ever learning the reasons, we had drummed into our minds during our Dominican formation that we must be very careful of all with whom we had the slightest contact, must avoid people whose indecorous lives would scandalize others and tar us; we constantly must be aware not so much of our mission (and certainly not of the literal teachings of Jesus) but of the public black suit and clerical collar we wore. Who could so plan that each activity, each situation (ministry to the indigent, listening to an abused wife and mother) would not eventually have some slight drawback, thus rendering the entire enterprise evil. Prudence was the virtue of that era and scandal was the sin. Thomas Aquinas, however, taught that prudence did not mean doing nothing but doing something in the right way, and the vices of ineptitude and sloth were the real scandals in the church. During the seven years of my education, teachers never discussed what the local church actually did; religion had to do with the correct order of administering sacraments to a repentant atheist hit by a truck or with the indignity of so much blasphemy in society. Lay people made up a church where many went to the rapid rites of Sunday Mass late and left at communion, where only those dying were brought the sacraments of the sick, where mixed marriages and divorce brought lifelong isolation, where almost no sermon contained an insight into what the Bible actually said, and where few, even priests and nuns, read a book about the meaning of Christianity for today.

New priests were to be privates in a vast army, ready for any routine position, fully disinterested, affable but tough company men. Of course, this lack of attention to human individuality could not escape having consequences: Talented people were frustrated, while the devout let themselves be saddled with impossible jobs; too often the wrong people became rectors of seminaries and bishops. Since there was almost no screening of candidates, a certain number of men who were emotionally ill—some by nature, some by religious conversion, and some by life in the church—assumed the church's service. Some had good will or a sense of sacrifice but no inclination to a life of helping others. Thus, a decade later, the church witnessed no small breakdown among its personnel.

Living in a Medieval World

On the last day of August 1956, the year of seasons and liturgy had finished its course and I left the novitiate in Minnesota for three years of studying philosophy near Chicago. The drive down through Wisconsin took me from the liturgical world of the novitiate to the first years of academic preparation for the priesthood: three years of philosophy (logic, psychology, the philosophy of nature, ethics, and metaphysics) would be followed by four years of theology in Iowa. My college education had been largely in languages and history, and I knew nothing of philosophy; in fact, I had absolutely no idea of what it treated. During the seven years of philosophy and theology, the monastic liturgical day included four hours of class every morning. To catch our religious interest, apologetics and ecclesiology were taught during the years of Aristotelian philosophy, as were brief courses on practical areas such as educational theory, preaching, and the theory of art (presented without any visual contact with any work of art). Our education consisted in translating and reading Latin texts, memorizing the main points of textbooks (also in Latin), and passing oral exams in Latin. Struggle for enough sleep, good and poor meals, a rare relaxation for ice cream, popcorn or a movie, silence, sports, attention to minute details, isolation from society—they composed an austere world. Intellectually we were learning about a field, medieval and Greek thought, that the church claimed to be universal and foundational, to be the teacher and backdrop for everything, a field whose neglect had furthered all that was wrong in modernity from economics to physics. Philosophy's meaning, its relevancy, however, eluded us. Psalms, antiphons, and hymns alternated with logic and definitions as the liturgical year ran around its circle of penitential introductions and festal climaxes.

The absence of time was reinforced by language, or rather, by the absence of language. In Roman Catholicism the Latin language had long been in worldwide service; it had an impressive theological and philosophical pedigree but no contact with daily life. Latin was the language of education in the Dominican seminary. Our classroom Latin was similar to that used by Bonaventure or Thomas Aquinas in the thirteenth century at the University of Paris—although class discussion could be in English. *Principia* and *leges* were unchanging; a *qualitas* or a *relatio* remained such forever. If Latin was the language of classroom and liturgy, and so for us not completely dead, nonetheless, its grammatical difficulty and its intrinsic abstraction as well as its total removal from contemporary culture kept our education at a distance from life. A number of professors, however, did not teach in Latin either because of an absence of a facility with languages or because of the presence of pedagogical sense.

My happiness in this world came from my fellow students: They were bright, full of energy, interested in people, hopeful, already mildly critical of the church's establishment. Liturgy and prayer and community life provided doors by which we might at times leave neoscholastic thought. The liturgy offered symbols—the procession, the candle—for a day too filled with definitions, while in the approach of Dominican spirituality we learned that prayer and mediation deepened faith not by proofs but by emotion and love, and that grace was ordinary, as God offered to each his presence in immediacy and intimacy. Three, five, seven years passed. We did not leave the grounds or visit home. Without newspapers and magazines, without radio or television, we inhabited islands in the Chicago suburbs and the Iowa hills. Seven years of no information, no outside cultural contacts or lectures: I remember casually learning from a visitor that Juan Perón had ceased to be dictator in Argentina two years earlier.

Modernity had been repeatedly condemned by seminary teachers or by papal bureaucrats, but it was not always clear what the modern ideas were or whether any Catholic held them. That reaction against European culture after 1750 was already—this was unknown to us—being challenged in a positive way by scholars, lay leaders, and activist priests in the churches of Europe. American Catholics dutifully learned in boring classrooms how the making of the modern mind was erroneous and destructive, and yet, we all lived in a world of cars, hospitals, and radios, and soon of television and jet travel. Dominican life like most of American Catholicism was involved in the impossible attempt to fashion, to sustain a Gothic world. That nostalgic enterprise was very much an aesthetic one, and yet art itself was rather disdained: Classical music, painting, sculpture, and theater were a waste of time, effeminate. We left the priories rarely, and we certainly did not go to any lecture, concert, or museum during the three years in Chicago (the seminary houses had record players but the scratchy records were old).

That time which was no time passed, sometimes with an excruciating slowness. The sameness of years was punctuated at times by stricter rules by which superiors were reacting to the failures of priests, alcoholism, and indolence, about which we knew nothing. Monastic time as an absence of existential time gave our personal times no hearing, no space; we were trained to submit any individual concerns to liturgical prayer or metaphysics, to the Latin texts of the Bible or the will of superiors. Mere chronology ignored the origins of dogmas, the creative milieus of liturgy, the mutability of ethical norms, and the transitoriness of church laws and structures. It even muted God's salvation-in-history on earth that was the very narrative of the Bible.

In America during the 1950s, history had stopped, time had no face, Catholics multiplied; talented priests and nuns were anonymous servants of more and more parishes, colleges, and high schools. The world would stay the same. The experience of only a dozen years after World War II was accepted as normative and permanent. But that brief time was passing. Soon nothing could hold back the aggressive force of history.

At the School of Thomas Aquinas

The philosophical theology we studied year after year was neoscholasticism, the thinking of the Catholic Church from 1860 to 1960. Scholasticism is the thought of an age, the philosophy and theology from the thirteenth to the fifteenth centuries. Great scholastics such as Albert, Aquinas, and Duns Scotus applied Aristotle's principles and terminology to Christianity. Three times the church approved scholasticism—in the Middle Ages, after the Renaissance and Reformation, and in the late nineteenth century. Neoscholasticism was a revival begun in the 1850s and imposed by canon law and papal encyclicals. Instructions from different popes urged that only Aquinas's philosophy and theology be studied because it was the correct antidote to Protestantism and modern thought. The late nineteenth century had rediscovered Aquinas much as during the Renaissance owners of villas came across buried classical Greek and Roman statues. By the early twentieth century a collection of abstract axioms, more Aristotelian than

Christian, exercised a monopoly over the church's thinking throughout the world. Timeless philosophy became ideology when Dominicans started a seminary in Africa around 1950. They solicited for the Africans Latin neoscholastic textbooks written in Austria a half century earlier. In Catholic seminaries and colleges, a young American might find that the only text on Christianity or moral theology was a translated, abridged version of a seminary book by a German or French cleric written decades earlier. My seminary studies took place during the last years of that neoscholastic revival. We Dominicans were taught to note that the vagaries of the Franciscans unwisely centered on love and that the misdirections of the Jesuits pretending a fidelity to Aquinas overemphasized human freedom. During my first week in the seminary, the professor introducing us to philosophy made two startling observations: Everything a priest needed to know was found in the writings of Aristotle, and the church was excessively tolerant in permitting Jesuit or Franciscan scholasticisms to be taught at all. Modern scientists attacked the principle of causality because, the professor of metaphysics observed, accepting that axiom would lead along a chain of unstoppable logic to the infallibility of the pope.

During the first half of the twentieth century, most priests in America received some neoscholastic indoctrination in philosophy and theology. That simple philosophy with a black and white logic emphasized laws that had no exceptions: the laws of logic, administration of the church, abstract moral rules, and obscure rubrics for liturgy. The church had somewhat exchanged the gospel for Greek antiquity and its Aristotelianism held no interest for scientific America or for ordinary Catholics.

That neomedieval expression of metaphysics and dogma, however, was not always the teaching of great figures such as Aquinas, Bonaventure, or Scotus. At times it contradicted Aquinas or Aristotle; the sparkling activities of nature and grace typical of those great minds were imprisoned in static arrangements of recent Catholic philosophers.

Philosophy—were we studying anything connected to religion? In those first months, it was difficult for me to make much sense out of philosophy. Natural philosophy had nothing to do with any course in chemistry or biology. Philosophical psychology never mentioned addictions, the personality, or the ego of Freud and was not employed in hospitals or clinics. What was philosophy? The connections to Christianity were tenuous and there were no links to American culture. My soul—some had said it was naturally Aristotelian—was American and pragmatic. I soon stopped peering into my mind to catch a phantasm emerging or breaking a leaf to search for prime matter, and after some months I concluded that schemata of impressed species, expressed species, substance and accident, matter, form, and privation were not to be read like a manual for driving a truck. Years later I realized that they were mental plans, ways of understanding things, forms or models with some mooring in external things. The form of that particular sparrow sitting on a post in the snowy winter existed always as that sparrow or its biological complexity and never as a form and matter. Causes do have effects, but nowhere in the cosmos is there a formal cause or an efficient cause. Ultimately, even in Aristotle's explanation of reality, there was only that eagle chasing that fish.

I sought distraction from philosophy by reading Aquinas's *Summa theologiae* and surveys of the different approaches to Christian life in the various religious orders, the history of spiritualities from Irenaeus to Thérèse of Lisieux. Manuals on apologetics intrigued me because I hoped to find some good fights there, but the arguments demolishing scientists and atheists were in Latin, and the vanquished were figures from the past: Cartesians, Kantians, and the easily defeated Auguste Comte. None of them had much influence in Dallas or Minneapolis. In ecclesiology, we learned that the church existed essentially in the pope and bishops; families, teaching nuns, the ministry of a parish, or the efficacy of a foreign mission were not mentioned. The mechanics of church authority intrigued me, as did the intricate degrees of relationships between an all-powerful pope and the lowly vicar-bishops or an ecumenical council (never to be summoned again). The popes from 1850 to 1950 continued the directions of medieval neo-Platonism and Baroque centrality, and all authority was exercised downward. Those recent popes were, in fact, the most powerful bishops of Rome in history, and lesser authorities imitated papal authority: Bishops and pastors, mothers-generals and abbots delegated downward, their wisdom closely linked to the will of God. Questioning authority in any way was not only disloyal but philosophically unsound.

Our professors were knowledgeable in Aristotle and Aquinas, some remarkably so, but they were largely without education or experience in the world outside the neo-Gothic priories. Most had received their graduate education at the Angelicum in Rome, a school located not far from a Vatican still angry at Garibaldi and recently enthusiastic for Mussolini, a Vatican not really in favor of democracy. Although they were good priests, they did not see far beyond rapid Masses, confessions without counseling, sermons without import.

For four hours a day, five days a week, for three years, Aristotle and Aquinas were explained to us. There were benefits to Dominican education, presenting a great tradition and giving a Catholic background in realism over against a religious and secular world dedicated to introspection and self-autocracy, relativism and the dominance of science. The Dominican Order had for six centuries been based upon the healthy theology of Aquinas. It was a realistic, optimistic perspective in which human nature was the image of God, and grace came as a further gift from the good and wise Creator. God's revelation in Jesus was real, complementing the goodness of the universe, and Christian life led spontaneously to love. Aquinas saw beings, from violinists to viruses, glorying in God's gift to them of being-a-cause. The Dominicans had not given up on the life of a friar or a priest being human, and divine contact enhanced human life. The dignity of a person lay not in having blind faith or neurotic virtue, but in being an active believer motivated by faith and love and empowered by the gifts of the Spirit. The clear Latin of Aquinas's theology brought not so much logic as balance and health, human love and divine assistance.

Still, I was troubled. Where did this lead? Where would it lead me? What could anyone do with this abstract past thought? What ministry in America would it further? Our education in philosophy, psychology, aesthetics, and rhetoric was a wonderland where Thomas Aquinas was more prominent than Albert Einstein or Jonas Salk or Fulton Sheen, and where Isaac Newton might still be proven wrong. But would we ever meet those ideas in people alive today?

Young people want to be with other people. What do we say to others? What do we do out in society for the gospel? Lacordaire, the dramatic preacher at Notre Dame in Paris and the restorer of the Dominican Order throughout the world in the 1830s, wrote: "After we have lived through eighteen springs our years expand and we suffer under desires which have for their object neither love, nor sex, nor glory, nothing which has a form or a name. The young feel oppressed by aspirations which have no form or goal, and they want to run away from the realities of life as from a prison or a strangled heart."[1] The heroic lives of the saints and of great Dominicans were still being brought to our attention but without any possibility of imitation now or in the future. My older fellow students boasted that they read nothing but novels in their spare time and that their education was useless. In a pastoral and ecclesial sense, that was correct. So much neoscholasticism brought a malaise, a presumption that learning itself was tiresome, that Latin axioms answered every question. An emptiness crept in, coming not only from celibacy but from the absence of things. There were few objects, individuals, colors, people with which to interact. Years later, I would come to see that there was value in learning Aristotelianism, but I would also come to the conclusion that all of Aristotelian philosophy could have been taught in two semesters. Our education, the years of repetition and abstraction, left us uneducated. At best we might be ready to teach philosophy but not to be a pastor and to preach.

Behind the bland timelessness of Roman Catholicism was a tight, subtly violent constraint. Although Aquinas was an intellectualist who looked for reason, plan, and harmony in everything, the church too often was the schoolteacher of blind obedience and subservience to an ignorant, authoritarian will. Church authority should have been, as it was for Aquinas, a loving plan of a wise God and not obedience to a feared will of God (or of a bishop). Since a will is blind and since no one knows the will of God, the will of church superiors was unlimited. Misdirected calls for obedience ranged from the novice-mistress in Kansas who decided the novice with leukemia was not really sick to the pope who condemned studying the historical context of Thomas Aquinas's theology. The church was run by cliques; the worldwide church by high ecclesiastical club members in the Vatican who were appointed and appointed one another. The religious orders ended up with a small number of members or a dynasty that distributed and controlled positions of governance. It was not unlike the rule of political bosses and just as rigid and condescending.

Within the Dominicans, some democracy had existed for centuries, but those forms eventually had been reduced by privileged, lifetime positions. After 1850, everywhere in the church, authority became control. The very goal of its ministry seemed to be obedience, and unwise decisions were discernable—in the European loss of the working class, in the lack of advocating gospel values before, during, and after two world wars, and in America in the mismanaged institutions conducted in ugly buildings and in the number of Catholics who had turned their back on this organization that sometimes ran on values rejected by the gospel. Removals of people, prohibition of books, censures, suspensions, dispensations–thus the church became a cause of suffering, not its remedy.

We learned vast amounts of material summarizing Aquinas and Aristotle. We could extemporize on our feet disputations in Latin in the February mornings and play in a hockey or basketball league that afternoon. As in all camps, hospitals, or prisons, humor helped us survive our difficult schedules. When a member of the priory dropped dead from high blood pressure, one professor of philosophy observed a few minutes later back in the classroom that this was a striking example of substantial change. The entire fabric of neoscholasticism shook when a young Dominican exchange student from Spain with a background in physics, not convinced of the links between terrestrial and cosmic forces in a long line of causality ending with God, shouted: "Who pusha the moon?" When the first plane took off from the newly opened O'Hare airport, not far away, our professor of metaphysics, who did lead a contemplative philosophical life, observed: "There goes the product of a fallacious physics."

Philosophy led to four subsequent years of theology. Our basic text was the *Summa theologiae.* During the eight semesters of theology, we were led for two hours each day slowly, section by section, and at some time during those four years we prepared ourselves for short quizzes on the 4,500 articles in Aquinas's masterpiece. Supplemental courses in moral theology and canon law addressed the administration of the sacraments and the problems of the confessional. Theology, too, avoided issues such as nuclear war or divorce. Liturgy was rubrics; preaching was voice projection; no courses discussed issues facing people in Chicago or Paris. We were encouraged to read famous preachers as a way of improving style and vocabulary. But why was preaching so universally poor? Would reading the sermons of Bernard of Clairvaux or Bossuet make me a better preacher? I had my doubts. Classics in rhetoric did not solve the problem of sermons empty of content, of addressing today's issues.

The young expect change. In the American church, young people were too intelligent and too honest to imitate and continue the drills of a clerical troop whose priestly routine had made meager ecclesiastical honors and rich dinners exciting. In retrospect, whether Vatican II arrived or not, change, exodus, and conflict on a large scale would have been inevitable. By the second year of our studies, many—farmer's son or Purdue graduate—suspected that this education was so limited as to be humorous and that there was an arrogance in insisting that what we received every morning in classes was the only way to view culture and science, the only way to present the gospel to all societies and in all centuries. Had the church, seeking a bulwark against modernity in the neoscholasticism of ungifted clerics from 1850 to 1960, itself become a mental system, an idealism?

With my classmates I wondered: What was theology? Was it knowing definitions from the past? Was theology something like sailing or swimming: You knew how to do it and then, heading out into the water, you met waves and fish and boats? Regardless, theology had no important role in running the church institutions in the United States for which priests and nuns were destined. Television and satellites arrived, and yet hypostatic union was the only explanation given of Jesus of Nazareth, although it was not easily intelligible to someone who did not know Greek. We students began to wonder if we wouldn't have to fashion our own theology, fashion our own ministries in the church. After all, Aquinas had been a courageous and original mind engaged with his times (which were clearly not ours), and his sustaining insight that grace lived within human nature and human culture could only lead to a theology and ministry for our own age.

Meanwhile, European Catholics across the Atlantic were finding new approaches to religious education and participation in the liturgy, developing ideas and experiments that were preparatory for Vatican II. In France, the thought of Aquinas was at work in new ways: in an historical appreciation of medieval thought, in understanding the purpose of his many writings, in sketching the long history of interpretation following his life, in applying his principles to church situations. In the novitiate, however, we had been taught that the papal censure showed the French Dominicans to be irresponsible eccentrics with new and questionable ideas. Although a few books by the historians Martin Grabmann and Étienne Gilson were in our library, we were not encouraged to read them for they held methodological and metaphysical errors. The Dominican expert on the purpose and structure of the *Summa theologiae,* M.-D. Chenu, was ignored as a dangerous Frenchman deservedly removed from his position as head of the Dominican school south of Paris. We did not know the French Dominicans were advocating modern architecture for churches and priest-workers for factories. Some European theologians held a view that parish liturgy and life should speak to the parishioners and that the metaphysically suspect experience, renewal, and relevance were vehicles of grace. Bringing together ordinary life with Christianity, however, brought suspicion. For our teachers, the Europeans' pastoral plans were unusual and so understandably the object of Vatican censures. The novice master had mentioned how French priests in adjoining chapels coordinated private masses to begin and end at the same time. He was, of course, describing concelebration, something to be introduced ten years later by Vatican II. Creativity was smoke indicating the fire of heresy and disobedience.

Summers without Days

Season followed season. For me, Dominican life was the real world, the only world. The summers of the late 1950s and early 1960s had a particular isolation and value. July and August were spent in the Upper Peninsula of Michigan at what was called "camp," a collection of pine-log buildings on Green Bay constructed by seminarians 25 years earlier. Water for cooking came from Lake Michigan that was also the place for bathing. We chanted the hours of the liturgy in a pine chapel. After half days of sailing or fishing, we might watch the Dominicans with monastic names such as Ceslaus and Urban play softball teams from the local bars. The sun rose dramatically across the lake and at night set to give place to a brilliant Milky Way of stars. On the shore, we experienced a time for recuperating from long hours of Latin prayer and philosophical memorization. Little radio, rare newspapers, and no magazines entered this isolated world.

During those summers, the autobiographies of Augustine or Teresa of Avila became real to us. Some of us read the fiction of Bernanos, Mauriac, Greene, and Flannery O'Connor, stories where grace and sin were not packaged ecclesiastically but burst out of the intricacies of human life. The ambiguous individuality of Mauriac's and Greene's fallen heroines and heroes was different from the black and white of Aristotelian vice and virtue. They searched for something transcendent, if not for a church or a dogma; their dramas were religious but not abstract. In Bernanos's *Under the Son of Satan* and Thomas Mann's *Doctor Faustus,* the devil appeared (something not usual in America of the 1950s), while grace wrestled with sin in ordinary life in *The Cypresses Believe in God* and *Kristen Lavransdatter.* Fiction had gone ahead of theology. The paradoxical stories of grace and sin in Greene, however, were not fully intelligible to more than a few educated American Catholics. Secular critics did not understand how Catholicism, full of rules, could be the milieu of so much struggle and redeemed failure. Those novelists' links with the new European theology were little grasped; only in the 1960s, when the writings of the great theologians fashioning Vatican II reached America in translation, did the theologies behind and within Mauriac, Greene, and O'Connor emerge.

Sitting on the sunny shore of Lake Michigan, I could not link the congested, sin-filled world of French Catholic novelists with American Catholicism. Europe seemed claustrophobic, in retreat from its own age battered by two world wars, while in America there was only a kind of ignorant but happy routine unmarked by any unusual event, demonic or graced.

Like many American Catholics in the 1950s, the only contemporary religious influence on my life was Thomas Merton. Reading *The Sign of Jonas* in the last weeks of my senior year in high school—I did not then read books other than textbooks for class—prompted me to enter the Dominican Order. It is astonishing how many Americans he influenced, leading us not only to the Trappists but to dozens of congregations of men and women. His pages drew people to think about something more in life—to become mystics, poets, teachers, activists. First and foremost, Merton was a fine writer. His prose was always personal, moving; he could write about praying to God while walking through the dogwood without communicating an embarrassing self-preoccupation.

The journal was Merton's special genre: their entries described picking sweet corn or keeping quiet when a fellow monk said something foolish, or prayer during a morning storm when theological words and biblical pictures faded. His reflections and autobiographical jottings were never maudlin; his meetings with God's grace held a directness that was not so much humble but unassuming. "The life of every monk, of every priest, of every Christian is signed with the sign of Jonas, because we all live by the power of Christ's resurrection. But I feel that my own life is especially sealed with this great sign, which baptism and monastic profession and priestly ordination have burned into the roots of my being, because like Jonas himself I find myself traveling toward my destiny in the belly of a paradox."[2] His journals gave me permission to think about daily life and to see more deeply into what was ordinary.

Merton was a modern person. He had not imbibed Catholicism through parochial schools and parish devotions; he had attended Columbia University. He was not only a Trappist but a published poet, a writer of books that hundreds of thousands of people chose to buy. He was not caught in the American Catholic diffidence toward art, history, and science. Merton didn't seem to take his seminary education—a shallow neoscholasticism had also infiltrated the abbeys of Citeaux—seriously enough to be irritated by it. Anyway, the Trappist preparation for the priesthood was mainly based on the fathers of the church, and they kept neoscholasticism at a distance. Monastic contemplative life led him into liturgical, patristic, and mystical explorations of different, freer worlds of symbol and ecstasy, while his outside friends sent him the books of Romano Guardini, the poems of Rainer Maria Rilke, and the novels of Boris Pasternak. What an exciting life he seemed to live each day—and yet he was a Trappist monk, and the excitement came only from a sudden rain or a flight of geese. I entered and left the novitiate an avid reader of Thomas Merton.

If in *The Sign of Jonas* I found a model for living each day in the cycle of seasons and feast days, in *Seeds of Contemplation* I found an understandable depiction of silent prayer and the stages of meditation that Dominicans were to join to the active life of church ministry. Merton's psychology of contemplative mysticism agreed with the Dominican theology of the silent ordinariness of grace. Was there a better introduction to the spiritual life than the commonsense theology found in the pages of the early Merton? His observations on humility ("...becoming transparent to grace like a window to the sun") in contrast to the enthusiastic purveyors of religion ("they always have a message with a capital 'M'"), his search for identity in meditations whose words recalled similar lines from Aquinas and Meister Eckhart, and his instinctive withdrawal before phony religiosity appealed to American readers. "Religion is not a matter of extraordinary experiences, and that rot. The most important thing is a really simple and solid living faith. I think the thing that matters for people is simply to live in an atmosphere of reasonable and alert faith and love for God and for other people, and in that way everything gets quite soon to have a simple meaning."[3] He was a forceful and rare corrective to some unhealthy Catholic spiritualities that had controlled convents and rectories since the mid-nineteenth century. He was a guide out of the frustrating sameness dense with depression and conducive to alcoholism. If some Dominican, Jesuit, and Cistercian authorities with limited education and imagination found him doctrinally imprecise, his theological instincts in fact were true: He saw the distortions of phony piety and understood the insights of great theologians. By 1960, he recognized the need for new directions in the Catholic Church and for a prophetic critique and transformation of society.

●

Winter brought a horizon different from the summer shoreline of Lake Michigan; the landscapes of Illinois and Iowa were lonely for colors and people. Cold, snow, long liturgies of Lent, monuments of an ancient intellectual life on the shelf made the young Dominicans frustrated over the absence of contacts with people. Did our superiors already worry that this next generation might not easily adapt to apostolates filled with routine and empty of creativity? If an offer came to go to some distant land where painful martyrdom was likely, most of us would have volunteered with a happy feeling of being set free. The angels, we had learned in philosophy class, were living in *aevum,* a time placed somewhere between history and eternity. So were we.

---

1.   Cited in C. C. Martindale, *The Life of Monsignor Robert Hugh Benson* 1 (London: Longmans, Green and Co., 1916), p. 78.

2. Merton, *The Sign of Jonas* (New York: Harcourt, Brace,1953), p. 11.

3.   Merton, *Road to Joy* (New York: Farrer, Strauss, Giroux, 1989), p. 62.

● ● ● ● ● ● ● ● ● ●

CHAPTER TWO

Something's Coming

The years before 1962 bring forth from my memory days much the same, years without difference as texts from philosophy and theology were memorized, the Gregorian chant for Masses sung, and the happenings and people of the world left unobserved. The winters placed a cover of snow over land waiting patiently, while summers let the sun shine down on fields of crops until a long twilight yielded to the humid nights with their woodwind band of insects. In monastic life and in Eisenhower's America, I expected all days to be the same.

Something's Coming

In 1961, and in the first months and summer of 1962, just before the commencement of Vatican II, however, there were intimations of change. My first months as a priest were unfolding, and like many of my young fellow Dominicans I had been longing to break out of various routines.

At that time the American Catholic Church's most public member was Ed Sullivan, and a rare contact by the church with contemporary culture involved the "Singing Nun's" hit tune about St. Dominic, sung in French. Bishops and provincials did not encourage intellectual pursuits except to fill a position in a seminary or college. There was no need to call attention to Catholic oddities in Protestant America, and there was no public discussion of the local church although a constant refrain by parishioners on how little their pastors and parishes actually did had long existed.

American Catholicism was a tight, obedient branch of Italian and Spanish ecclesiastical organization with some French and Irish modifications from decades earlier. This European model imposed through devotional and theological textbooks produced little life, and what was vital came from American enterprises in working with young people, the poor, or married couples. A Roman horarium or a Spanish custom, when imposed on modern Americans, brought impractical situations and personal ulcers. For instance, eating the main meal at noon rapidly and in silence only impaired monastic life; in a different context, in our large Dominican priory and school we had a laundry room as large as a house. Its industrial washers and dryers were manned for several days each week by lay brothers, members of the community who were not priests and who in those years did manual labor. When, after 1965, those brothers entered more direct ministries of education, the laundry apparatus was replaced by four washing machines and dryers in which the 80 Dominicans were quite capable of doing their own laundry.

Dominicans were ordained a year before the completion of their theological studies and on weekends were sent out to help in parishes from Illinois to Minnesota. For my trips to crowded parishes in Madison, Rockford, or St. Paul during the summer of 1962, I had a constant struggle to write the Sunday sermon. There was nothing to say: no problems, no connections between the gospel and American society, no choices concerning unhealthy or salutary directions in life or in the church. At my three Masses on hot summer mornings, moving quickly but still respectfully through the fixed passages of Latin, I mediated between heaven and earth, brought grace to matter and to lives. Preaching, however, was another matter: It was in English, to people in front of you. Were the liturgical readings for the Sundays after Pentecost more than unexciting aphorisms from Paul and frequently heard parables from the gospel? Metaphors from a distant middle-eastern Bible-land and abstract Latin nouns of redemption and salvation had little impact. Faith, sanctity, redemption, penance, church—what could I say? We all knew the catechism's words and the church's phrases. Society seemed to need nothing from an inspired Bible; Calvinist respectability reigned at home, while Communism was a disturbing but distant foe. Catholic parishioners looked up at me in the pulpit—fans worked to counter the heat of August—and waited patiently through the epistle and gospel read a second time in English, and then through my abstract sermon. They waited for the moment to receive communion and for the end of Mass, for release from the tedium of the words and the ecstasy of the sacrament.

The Catholic population was always growing in the 1950s and 1960s, moving away from the ethnic neighborhoods of large cities to the suburbs where new parishes were springing up. Catholics were becoming better educated, more affluent, more American (some in Wisconsin or Iowa had even joined the Republican Party). Unfortunately, too often bishops and mothers-general, answerable to no one, built more schools and convents and churches in the wrong locations and on the wrong scale, in an artistically bland mix of terrazzo and brick. A Catholic diocese or parish dealt with quantity, many Masses attended by thousands of people. Insights into Christianity or pastoral programs for different kinds of people were not needed and might only disturb this changeless expansion. In a year, all that would change.

In parishes along the upper Mississippi, in small and large cities overflowing with families, I met in the summers of 1962 and 1963 people searching for something more, thirsty for religious ideas beyond an old catechism, reaching out to find some kind of parish activity other than collecting canned goods. The civil rights struggle had appeared on television, and the poor were suddenly visible. Small groups came together to read a book about the motifs in the gospel according to John or to help single mothers with undernourished children. In Minneapolis, after the crowded Masses in the parish gymnasium as well as in the church, the younger priests went into the inner city with its other church composed of the new urban immigrants, Hispanics, and Native Americans; in Rockford, parishioners had discovered the poverty of immigrants from the South; Bible study groups flourished in Madison, and you heard of a parish in Minneapolis reciting Lauds and Vespers. Those intimations of a deeper Christianity coincided with the election of Kennedy and with the preparation for Vatican II. Still, how would a church where history had been replaced by endurance, where Jesus' teaching waited behind Baroque statues, receive the slightest change?

Three months after my ordination in 1962 Vatican II began. After early debates over church and revelation, the bishops assembled from around the world rejected the drafts prepared by Roman bureaucrats for conciliar documents, and the stage was set for the entry of other approaches to Christian faith and Catholic life. An American writing under the pseudonym of Xavier Rynne reported in *The New Yorker* of intrigues at the Council, gossip and political maneuverings that American Catholics could not imagine existed in their church. I was helping out in a Dominican parish in December at the end of the first session of the Council. Being the youngest in the house, I was entrusted with the short period of reading aloud at the evening meal, a common practice then in monastic communities. The community was reading Rynne's final report of that first session in which he described how cardinals were conniving to block open theological discussion at Vatican II.

The provincial residing at that priory angrily interrupted my reading to say that this was all made up—such things did not happen in the church. A fog was lifting, and through the damp mist one could see the church on the coastal edge of four centuries setting out to sea.

As I mentioned, the Roman Catholic Church in northern Europe was living in real time, although we did not have much access to its books and articles. The French Dominicans discussed ancient icons of the Trinity with the Eastern Orthodox, conversed with Calvinists and Marxists, introduced procedures in which people prayed the Latin responses at Mass, and published religious textbooks planned especially for children. In Europe, schools and scholars saw Thomas Aquinas not as an apologist but as an inspiration for renewal and dialogue. Dominicans pursued the historical unfolding of Aquinas, while the Jesuits studied his relationship to modern philosophy. M.-D. Chenu, at the Dominican seminary near Paris, had unlocked the structure and context of the *Summa theologiae* of Aquinas and described the university life of the thirteenth century. Nonetheless, the Vatican had condemned Chenu's book presenting the Paris Dominicans' new school of theology where a historical knowledge of Aquinas furthered ecumenism, dialogue with the Orthodox churches, liturgy, and ecclesiology. History was dangerous: If one admitted the historical context of theological Paris in the thirteenth century, one admitted that there was no one, timeless theology. Cruelly, the pioneer of ecumenism, Yves Congar, learned in a Nazi prisoner-of-war camp that Chenu's book about their Dominican school had been censored.

In the United States, only a little of Christianity's riches was made known to American Catholics—for instance, Anton Pegis's selections from Aquinas or the popular collection of pages from Augustine, Bonaventure, and others called *Wisdom of Catholicism.* The ideas of John La Farge, Dorothy Day, Peter Maurin, and Canon Cardijn appeared in the *Davenport Register* or

America. Books on spirituality were general and European, conceived in the thin air surrounding a Portugese nun dying of
tuberculosis or an anonymous Carthusian in the Alps. Some
writers, such as Dietrich von Hildebrand, were attractive
because their style was not neoscholastic but their ideas about
prayer and the Christian life remained abstract, without contemporary examples and removed from American Catholicism.
Books by Christopher Dawson, Jacques Maritain, and Romano
Guardini—and these reached only a few thousand laity and were
often kept out of seminaries—offered new perspectives, but the
European sources and goals of those alternatives were hidden
from Americans. Thomas Merton knew an international array of
artists and thinkers open to their age and corresponded with
them, while Daniel Berrigan received permission to go to
France to study the new theology that he described in *The Bow
in the Clouds.* They were exceptions.

An occasional article on the European churches and their
art and theology appeared in *Jubilee* or *Worship;* volumes on
liturgy were published by the Benedictines at Collegeville or
by the University of Notre Dame. The pages of *Commonweal*
brought poems and sketches from younger writers and artists,
and *Jubilee* in pictures and texts opened up a world of mystics, lay social activists, and makers of mosaics joined to veins
of theology from Greek fathers and Russian mystics. The
Dominicans in the United States, however, dismissed Gilson
and Maritain because of alleged errors in the order of metaphysics, while Chenu and Congar were left unread. Our seminary library had the publications of the French Dominicans,
Vie Spirituelle and *Vie Intellectuelle,* and their articles could
give a glimpse of a free, exciting, contemporary theological
milieu, but you had to be able to read French. The vision of
Worship was seen as eclectic, aesthetic, while the *Common-
weal* culture and the attractive directions of *Jubilee* were not
encouraged. Occasionally, hints of diversity and vitality
entered our young and unformed intellectual world but not

change itself, and contemporary European books did not find their way into our seminary. Indeed, almost no books at all were purchased. The philosophy seminary held little beyond random additions from the 1950s, and the theology library increased its holdings only through books that arrived for review by a Dominican journal. By 1960, however, we knew the names of the few American precursors of a new theology: John Courtney Murray (on the cover of *Time* at the end of 1960), Gustave Weigel, a pioneer of ecumenism, and the Frenchman George Tavard.

In the 1950s, my fellow students and I, finding our classes sterile, read hungrily what little we could find about this wider world. The isolation of the church fed on ignorance and some arrogance. Who could have imagined that what the rare Catholic intellectual of those years found advanced—the congregation reciting Latin responses with the altar boys—would be only a prelude to great changes to come?

American contemplation and sacramentality drew mainly from nature. What else was there? A famous French biblical scholar who had spent most of his life amid the archaeological bazaar of Jerusalem observed, as we were looking west into Iowa from the hills above the Mississippi: "How boring! Nothing under the earth." (Actually, nearby were Indian burial grounds from the time of the Norman invasion of England.) The fields of corn, green in August, gold in October, brown and barren in December, undulating, falling into rocky gullies and woods because the great river had cut through the rock, had a geological history, and midwestern America held its sacraments in fields and valleys. If nature was alive and not dead like ruins, nonetheless, there were no temples in ruins, no church spires from ages past pointing to God. Growing up in this topography of rivers, lakes, and fields, I had no contact with what was waiting across the Atlantic: the city with layers of history, the church displayed in architecture, a cultural epoch revealed in art.

We were waiting. We did not know it but we were all waiting. Americans, not just Catholics but blacks and Hispanics, the young, the talented, were waiting for a wind. No longer defined by links with Ireland or Poland, no longer slaves or immigrants but living in a society touched by the migration of poor blacks to the north, by the issue of birth control, by education and television, Catholics were waiting. As the opening song in *West Side Story* mused, something was coming. What would it be?

Ready or not, my world along with the church was about to be replaced. The fixed pages of canon law and rubrics (by 1975 few would remember the church's code of canon law from 1917 or the Mass of Trent) were to be flooded by the waves of pastoral and theological newness. Things were about to change.

The Advent of Ecumenism

A first arrival was the ecumenical movement, and its spirit visited Iowa early on. At the beginning of my sixth year of study for the Dominican priesthood, in September 1961, a first year seminarian at Wartburg Lutheran Seminary in Dubuque walked over to the Dominican house of studies and inquired about taking a course there. Although this was a journey of less than a mile, he passed that afternoon through four centuries, from the time of the Protestant Reformation to the 1960s, moving through periods of hostility between Catholics and Protestants that had marked Europe's past and colored Iowa's history.

Growing up in Des Moines in the 1940s, I took for granted Catholic and Protestant separation and mistrust. Catholics had their own schools and hospitals, and they avoided not only Protestant churches but their weddings, boy scout troops, and the YMCA. In the late 1940s, walking home after school at St. Augustine's, I sometimes saw advertisements at a Protestant church for a lecture by a former priest, an evening's exposé of the secrets and perversions of Roman Catholicism. This very American tension between Protestants and Catholics seemed destined to last forever.

Quickly, some Catholic and Lutheran seminarians began to establish contacts between the Dominican school and the nearby Lutheran and Presbyterian seminaries. Protestants attended the monastic evening worship service of Compline, while Catholics shared duplicate library books. Dominican seminarians were not permitted to attend the worship services of other churches. Gifts of Protestant books, however, had little value, since prior to 1965 all theological books by Protestants had to be kept in a separate room in the library. Catholic libraries locked up books by non-Catholics on religious topics along with books explicitly listed by the Vatican on the Index of Forbidden Books (e.g., Voltaire, Darwin). Nicknamed the Inferno, this nether region usually held little of interest (Croatian or Italian Catholics had not been much shaken by David Hume). That same fall something new occurred when the Dominicans were asked to give a demonstration of Gregorian chant for the organists and choir directors of the local Protestant churches. When the concert and lecture received wide notice, the event became an open house that 300 people attended. Couldn't this open-house model be offered to other groups? Requests multiplied, and the following year more than a thousand people from Protestant parishes and schools in northeastern Iowa came to hear an introductory lecture about Catholicism and to attend the solemn High Mass.

In October 1961, an important visitor came to the Lutheran seminary. He was the internationally known Danish theologian Kristen Skydsgaard. Soon to serve as a Protestant observer at Vatican II, he had just attended one of the first ecumenical meetings in the United States held at the University of Notre Dame. Skydsgaard concluded his talk at that conference: "The church is seen as an eschatological magnitude. It points beyond itself to that kingdom that is yet to come. It appears in this world in hiddenness and ambiguity, always under 'the sun of Satan,' tempted to apostasy and emancipation and yet under God's mighty promise. God himself will accomplish his kingdom, that kingdom of which the church is the beginning."[1] One or two Dominicans were at the conference, and the Lutherans and Dominicans invited him to Dubuque.

The Danish Lutheran theologian came to lunch in the Dominican refectory. Afterward, he pointed out what an opportunity there was in Dubuque for ecumenism among the three seminaries from the Lutheran, Catholic, and Presbyterian traditions. Shortly after Skydsgaard's visit, the professors held an informal meeting to plan for theological discussions among themselves. In classes, students were assigned topics in Protestant theology. Naturally, there were a few teachers from each tradition who opposed this outrageous novelty. Were not Protestants secretly receiving communion as they attended Sunday Mass at the priory? How could Catholics sing "A Mighty Fortress Is Our God" at ecumenical gatherings? The Kennedy presidential campaign had shown that anti-Catholic views ("slaves of the pope," "ignorant immigrants") were still strong. American Catholic seminary professors were ignorant of the Protestant Reformers and of modern theology, while their Protestant counterparts had little more than prejudices about what Rome taught concerning the Bible or Mary.

The faculties of the three Dubuque seminaries began discussions of theology. The minutes of the first one in February 1962 recorded their careful procedure: Each meeting would begin with a minute of prayer (silent to avoid sticky situations such as the Protestant ending of the Our Father); a Protestant faculty member would be addressed as "Doctor," with a Catholic one addressed as "Father." The subject for the first theological discussion was not timid—"Theology and Dogma"—but those ecumenical discussions would not be made public.

Thomas O'Meara in his Dominican habit outside Wartburg Lutheran Seminary, Dubuque, in 1963. The inscription on the building reads: "God's word and Luther's teaching go forth now and forever."

The months of 1962 and 1963 showed how fast attitudes could change and prejudices fade. The seminarians, particularly the Lutherans, pushed for progress and more ecumenical events. One comical incident illustrates the era's anxiety. Wartburg students wanted their choir to sing in the auditorium of the Dominican priory. This seemed imprudent to our superiors, but, badgered by Catholic and Lutheran students, they agreed and fixed the date. As the day for the concert approached, someone noticed in horror that the day chosen was March 17. It was risky enough to have Lutheran singers performing in a Catholic institution, singing phrases about "justification by faith" to tunes by Bach—but on St. Patrick's Day! There had to be a show of Catholic identity and detachment, and so it was decided that at a reception afterward soft drinks would be served, but no cookies.

In 1964, Dominicans began to work with Protestant clergy and seminarians on various projects. When one of the most severe floods in the Mississippi's history occurred, Protestant and Catholic seminarians together built dikes protecting parts of the city. A clerical official, who devoted sermons to the importance of priests wearing and caring for gleaming black shoes, described this cooperation as the beginning of relativism and indifferentism. Wouldn't ecumenism dilute church allegiance and bring about a Christianity missing any doctrine or identity? Just the opposite happened: Knowing about another Christian church deepened an understanding of one's own tradition. Ecumenism led not to indifference or conversion but to a view of Christianity beyond piety and prejudice, to an experience within Christianity of different approaches to the message of Jesus Christ. Teachers in the three seminaries in the 1960s found in ecumenism a mission, a ministry to spread the word of church dialogue. Groups of professors from the three schools began to go out to the small cities of the upper Mississippi valley to speak in churches about the new positive relationships among Christians. Over the next decade, by example and word the seminaries changed the religious climate of the surrounding midwestern states.

The changes of the early 1960s included: Martin Luther King appealing to American justice and equality to find civil rights for black Americans; John Kennedy inspiring the country as president; Pope John XXIII preparing Vatican II to bring renewal. *Time* and *Life* offered illustrated treatments of the popular Pope John and the opening of Vatican II, and suddenly Catholicism received a new, rather startling media prominence. Enthusiasm for change was growing amid lay people, nuns and priests, and

Catholics and Protestants. Young people greeted change enthusiastically, and people over 65 also welcomed it: They had grown tired of a church that throughout their lifetime had harangued and bored them, taken their money, and then put up ugly buildings and pursued foolish policies. Why preserve an immigrant parish when the immigrants were gone? No one, however, foresaw that the changes then beginning would last through more than four decades, that they would not just modify the Latin Mass or alter nuns' habits, but also would refashion more and more forms, at deeper and deeper levels.

Theologians, Protestant and Modern

A few years after the protoecumenical days a Lutheran friend noted, when I was describing my seminary education: "You really studied the Middle Ages." "Studied them?" I brusquely answered, "We lived in them!" At the end of my eight years of formation, however, events occurred that would lead me personally into the world and into my own time.

In the autumn of 1961, one of my Dominican teachers who had just spent a summer studying at Union Theological Seminary in New York, unusual at that time, assigned me to research what Protestant theologians thought about Mary as the mother of Jesus and the mother of God. What did the reformers think of the theology of the incarnation as stated in the councils of Ephesus and Chalcedon? My Lutheran seminarian friends made an appointment for me with the librarian at Wartburg Seminary—I was perhaps the first Roman Catholic to use the library. The seminary's central complex, although built out of Iowa sandstone, was modeled on the Wartburg in Thuringia where Luther had worked on his translation of the Bible into German while hiding from bishops and princes. Unlike the Dominican library that held few books in English and few books published after 1940 or written after 1600, this was a bright, modern theological library with a staff. I was shown lexicons such as Kittel's *Theological Dictionary of the New Testament* and *Religion in Geschichte und Gegenwart,* and European and American surveys of contemporary theology (Roman Catholicism was usually omitted—its thought was not important for the modern world). To learn about historical and speculative Christology, I was directed to Karl Barth's *Church Dogmatics,* Paul Tillich's *Systematic Theology,* and Rudolf Bultmann's *Kerygma and Myth,* as well as to the books of Gustav Aulen, Anders Nygren, and Skydsgaard. I was captivated by the different theological approaches, by their attention to the history of doctrines, their stern professorial tone and utterly different, even radical ideas. In the weeks that followed, I began to check out dozens of books from Wartburg and from the library of the nearby Presbyterian seminary, for instance, the commentaries of Luther and Calvin on Luke, Matthew, and John, and their writings on the early councils.

After each visit to the Protestant libraries, upon my return to the Dominican priory, I was obligated by the vow of obedience to bring all books without exception to the master of students to receive permission to read them. If the student-master was not in, I had to leave the books outside his room until he returned. For me to place those books in my room was indirectly to give a place in an orthodox world to heretical writings, at least, to those "materially heretical." My ecumenical interests, however, were looked on with approval by my superiors who were now meeting with their Lutheran and Presbyterian counterparts. Soon, they suggested I write to the Vatican for a rescript granting me one permanent, global permission to read all books, past and present, by Protestants. The desired document, written in a flowery Latin and mentioning my prostration at the feet of the pope, soon arrived in Iowa. It cost under two dollars. I was in business.

To an Aristotelian mind, Luther appeared revolutionary and annoying. Creative, opinionated, one-sided, he sought not theological consistency but personal impact. He had not initially intended to be a rebel against Rome but saw that an age was ending and decided that the gospel deserved to be reborn. Luther led me into a world quite different from Aquinas, one lacking a system, one where the Bible, Paul, and Augustine presided, one that expected church teaching to move people. A revolution was occurring in 1962 as one had in 1518. How fortunate it was that in my first experience of extramedieval thought, along with Barth and Tillich I was initially introduced to Luther. I could have been given only American religious thinkers whose Puritanism or vague religious psychology had less and less to say in the 1960s.

I sympathized with Luther's heroic and insightful break with a scholastic and Vatican monopoly, but I learned that there were several Martin Luthers. Books in the 1920s had viewed him as a proto-Kantian; the mood of the 1950s saw him as the first existentialist. To make matters more confusing, Heiko Obermann's writings had just located Luther in the late Middle Ages, for Luther's view of Christ, pastoral issues, and worship could be, for better or worse, quite medieval. A genius, he was a witness to and a product of his *Zeitgeist* and also a precursor and creator of the modern world. Luther was a pastor and a theologian, a success in the correlation between situation and revelation, a visionary in seeing an alternative to medieval scholasticism, even a mystic. Some of those viewpoints, I learned with surprise, made Lutherans uncomfortable.

Who was Martin Luther? The Protestant par excellence? Luther was certainly not the Methodist anti-Catholic G. Bromley Oxnam or the Baptist preacher Billy Graham. Lutherans seemed to have an antipathy for Protestant charismatic sects or for the word *mystic*. What then was Protestantism? Much of American Protestantism owed little to Luther, and Lutherans were quite different from Southern Baptists and Disciples of Christ. This reformer liked church order, advocated a eucharistic real presence, and urged the confession of sins. I learned, too, that great thinkers could only be understood within their historical context, and such an understanding, far from reducing their genius, would extend it. Oddly, I first grasped the value of the historical context of a thinker from books about Luther and his age rather than from the writings of Chenu or Gilson on Thomas Aquinas.

A large, imposing bronze statue of Martin Luther stood on the campus of Wartburg Seminary. We Dominicans, fellow members of the Order of Johannes Tetzel whose sale of indulgences had driven Luther to reform and of Sylvester Prieras whose advice to the Medici pope, Leo X, was to dismiss Luther's too biblical and Augustinian ideas, were cowed by that statue. Still, the Dominicans had also produced the beneficent and attentive Cajetan who talked with Luther at Augsburg. The Lutheran seminary had a unity of life not unlike Dominican life. Despite voluminous Lutheran literature protesting monasticism, Wartburg was a kind of monastery, a cloister of buildings that housed spouses and children. As the liturgical cycle of Catholic feast days moving from Matins to Compline balanced scholasticism, so the hymns and sermons expressed Luther's preaching and theology.

In my third and fourth years of theology, classes were repeating the slow journey through the *Summa theologiae,* and that offered me hours to explore new worlds. During the lectures being delivered from professorial notes composed a decade or two earlier, I hid the books of Barth and Tillich behind my black, leather copy of the Latin *Summa theologiae.*

Karl Barth, Rudolf Bultmann, Emil Brunner, and Paul Tillich dominated American Protestant theology in the 1950s and into the 1960s. Bultmann applied a literary analysis of form-criticism to the Synoptic Gospels with the radical result that history was changed into stories and literary forms given the name of *myths.* His interpretation of Christianity was a pastoral plan where every supernatural event and every dogma expressing God in history had been removed for the sake of "modern man" who, captivated by mathematical natural science, could no longer believe in any special presence of God in history. For Bultmann, Martin Heidegger's philosophy of existentialism expressed well (even better than did the language of the New Testament) the core of revelation, and the philosopher's existential analysis turned Christian revelation into existential psychology. What more was needed? Bultmann was the mentor of liberal Protestant attitudes to the Bible and to the historical teaching of Christianity. Evidently, the modern problem for Protestantism was whether there was any historical revelation at all. Was liberal Protestant theology more than new terminologies? More than the reduction of grace and revelation to psychology?

American Protestants in 1960 viewed the Catholic Church as a warehouse of antique rites and pieties, although European Protestant scholars knew that Catholicism was more than a neo-Gothic castle, and in the first half of the twentieth century European theologians usually included some critique of the Catholic castle of superstitions. Paul Tillich's understanding of Catholicism, however, was moderate, accurate, and useful. The Catholic ethos, he said, does tend to be a *heteronomy,* a subjection of people to church authority, strict and severe, and, too, the Catholic spirit or thought form, the *Catholic substance,* can be guilty of the fundamental Protestant charge that it confuses the human and the divine. On the other hand, Protestantism, Tillich observed, could end up as little more than an austere critic, a church where autonomy allowed no teaching or symbol to withstand total freedom and individualism. "The Protestant principle is an expression of the conquest of religion by the Spiritual Presence and consequently an expression of the victory over the ambiguities of religion, its profanization, and its demonization....It alone is not enough; it needs the 'Catholic substance,' the concrete embodiment of the Spiritual Presence."[2] The *Protestant Principle* needed the *Catholic Substance,* the sacramental. Both sought maturity in *theonomy,* a transparency of the cultural form to the divine, of the existential to "New Being" or "the Power of Being."

In Tillich, I came across ideas on religion related to culture. Modern art, psychology, expressionist theater, or opera were not danger but channels for the divine presence. Religions were the products of cultures. "Religion and culture are not separate. While most of human life stops short of revelatory experiences, religion and culture lead to the depth-question."[3] Philosophy, as well as art and theology, was the expression of culture. Art and theology were sometimes related, both employing the forms of one age. Through both time flowed. Theology, like culture, had new catalytic moments, and Tillich used the Greek word *kairos*—St. Paul had used it to indicate the moment of the birth of Christ—for times of creativity and impact. There were births and deaths in culture and theology, forms and limits, variety and innovation. "Religion is the directedness of the spirit toward unconditioned meaning; culture is the directedness of the spirit toward conditioned forms....As the substance of culture is religion, so the form of religion is culture."[4] American Catholics needed Tillich to assist them in making sense of their own reality and history.

After five years of school in the Order, my classmates and I were still trying to figure out how theology served church and society. We argued over what theology was. Was it the same as philosophy? Did it have any audience? Tillich's method of a correlation of God's revelation to a human age and society broke out of a self-centered circle into a dialogue with the present. There are two poles in the correlation: The first is the revelation of God; the second is the situation that the Christian, especially the Christian teacher or minister, must address. "Theology, as a function of the Christian Church, must serve the needs of the Church. A theological system is supposed to satisfy two basic needs: the statement of the heart of the Christian message and the interpretation of this truth for every new generation."[5] Here was a view of theology that was pastoral and cultural, psychological as well as metaphysical. Had this not been the theological method of every great theologian? Aquinas's prologue to the *Summa theologiae* described the relational situation he faced as a teacher in an educational system that he observed was repetitive, disorganized, and boring. Aquinas interpreted faith through Aristotelian science at the universities of Paris or Padua in the thirteenth century, just as Tillich approached a general, contentless revelation through contemporary existentialism. For Catholics, the correlation of people and gospel would mean big changes for theological education and ministry. It was not enough to memorize past Latin texts. One must think, imagine, and relate the past to the present.

To my surprise, I found that a few Catholics had written essays on Tillich in the 1950s. Weigel, remarkably knowledgeable in Protestant theology, saw Tillich as a high point in Protestant theology and of particular interest to Catholics because of his appreciation of the history of philosophy and his view of theological correlation seeking to make Christianity coherent to today's world. The Jesuit posed critical questions. Did Tillich's existentialism eliminate God's revelation and the church's tradition? Was his theory of symbols adequate to express with any degree of realism historical events and religious truths? Still, the two theologians appreciated one another's views, and Tillich wrote responses to Weigel's articles.

During the summer of 1962, after my ordination, it occurred to me that a volume of essays on Tillich could be collected from articles written by Catholic theologians, American as well as European, a book of essays such as that edited by the Protestants, C. W. Kegley and R. W. Bretall. I wrote brief letters to Avery Dulles, Kenelm Foster, Tavard, Weigel, and others asking to reprint essays already published, and when they quickly responded affirmatively, I solicited some new essays. The Dominican publishing house Priory Press accepted the book, *Paul Tillich in Catholic Thought.*

A few months later, Tillich was contacted at the University of Chicago about writing a response to the essays by Catholics, and he agreed with enthusiasm. He worked on "An Afterword: Appreciation and Reply" during the first months of 1964, even writing responses to the different essays when he was hospitalized. Hannah Tillich said it was something "Paulus" wanted to do, and the piece was eventually completed with *Paul Tillich in Catholic Thought* appearing in the autumn of 1964. J. Heywood Thomas, a Welsh theologian whose *Paul Tillich: An Appraisal* had recently been published, wrote a "Foreword." The introduction to the volume explained:

> The following pages represent an appraisal by contemporary Catholic theologians of Dr. Tillich's theology....These studies, arranged in an order somewhat similar to his theological system, touch upon the fundamental areas of his thought: the nature of revelation and theology; its relationship to human thought; Jesus Christ; the Church and the Christian. The purpose of the volume is not, ultimately, critical; its purpose is to explore the truth and relevance of a theologian's understanding of Christianity and the causes for his success in forming our contemporary scene.[6]

I went on, with the brashness of youth, to introduce a contemporary Protestant theologian to a Catholic audience for whom theology, for too long, meant pages indifferent to living issues.

> Tillich's ideas and terms are new and, as he wishes, contemporary. The judgment of right and wrong in relation to Catholic theology should be made only after the meaning behind the words is explored. Dr. Tillich's desire to be relevant, his prominence, and his respect for coherence should lead us to expect that he has something to offer anyone interested in shepherding the space age. The Catholic reader may recall that Paul Tillich has been asked to speak as today's theologian before many eminent gatherings because he has worked for the present and the future. The tragedy of being out of touch with man and his

life can never prevail over the revelation of Christ. But irrelevance is a perennial threat to theologians.[7]

All written before 1964, the essays on Tillich reflected the first months of Catholic ecumenism in the United States. Some are Roman Catholic in static and unimaginative ways; some compare Tillich with an aspect of neo-Thomism where the focus is more philosophical than theological; all were written before the second session of Vatican II. The act of dialogue, however, was new. American Catholics were conversing with an internationally famous Protestant theologian who had been on the cover of *Time.* In May 1963, Tillich was invited to address 250 guests at the celebration of the fortieth anniversary of that magazine. Ecumenism had entered; change had begun. Tillich wrote of a new moment, "a *kairos,* a moment full of potentialities, in Protestant-Catholic relations...,"[8] and his "Afterword" (among the last of his many writings) ended with the words: "I want to repeat that I did this reply with the same joy about a fruitful dialogue with which I read the articles. One thing I learned in doing so is the necessity that we learn more about each other's thought, the classical as well as the contemporary....But fundamental differences cannot be removed and must be acknowledged. Only the divine Spirit and historical providence can overcome the splits amongst those representing the Spiritual Community which transcends every particular church and every particular religious group. A dialogue, done in 'listening love,' can be a tool of providence and a channel of the divine Spirit."[9]

The book was launched with a reception in Chicago at a Dominican house that was the press headquarters. The volume was also published in England. It was said that Franco's censors blocked its publication in Spain. In a circular letter in December 1964, sending German-speaking friends greetings for Christmas and the New Year, Tillich wrote:

In 1964 three books by me have appeared: the third volume of sermons with the title, *The Eternal Now,* just
appearing in German as *Das Ewig im Jetzt;* second, five
articles under the title *Morality and Beyond;* thirdly *Systematic Theology* Vol. III. Moreover two new books have
appeared on my theology. The first is from a young American theologian who studies under Barth, *The Systematic
Theology of Paul Tillich* with an interesting "Forward"
from Karl Barth. The second is *Paul Tillich in Catholic
Thought.* It is edited by Dominicans, and contains fifteen
essays by various Catholic authors and an extensive
response by me. It was recently dedicated with a "Cocktail
Party" at the Dominican house.[10]

Tillich died the following October in 1965.

Paul Tillich was not the first Protestant partner for
Catholic ecumenists and theologians; Karl Barth was.
Although he had periodically ventured forth from Switzerland with denunciations of Rome, Barth seemed to Catholics
to be free of liberal Protestantism's denial of traditional dogmas. By 1962 Jérôme Hamer, Hans Urs von Balthasar, and
Hans Küng had written books about him. Nonetheless, the
thick volumes of Barth's system soon disclosed their own
scholasticism, their own isolation. A mixture of the Bible
and selections from the history of doctrine, Barthianism separated too much the human and the divine, posed grace and
nature against each other, and so its view of sinful people
and salvation was alien to Catholicism. Why did Tillich have
such success among Catholics? After all, his was a liberal
theology. The Christology in the second volume of *Systematic Theology* was thin and heterodox—an existentialism
reduced the presence of the word of God in Jesus to his
death on Calvary, while the resurrection and the Holy Spirit
were only symbols expressing a vague belief in an unclear
presence. American Catholics were attracted to Tillich not

because he offered novel but empty expressions of the incarnation and Trinity, but because he appreciated Greek and medieval philosophies and took into account the full history of Christian thought, not just approaches that began with the Protestant Reformation. Tillichian theonomy and Catholic sacramentality were similar. Catholics saw a different Tillich. In the auditoriums of Harvard and Chicago, Tillich, although a liberal Protestant with little direct experience of Catholicism, pointed Catholics in ecumenical directions, helped them express in contemporary ways their own multiple relations between culture and grace, and expressed an existential personalism prominent in American life, an "interaction between destiny and decision which determines the religious condition of every human being."[11] In his later books, there was a view of the kingdom of God that echoed Karl Rahner's theology of grace outside of Christianity in human religions and resembled the pages of Teilhard de Chardin whose works after his death in 1955 were finally being published.

I had learned that Luther's revolt against the late medieval church and state was similar to today's questioning of rigid canon law and metaphysics. I had seen that Barth wrote beautiful paragraphs on the power and depth of revelation and that Tillich gave a living cultural context to it. Nonetheless, Protestant theologians in the twentieth century too easily reduced realities to words, to pictures (the Bible), or to ambiguous existence (modern psychology). Was modernity incompatible with revelation as the numerous documents issued by the Vatican over the past century had stated? Could faith today be more than a psychology of the self, a self empty of revelation and transcendence? Was Protestantism continuing its late medieval and Reformation breakthrough or was it facing one crisis of self-understanding after another?

From Ecumenism to Modernity

At the end of my theological education, ecumenism was spreading through the states along the upper Mississippi. A healing of long enmities began as pastors and people in towns and colleges in Iowa and Wisconsin met, discussed beliefs, and learned about one anothers' ways of worship. In the seminaries in Dubuque, Catholic, Lutheran, and Presbyterian faculty and students not only discovered the truths in other traditions but began friendships that lasted for years, for a lifetime. After the first session of Vatican II, the timid archbishop reported on the Council in the chapel of the Lutheran seminary. An eschatological time had arrived in which Catholics sang at Lutheran Vespers and Presbyterians drank beer. New ideas from contemporary theology drawn from books and discussions ran through my mind, while beneath them moved the harmonies of Lutheran chorales heard for the first time.

The young theologian Hans Küng had published a sensational book in 1962. In America, *The Council, Reform and Reunion* became a best-seller. It was a program describing what the upcoming Vatican Council should do. We read the book in the refectory, and its suggestions shocked our professors. Many, even most, of its proposals (downplaying Baroque devotions and canon law and developing theologies that dealt with contemporary issues, Mass in the vernacular) seemed daring and impossible to me but eventually would be enacted. Riding the wave of international fame, the 34-year-old Küng arrived in the United States for a lecture tour in the spring of 1963. Iowa seminarians were bussed to Chicago to hear him speak in a convention hall holding thousands. Theology was moving from the back page to the headlines, from a darkly lit church to a packed arena. Küng's ideas were important for leading American Catholics out of their backward and defensive state. His talk on "The Church and Freedom" began with a comparison of Communism and

Catholicism. Both take as their starting points that the world is "in a bad state," claim to have the only solution, and center on a strict authority. "But the church which proclaims the Gospel of Jesus is meant to bring men true freedom." The church must cease being the prison that it appears to many and become "a sanctuary of the free Holy Spirit," renouncing the cowardice of unfreedom and the error of persecution. "Freedom in the church," he concluded, "has to be won over and over again."[12]

Responding to the bestowal of an honorary doctorate at St. Louis University, Küng said: "This honor and this support belong not only to me, but also to the many theologians who fight with me in the front ranks for the renewal of the church and of theology....I have only a small request in conclusion: the doctor of theology begs you to say a little prayer that the doctor of law may remain a humble servant of the church and of her Lord." After one lecture, a Chicago chancery ecclesiastic declared: "We will be picking up the pieces of that for years!" Prophetic words: Walls were crumbling. Later, back in Tübingen, the Swiss theologian wrote "a word of thanks" to American Catholics, people who had rarely heard that word in their parishes. "What I found in the United States was not only a tried and proven Catholic life. I found a church which has visibly awakened to a new life, a new strength, a new hope since the first session of the Council."[13] At the same time, three important American theologians, practically the only American Catholics engaged in contemporary religious issues, Godfrey Diekmann, O.S.B., and the two Jesuits, Weigel and Murray, were banned from lecturing at The Catholic University of America in Washington and from speaking in the Archdiocese of Los Angeles. Freedom would not come easily.

Ecumenism gave access to the modern, Protestantism presented biblical themes, and Vatican II began church renewal. How could church and faith come close to the flames of the

Reformation and modern philosophy and not be burned by them? Weren't all liberal theologians the prodigal children of Hegel? Bureaucrats in the Vatican had long viewed modern philosophy and Protestantism as much the same. And yet the life of Catholicism must eventually reach out and speak to the world of secularity. Subject, history, freedom, science, person, and social participation composed modernity and could not be avoided. Freedom, however, was a confusing and frightening word. America was the land of the free, but to enter a Catholic institution was to renounce any freedom whatsoever. Küng had said around the country that the New Testament offered a freedom of the Holy Spirit, one different from modern libertinism but no less real. Freedom, experience, life, and community were coming back to life.

Tillich's *kairos,* meant the right historical moment when one cultural epoch ends and another begins: Thomas Aquinas's Paris, Fra Angelico's Florence, Beethoven's Vienna. The planning of Vatican II liberated the great theologians in Europe and brought a new era. The 1960s would bring changes not only for bishops but for Communist Party leaders, for politics in Latin America, and for liturgies in Africa. Would this new time in the church be as significant as that after the Council of Nicaea or the Council of Trent? For a few—in 1960 they might be enthusiastic about the poetry of John of the Cross or the prints of Rouault but they could go no further—the changes would be too many. Educated converts or academics content with a restored Romanesque church found the Spirit loose in the world frightening, but most Catholics around the world would embrace the efforts of people, teachers, churches, and communities to seek out and present in ministry and liturgy circles of grace at work, at play in the streets of the world.

Regardless, by chance or predestination, choices made largely by others plunged me into a time of dramatic change.

To Europe

Chance, Aristotle observed laconically, is the intersection of two independent lines of force. Providence, Thomas Aquinas explained, is the actions of all the natures in the cosmos moving symphonically toward their goals; and then, predestination is a special providence for intelligent creatures, not the capricious act of a mean God dividing humanity into the saved and the damned, but God's pervasive love intent upon a deeper life and meaning for each person. A woman meets a man ten years after prior events separated them. Will this moment be important to two people or to millions? Is it chance? Providence? A Hitler, a Churchill, an assassination, a storm—are they all God's will?

During the summer of 1963 as my seminary education ended, my Dominican superiors, with no warning, made a decision about me. Someone in the Province should know something about Protestant theologies, something about philosophy and theology after 1300. Since I had annoyingly and persistently been interested in Luther and Tillich, I was to be sent to Germany for doctoral studies. That decision was a result of the ecumenical cooperation between the seminaries. A German university seemed to be the right place for studies because those universities had long worked at understanding both German theologies and churches, Lutheran and Catholic. Also, the professors of the German schools were influencing Vatican II, and there one would hear the best and latest ideas on both ecumenical dialogue and church renewal. Tübingen, in southern Germany, was the obvious choice because that university had two faculties of theology, one Protestant and one Catholic. In the Protestant seminary, in 1795, the future philosophers Schelling and Hegel shared rooms with the young poet Hölderlin; there, the Protestant Tübingen school from David Friedrich Strauss in the 1830s on pursued a distinguished if radical critique of the Bible, attempting to isolate the core of Jesus' teaching and concluding radically that the narratives of the gospel were a creation of human consciousness, that is, a myth. There, too, the Catholic faculty at Tübingen—of which I had never heard—had an illustrious, if more traditional, history, and its ideas past and present were influencing Vatican II. At Tübingen, Catholicism had found in the Romantic philosophy of Schelling—he saw the world as realizations of an ideal form and society as a living organism with many activities—a model for understanding the church and liturgy. The church was a living body, an organism with various vital gifts and ministries, and the liturgy was the community's self-presentation, similar to art. Karl Adam and Romano Guardini, whose books were popular in America, had taught at Tübingen. Through the books and lectures prescribing what the Council ought to do, Hans Küng had just made his university known in the United States. It was the right place to study ecumenism and Protestant theology, and Catholic theology for a new era.

As I was in the process of sending the documents necessary for registration at that university, my superiors panicked. It was dangerous to have someone studying outside of Rome—I was the first American Dominican to study in Germany and one of very few to study outside of Rome—and I learned that I could not go to Tübingen because there was no Dominican house there, but I might choose any German university whose city had a priory. I soon came up with Munich because a professor at the Lutheran seminary recognized the names of its faculty members who taught scripture. I wrote to that university about requirements for entrance and contacted the Dominican priory, and when both responded positively I faced the hurdle of shipping a trunk of clothes across the Atlantic to Germany. Then, in August, *Time* magazine reported that Karl Rahner was moving to the University of Munich, and this buoyed up my spirits against the loss of picturesque Tübingen and the meteoric Küng.

One problem facing me was that I knew almost no German. I had studied the language in college eight years earlier but remembered few words. What a language: assembly lines of words marching out with a Teutonic independence but lacking obvious English cognates. (Why was *Aufzug* an elevator, *Anzug* a suit of clothes, *Zug* a train, but *Bezug* a relationship?) How could anyone have facility in a grammar where adjectives and articles were declined and in two different groups? But I liked the language and its atmosphere. In German class, we had translated pages printed in the old Gothic script and were introduced to short stories by Thomas Mann. Without understanding much, I read, in English, *Buddenbrooks* but set aside *The Magic Mountain.* Clearly, German short stories and plays were about serious, philosophical, and theological aspects of life.

●

In the late summer of 1963, as I packed for Europe, at the end of my first year as a priest, there were tremors of change. The opening session of Vatican II had taken place; in the South, the civil rights protests began; the Cuban missile crisis came and went; and ecumenism expanded in the Midwest. Nothing, however, prepared me for a journey that was more than a transatlantic trip. Beyond my apprenticeship in the seclusion of Iowa and the restored Middle Ages of the Dominicans, I was about to be thrown into a current as fast as any in the Mississippi, into the river of time headed for the rapids of epochal change, not to be an actor but an observer.

With little experience of the United States I began four years of living in Europe. During that time I did not return to America. When I did, although I knew well the train schedules linking Munich, Paris, and Rome and the names of cheap places to eat in Venice and Salzburg, I had not yet seen San Francisco, Boston, Miami, or Seattle. Waiting in New York at Idlewild Airport for the Pan Am flight to Rome to take me to Europe, in a youthful and incoherent explosion of enthusiasm, I blurted out to two Maryknoll nuns on the same flight that, with the second session of the Council about to begin, flying to Rome was like traveling to Nicaea.

●

My journey from the Mississippi to the Tiber and on to Munich's Isar was to be a trip among the rivers of culture and in the landscape of my psyche. For me, time and space were about to become alive and to reveal. Over the Atlantic in September 1963, temporality and space would alter not just in longitudes and time zones but in their inner nature. At the end of the transatlantic flight, experience and history, my new mentors, stepped forth to meet me, ready to show me Europe and ages past, but also worlds being born, worlds yet to come.

---

1. Skydsgaard, "An Evangelical View of the Church," in *The Church as the Body of Christ* (Notre Dame: University of Notre Dame Press, 1963), p. 41.

2. *Systematic Theology* 3 (Chicago: University of Chicago Press, 1963), p. 245.

3. Tillich, *What Is Religion* (New York: Harper and Row, 1969), p. 72.

4. *Ibid.,* pp. 72f.

5. *Systematic Theology* 1 (Chicago: University of Chicago Press, 1951), p. 3.

6. *Paul Tillich in Catholic Thought* (Dubuque: The Priory Press, 1964), pp. xx f.

7. *Ibid.,* p. xxiii.

8. *Ibid.*, p. xxi

9. *Ibid.*, p. 311.

10. R. Albrecht, ed., *Paul Tillich, Ein Lebensbild in Doku-menten, Briefe, Tagebuch-Auszüge, Berichte* (Stuttgart: Evangelisches Verlagswerk, 1980), p. 362.

11. Tillich, "Appreciation and Replay," in *Paul Tillich in Catholic Thought,* p. 301.

12. Küng, "The Church and Freedom," in *The Common-weal* 90 (June 21, 1963), p. 343ff.

13. Kung, "A Word of Thanks," in *America* 145 (June 8, 1963), pp. 829, 827.

CHAPTER THREE

● ● ● ● ● ● ● ● ● ●

The Lessons of Rome

Flying to Nicaea! My destination was Germany and Munich, but I flew first to Rome. I wanted to see as much of Europe as possible and did not want to pass up spending a few days in Rome, particularly with the Ecumenical Council about to reconvene. Vatican II was to assemble for a second session under a new pope, Paul VI. So my journey to Europe brought me first to Rome.

Signs along the bus route from the Roman surburb Fiumicino to the main railroad station—the airport itself was named after Leonardo da Vinci—gave enticing intimations of history: there was Ostia Antica, the port of Rome where Augustine and Monica had had their vision of heaven, and further on the basilica of St. Paul outside the walls on the spot of the Apostle Paul's execution. Inside Rome, the streets passing through neighborhoods of ochre buildings adorned with lines of laundry were disappointing, and the September day, though overcast, was hot and humid. Jet lag induced a restless sleep during the afternoon, as the fountain in the courtyard of the Dominican school splashed in the background. Then, I went out to a restaurant where I ate pasta and drank too much Frascati wine and slept again until dawn. The bed had its own ancient arrangement of heavy sheets and a rolled-up pillow.

I spent my first days in Europe at the Angelicum, the Dominican graduate theological school and seminary. It was named after Thomas Aquinas but called the Angelicum because Aquinas's theological acumen had resembled that of an angel. With a few eccentric scholars, some inedible meals, primitive toilets, officious porters and sacristans, the "Ange" lived up to what I had heard of it from my teachers who had studied there. A year or two before it had been an almost obligatory school to which Dominicans came from all over the world to gain expeditiously a doctorate. The study of dogmatic theology rarely ranged far from collecting passages from Aquinas on some major or minor topic and ignored other theologians from Origen to Maurice Blondel. Historical contexts and contemporary problems were neglected, for this was a citadel of a strict neo-Thomism where the salvation of Jesuit Suarezians was in only a little less doubt than that of Protestant Hussites. On the eve of the Council, one of the Dominican professors at a meeting of advisors to the Vatican had bemoaned the variety and looseness of theological opinions tolerated by the church, views held even in Rome, views such as those of the Redemptorists in moral theology or the Jesuits in the psychology of grace. He devoutly hoped that the Council would proclaim lists of clear positions on canon law and doctrine so that those vagaries opposed to the Dominican school of Thomism would end. Most of my teachers in the Midwest had received their doctorates from the Angelicum in philosophy, theology, and canon law. What soon amazed me was that American Dominicans had lived in Rome without becoming interested in history or art. Their graduate studies had been repetitive, boring, more memorized scholasticism, and the two years were physically and psychologically difficult, the life of prisoners whose goal was survival. Sadly, poverty, isolation, and rigidity of daily schedule—even in a cloister arranged around a fountain and palm trees and perched above the Roman forum—had for most blocked out the history and beauty around them.

Walking into History

After Prime and Terce and my private Mass in Latin—an eccentric sacristan, not unlike the one in Puccini's opera *Tosca* urged me in Italian to perform the ritual rapidly—I ate a breakfast of hot coffee and hot milk mixed in a large bowl served in a subterranean room. Wearing my black cloak over the white Dominican tunic and hood (at that time members of religious orders still wore their habits on the streets of Rome), I walked out of the grand, marble-floored Baroque building of the Angelicum into Rome, my first day in Europe.

The light of the sunny Mediterranean morning made the city shine; green umbrella trees and pines framed marble arches whose carvings were old when Constantine was emperor. I had a map of Rome and turned left to the Roman forum. Walking down the steps under dark arches and past the empty stalls of a Roman market built in solid red bricks in A.D. 110, I entered Trajan's forum dominated by his high column depicting in detail Romans administering their conquests on the Danube. Perhaps on Trajan's column, whose figures were so sharp and vital, I was looking at my Celtic ancestors. With their long hair and pants, and with a certain diffident attitude, they were listening to the Romans lay down the law. Amid fragments of temples and forums, I walked for the first time into history.

I met the past, or rather the past took me in, for it was very much alive and welcoming. Beyond the forum of Julius Caesar lay the older forum of Rome, which held foundations of sacral places from the time of the Etruscan Tarquinian kings who ruled five hundred years before Christ and in which, 200 years after the Crucifixion, a triumphal arch of Septimius Severus dominated. My map pointed out the ruins of the house of the vestal virgins and of the Curia, the senate of the Roman Republic. Impatient, I headed toward my first church in Rome. Grand and overdecorated, it was Baroque—I could not yet distinguish one style of architecture from another—and the placard on the wall indicated the seventeenth century—not old at all! The statues in the musty interior beneath high windows of yellow light seemed to be messengers, even friends from other times about which I was to hear more.

In the next hours and days, the periods of Christian history appeared. I expected Rome to be mainly Roman from the era of Julius and Augustus Caesar, or medieval. It was not. A guidebook and the placards in the churches, sometimes incorrect, helped me to begin to sort out the jumble of imperial ruins, seventh-century mosaics, and Baroque forms that surrounded me. Soon I came across the Mammertine prison, the prison of Vercingetorix of Caesar's wars, of Sejanus who had been the head of the secret police of Tiberius, and of many other distinguished condemned figures awaiting a dawn that held for them a beheading or being shot full of arrows like Saint Sebastian or Marcellus in the popular novel and movie, *The Robe.* Was it in this prison that two men, Peter and Paul, prior to their executions by cross and sword, spent their finals days, unnoticed by the politicians and businessmen hurrying to appointments? Some scholars thought that early Christians would not have been housed in such an important location, but like many ruins and excavations in Rome the Mammertine was part history and part tradition, both museum and chapel. The few rooms the tourists saw were only a small area of what must have been a huge layout filled with the miserable, the desperate, criminals and prisoners of war, perhaps even with Christian preachers.

After those first days looking at Augustan columns rising amid flowers and trees or at candles framing a Byzantine mosaic, I would never again see the past as a ruin or as a relic of a time that was finished and over. Curiously, my great drive to learn about the present first met in Rome the past.

Still, to understand a new time in the church was not opposed to learning about time past. The past fashioned the present, and in a history of salvation the past never really ended. Couldn't liturgy and art, as they had in 560 or 1560, illumine and mold culture and Christianity in the 1960s? I had been prepared by years of processions and statues, candle-lit churches and sacraments to look at matter and color as places where the divine might be present. A Catholic upbringing had shown how Jesus lived on in the liturgy, how the lives of past saints could inspire one to be a Christian in secular America (Tarsicius, a boy carrying holy communion to the Christian prisoners, was stopped, teased, beaten, and killed by Romans). Moreover, the Dominican Order had flourished in Gothic Paris and Renaissance Florence. What better place than Rome to see the incarnations of time. I had nothing to fear from history.

A building, a piazza freezes an epoch. Styles intermingle and converse, and people live among them. Marble slabs had been borrowed from the Roman forum to build churches. The mosaic of Christ at Sts. Cosmas and Damian—its lines and colors seemed to be of paint rather than of glass—shows an Eastern iconography, a Byzantine theology of the emperor of the world. The smell of Roman churches was different—a mixture of mildew and incense, of old varnished wood and faded vestments and drapes, as well as of old men and women with their fears. Outside, sunlight slanted off the great domes of St. Peter, San Andrea della Valle, and San Carlo al Corso.

The Roman church had seen much history, one that is not a line of progress but a celebration of cultures, which offered the church its forms for life. Even God's word came to earth in a particular time and people, expressing itself in Hebrew and Greek. The church belongs to time. History is always lighting up life, offering stages for existence and forms that are sacraments from the past. Time gets into us, permeates us. We don't observe or make our history. We don't have a time. Time and history have us.

Rome means many things: a city, a world culture, a religion, a church. Existing as *urbs, the city,* Rome is a particular city, and it is *the* city. This city brought to empire an urban center, and Cicero described the whole world as a city where gods and humans dwelt together. "Come to Rome," he wrote, "and live." Rome was a large and important force three centuries before Peter and Paul. After it had passed through the turbulent centuries of the Republic, the emperors—Augustan, Vespasian, and Antonine—expanded its marble precincts. Struggling through the Middle Ages, it was reborn a little in the Renaissance and more during the subsequent Counter-Reformation and Baroque periods. Rome created city patterns for the first century, and in the sixteenth century the popes and their advisors laid out boulevards linking fountains and churches to connect in a new style the areas of a large city.

When Vatican II was taking place, a century had passed since Papa Pio Nono; a third of a millennium since Bernini and the Barberini; 500 years since Luther was scandalized by the city's business of relics, and since the Medici popes' eyes lit up at some new project for art; 1,500 years disappeared with their months named after Augustus, Juno, and Mars, and since Gregory the Great in the midst of a collapsing world sent the missionary monk Augustine to Britain. And it has been two millennia since the executions of those unknown Jews now presented everywhere in the city as the princes of apostles. Further still, centuries run backward to Julius Caesar, to Sulla, to the tough disciplined shepherds of the Latin hills. Wild flowers, I noticed, were blooming in the corners of the Roman forum. Bees hovered over the petals of imperial purple, recalling the bees on the coat of arms of that patron of urban development and all the arts, Urban VIII Barberini. The bees sculptured by Bernini three centuries ago and the bees whose ancestors in this forum flew into the Curia to annoy Cicero meet in my mind and hover around the opulence and excitement that Rome contains.

The Business of an Ecumenical Council

In September 1963, when I walked into the Roman forum, it was autumn, a season of dying, but the times were giving birth. Pope Paul VI was continuing Pope John XXIII's Council, and John F. Kennedy was president. Europe was entering a new prosperity, and America seemed capable of leading the disenfranchised and poor into a better life on a new frontier. Technology was blasting off to the moon. There was as yet no Vietnam, Kent State, poor America, or fearful religious sects. In the streets of Rome, Protestant observers at Vatican II were saying for the first time good things about Catholics, while the theologians and bishops worked on the visible (the Mass in French or Urdu) and the invisible (the Holy Spirit at work in human religious history). Later, I read of young Hegel and Schelling bursting with excitement as they read Kant in the Tübingen seminary in 1795, appreciated the fall of the Bastille, and pondered the discoveries of electricity and chemistry. A new era was beginning then too. "The Kingdom of God is coming," they wrote to each other, "and our hands are busy at its birth." Vatican II was, as Pope John originally saw it, a renunciation of angry and defensive postures and an amicable acceptance of some basic directions of modern life. The pope evidently thought that his predecessors had condemned sufficiently the obvious problems of modernity such as atheism, state socialism, and relativism and that without compromising the gospel one could accept individual initiative, history, freedom, and the humane uses of science. There was a church, Pope John said, but it was too eccentric, moribund, and dusty. Bring it to life!

Someone gave me a ticket for the opening of the second session of Vatican II. I arrived at St. Peter's two hours early and found my section; as the liturgy attended by thousands slowly progressed we sat, then stayed on our feet, and ended up standing on our temporary benches to see. Of course, that morning I knew nothing of how anxious bishops, theologians, and curial officials were. Would the pope bring the Council to a rapid, bureaucratic end? Would he extinguish the very idea of change and return the Baroque of the church to its rococo port, where it would wait another century for the journey to lands of contemporary life? Would the will to end what Karl Rahner had called a clerical-fascist style by which the Vatican bullied Catholics and denied freedom of belief for others, the modus operandi that in Yves Congar's words was not far different from the approach of the KGB or the Gestapo, be repressed?

The address delivered by Pope Paul VI that Sunday to begin again the Council turned out to be an eloquent program for the church in the future. He began by greeting "with a happy spirit" those who had come from all parts of the world to this gathering of the church, a church that has been on pilgrimage for twenty centuries, one that contains immense powers and strengths, many of which are rather hidden in its depths. His themes were the renewal of the church, its role in seeking unity among Christians, and its dialogue with all people in our time. The goal was not to alter the essential life of the church or separate it from traditions that are vital and venerable, but to pass beyond other forms that he said are full of holes and collapsing. Jesus said that he would prune the vines so they might bring more fruit; such a process is needed today, not through more discipline but through more love. Indeed, the church should become a "church of love." In 1963, ideas that the church would support and share with humanity, that it would be joyful and loving were curious and daring. A church of the Spirit, the pope concluded, as it becomes more alive, will also be more clearly distinguished from profane society. It is to be a leaven, a life principle of salvation, but also a force amid human life. "To the large populations of youth, of new nations, of cities..., to all these and to each individual, the church directs its voice full of hope and offers the light of truth, life and salvation to all, for God 'wishes all to be saved and to come to a knowledge of the truth' (1 Tim 2:4)."[1]

As I left America in September 1963, I felt there not just change but newness. Now, in Rome, I sensed a force blowing away inhuman religion sustained by clerical and bureaucratic laziness, a force electrifying the atmosphere around St. Peter's. Bishops had found more to do than smoke cigars after rapidly confirming hundreds of children. They were no longer routinely making bad decisions, but studying and planning good ones.

In the evenings, the autumn wind whistled around the corners, blowing leaves down the Roman streets as I found my way to lectures by theologians such as Edward Schillebeeckx or Bernard Häring. I telephoned Kristen Skydsgaard who had stimulated ecumenism in the Iowa seminaries and was now a Lutheran observer at the Council. He invited me several evenings to come to the Danish Academy to hear, over a dinner of ham, bread, cheese, and beer, his experiences at the Council. In my journal—only its first pages did I conscientiously fill with the ideas and happenings from those days—I wrote my impressions: "Skydsgaard says it is impossible to write a book on Catholicism now. It is changing; it may be twenty years before one can say what the Catholic Church now is....He is happy with the schema on the laity. The bishops are still too scholastic. One Italian bishop said that the church is not built on the apostles. 'That is heresy!' Skydsgaard noted. Congar and Ghils did not like the schema on the laity, while more and more bishops have asked Skydsgaard to tell other bishops that Mary should be discussed not in her own schema but in a broader one on church or salvation-history. The Lutheran Skydsgaard and the bishops have many objections in common....The divisions in the church offer opportunities for a greater penetration of the truth. Only if both sides are studied will the full truth be known."

Skydsgaard had an important role to play as autumn progressed. On the feast of All Saints, November 1, 1963, Paul VI invited the Protestant observers to a reception, and Skydsgaard addressed the pope in their name. "We are following a path together; in other words we have not yet arrived." In the Council discussions, the Danish Lutheran emphasized the role of biblical salvation-history. Theology cannot be purely analytical and conceptual, and Catholic theology can no longer ignore the Bible and history. Was the Roman church's fear of history and diffidence toward the gospel coming to an end? Skydsgaard concluded: "A real Christian does not know what it means to stand still." Then the pope responded by taking up the theme of journey, a prominent motif in the Bible's history of salvation. Did Catholic universities, he asked, need a professorship in the area of the divine economy active in history? John XXIII and Paul VI had chosen a prophetic and future-oriented direction for the Council, building up the church not through condemnations and aloof audiences for elite groups, but by their warmth and interest in others.[2]

In St. Peter's basilica bishops from Latin America and Africa met together. They represented a new church, not European but worldwide. At the Council, the pendulum was beginning to swing to churches local and diverse away from Roman domination, which for centuries had relentlessly drawn all directive power to Rome. St. Peter's was itself the visible symbol of the self-understanding of the church from 1560 to 1960, stone illustrating a theology of the church. In Bernini's architectural space, the triple colonnade around the piazza, with its two fountains, led to the entrance to the great church and inside to the papal altar above the apostle's tomb, and then upward to the dome of Michelangelo. Bernini's ensemble could also proclaim the worldwide missions of the church: The colonnade and the piazza were seen as arms welcoming the world. For more than four centuries, the Roman center of the Petrine office had drawn increasing amounts of administration and authority to itself; every branch of church life was to be controlled or administered by the center. That process began with the forceful ascetic of the Counter-Reformation, Pius V, and ended with the

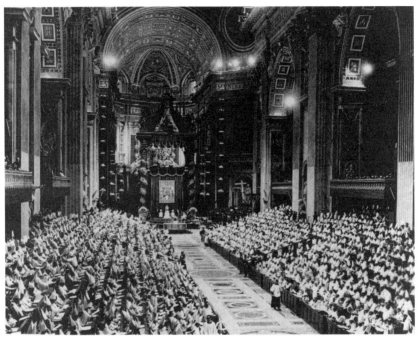

The opening of the second session of Vatican Council II in St. Peter's Basilica, Rome (CNS photo)

powerful *Pian* popes from Pius X to Pius XII. The documents and policies of each of these popes offered the mistaken theology that he was the direct pastor of every Catholic.

Now the church was on its way to becoming less "Roman." Ways of looking at Christ and the church were accepted that were not the products of a Roman neoscholasticism composed in timeless isolation from 1905 to 1960. Also accepted were the liturgies for Christians living after feudal rites and rococo devotions. In the 1960s, a movement toward some sharing of authority with bishops and a complementarity of ministries was beginning. In a church of communion and collegiality, local bishops' conferences would take responsibility for fashioning a richer Christian church along the Amazon or Congo and for giving some diversity to liturgy and education.

The time of the European theologians, which had started in the years after World War II, was finding an unexpected climax. Their teaching and writing prepared for and expressed the renewal of the Council. I occasionally walked past the great figures—Hans Küng in cassock talking to Africans in front of St. Peter's, M.-D. Chenu visiting informally after a lecture with Cardinals König and Döpfner, Rahner on his way to the press hall. I kept my distance—the leap from Iowa into those circles was too great. And, too, I felt that these figures, who were in fact modest and approachable, were separated from the rest of us not only by intelligence and fame but by a prophetic role given to them. The lookout crew of the flagship leading the rest of us into a new era must see further, anticipate more, work harder. I did not know about their own struggles and uncertainty. For instance, during the second session, Küng turned down Karl Rahner's suggestion that he work with the doctrinal commission because Küng saw little likelihood of that commission ever taking seriously the biblical themes of the church. French theologian Congar wondered whether the efforts of the Council would lead to anything even moderately new.

To me the Council was already a success; it corresponded to the energy and excitement of being young. There was no limit to people's expectations of the Council as its sessions went on, for once the Catholic Church had accepted the slightest change, more were inevitable. And the future? A new era, one of intelligence and maturity, of human service. Like many others I expected a utopia, the eschaton.

One day, while standing on a Roman street talking to a Dominican I had known in the seminary and who was now a theological advisor to African bishops, a black limousine pulled up. Yves Congar climbed out and handed my colleague a stack of papers and in strongly accented English said: "For the African bishops, *mon cher Père,...* and please hurry!" He got back into the limousine—I learned later it had been placed at his service by some government—and sped off. Initially,

Congar lived in the Dominican school where I had spent my first nights in Europe, but the theologian whose life's agenda was fulfilled by the Council's work found there a certain coldness and lack of support and so accepted in Rome the accommodations and assistance of government institutions.

For years, he had given talks all over France urging Catholic involvement in ecumenism. After spending the day teaching or writing his historical studies of the institutions of the church, in the evenings he went out and talked to small groups. From Paris to Jerusalem, he preached the eight days of sermons and prayers called "The Church Unity Octave" from 1935 to 1960. In 1955, he had preached those days of sermons and prayers in Rome—"in a small way," he said, meaning that it had been little noticed and poorly attended. His books, which prepared so much for this ecumenical council, had been forbidden a second printing by church bureaucrats. Now he and his ideas had returned to Rome. Without any feelings of pique, he had plunged into long days of work even if at times a neurological illness confined him to a wheelchair.

Not a few bishops and theologians at Vatican II kept diaries. Congar's are vivid and frank. As the summer months approached the beginning of the second session in 1963, he wrote that there had really been no vacation, for the "studies provided by the experts rained down like leaves in autumn."[3] The struggle to bring closer together scripture and tradition, an enterprise about which Protestant and Orthodox observers had much to say, had been long blocked by the neoscholastic picture of two independent sets of writings, both tightly controlled by church authority. Great figures in the nineteenth century, such as John Henry Newman and Matthias Scheeben, had prepared the way for the view that scripture was a living source for the community in each age and that tradition was not just past books but the entire life of the church pondering some belief. "From my own two volumes [on tradition]," Congar wrote, "it emerges that the present theological climate which is characterized by a return to the

Fathers, by greater freedom in regard to controversies of the past, and, finally, by ecumenism, requires a consideration of the intrinsic nature of tradition over and beyond...Protestant denials."[4]

Acquainted with ancient and modern theologians who viewed the church as a varied organism, Congar wrote of the need to pass beyond the conception of the church as a frozen institution. "The pastoral life of the church nowadays demands great breadth and cogency of information on all human and world problems. The church is certainly Catholic in the dogmatic sense of the word but not fully worldwide in the actual system of government. The people of the world will not be at their ease until they can express themselves freely."[5] Some feared any discussion of roles and ministries for Christians who were not ordained, but Congar bemoaned this un-Christian monopoly by clerics of church services, bemoaned a church directed by an ideology ignoring people, and by an administration that had no clientele. To counter that impoverishment, he wrote a book on the theology of the laity and a work critical of ambition in the church entitled *Power and Poverty in the Church.* The French Dominican asked in his diary: "Was the church to be a community of celebration, or a Renaissance court?" Paul VI implied something new, and in Congar's view the papal address opening the second session was "very closely knit and composed with great care," an emotional and personal expression of the themes of Pope John. He had successfully reestablished the council as an ecumenical event of Christ among people.[6]

The days and nights of Rome with their smells of times long past were strange to me—not at all like the humid heat of a midwestern August when the corn grew overnight or Indian summer's mixture of smoke and warmth. Outside a monastic seminary for the first time in eight years, alone in a foreign land, disengaged from family and friends, I had been drawn away from the poverty of medieval Latin propositions too weak to speak Jesus' gospel in the twentieth century—paradoxically this happened in Rome—to be a spectator and witness of the arrival of the new.

In later autumns, 1964 and 1965, I would come back to Rome before the German winter semester began, accompanying family and friends for a few days at the end of their European tours. After they left for America, there would again be time to observe the Council in action during sessions three and four. Press conferences were held in the afternoons each day in a hall on the Via della Conciliazione, the street leading down from St. Peter's to the Tiber. One afternoon I listened to Karl Rahner in his slow and precise German, interrupted by translation, explain to 500 reporters what had happened that day in the basilica. Leaving the hall and walking out into the late September afternoon, I passed an Italian priest in a cassock and a broadrimmed clerical hat muttering to himself, *"E tutto Kant; e tutto Kant."* "It's all Kant." "It" was, in fact, more Heidegger—it was also Thomas Aquinas in a new form. But clerics of those years were, as was I, ignorant of thought outside of neoscholasticism. The administration of ecclesial empire seemed oblivious to the city around it with a dozen different cultural-theological periods, and to a Roman clergy the Germans were still the barbarians, still eleventh-century Ottonians, the looting army of Charles V, or the cold and cerebral Protestants, inhabitants of a misty world that could produce Luther and Nietzsche. The new theologies of the Germans, Dutch, and French recognized the need for historical research and biblical themes, for more than quotes cited from past theologians and saints in church documents apart from their historical meaning or context. Every form, symbol, sacrament, dogma, theology had its origin and its history. The church for the conciliar theologians was a living, dynamic source of ideas and liturgies, a sacramental center for all kinds of sacramental forces. In accepting the church living among different peoples and times, the Council and its theologies were turning out to be more Catholic, more traditional, and less modern than the tired mental apologetics of the recent century that claimed to be timeless.

Vatican II was perhaps the first Council to be deeply aware of itself, of its own life, of the impact of its acts. The earlier Council, Vatican I, had influenced the structure of the papacy, but its impact on ordinary church life was minimal. Vatican II was conscious of its dynamics and destiny, of its choices for the world, and thereby the church became aware of its collective self, local and multicultural, and then of its place within the various human groups ranging from atheists to Buddhists.

Each day the bishops poured out of St. Peter's basilica into the broad piazza after their morning of change-making—agents of renewal, enthusiastic or truculent helpers of the Spirit, swimmers in history. Contrary to what they then thought, Vatican II was not to be a brief interlude but an opening leading to more and more variations, more difficult issues. Time, like the Holy Spirit, was to show itself to be more powerful than legal texts and Renaissance clothes. Places and peoples, schools and movements—all would be touched by a further Pentecost.

The Sacrament of Time

Rome met me in churches and temples, obelisks and fountains. Romanesque towers, fragments of Augustan theaters and amphitheaters, rococo palazzos rejected any notion of merely existing in one age. The city was a living backdrop through which the literature, philosophy, and mysticism from past eras touched those who listened. To read a letter of Clement, a Roman church leader of A.D. 90, on the Celio hill or Ignatius Loyola's letters to Francis Xavier in a piazza near the Collegio Romano was an ecstasy into a particular age.

The cloisters and gardens of schools and religious houses in Rome are strewn with marble fragments of columns and sarcophagi marked by Latin or Greek letters. Cultures collapse under their own weight and yield to the next emerging, youthful, cultural epoch. The world of the present does not take shape without the past: The old and the new live together without either out-lasting the other. There is no Rome without the layers of religion: complex, interesting, curious, superstitious, heroic religion, pagan and Christian religion intertwined. Each figure, whether it is the Roman officer on an arch or a Jesuit saint in the church, stands forth as an offspring of an age in which the Spirit worked. Secular or Puritan spirits do not much enjoy history and culture, preferring cleaned statues set up in museums to inspire civic virtue. Catholicism had preserved me from an American Calvinism that avoids the smells and soil of cultures: It had prepared me for Europe.

But what was the idea of Rome? Spirit in matter? Christian grace in architecture, paintings, and liturgies? The cult of the martyrs at the places of their execution and the relic bones with subsequent miracles? Sacrament and art, Christian grace penetrating pagan matter, intrigued me in Rome, for in them you could see, touch, and smell the Christian idea of life over death.

Walking from piazza to piazza, from church to church, I began to see how architecture directed my eyes and feet. Architecture and liturgy mirror life. Walking into a church you can see something of the forms inspiring and regulating an age: the house church, the basilica, the Romanesque monastery, the Baroque theater of devotion. Columns and aisles form and direct movement. The basilica's space of meditation and worship differs from, without opposing, the Baroque heaven on earth. Most American Catholic churches built between 1850 and 1950 were, in their basic style, basilicas, Gothic cathedrals, or Baroque pilgrimage churches. Re-creations from the recent past, they could be places of interior prayer but not easily places of gathering or ministry. The architecture and decorations of an age have their limits. If I had joined, a century after Jesus, a group of Christians hurrying to some room in a house lent to them for meetings, I would have been led into their circular gathering of community and worship. In a bare room I would have shared money, support, and food collected for a fragile community in a violent world. A Christian basilica is very different from a back room. It beckons me toward the front, toward a bishop's chair, toward the mosaic of the cosmic Christ on the wall. I am a part of a large group in A.D. 450 attending a liturgy centered on a bishop's sermon and upon the Eucharist of processions and crowds of Christians. Much later, in medieval cathedrals, the eyes spontaneously drift upward to the colored light of the windows, to the high columns where above the altar and the crucifix light implies the ineffable God, and the believer feels small, located in a benevolent hierarchical world and invited to mysticism.

An age introduces a particular cultural illumination. It arranges, spotlights, and hides a world around us. Culture is the setting of the spotlight's format, and philosophy expresses a culture. Does culture progress? Decline? Stay the same? Certainly, information and science progress. Improvement brings more materials and things but not always more wisdom. Cultural times are not winners in a competition but are simply striking ways of seeing. As long as we are staging a competition between Phydias, Michelangelo, or Rodin, we cannot understand any artist. Is Picasso more realistic than Giotto? Must Michelangelo anticipate the lines and colors of Cézanne? Ages are individuals: Raphael is not better than Monet, although he is different. This is not to say there are no periods in culture that are mediocre, but great epochs have their dominant motifs and thought forms embracing both poetry and metaphysics. Creations of time, they stand on their own. Each gives ways of seeing and each holds limitations. Lights on, lights off—a display of the forms brought by time.

In Rome, around each corner something new, small or grandiose, appears, and suddenly you say to yourself, "I see." Rome is a place of processions, of evening walks, of gathering and display. People like to walk as walks forecast their journey into the mystery ahead. Here, amid the great buildings of the

Caesars, lies the *via sacra,* the sacral route of religion and politics, while across the Tiber the pope processes into St. Peter's for liturgies. I stepped into the movement of life by being born, by being baptized, by entering the Dominicans, by living at this moment. Now the church is processing into its own time, ceasing to be only European and passing beyond the Greek and Roman, the Celtic and German to be African, Asian, American. In a second procession, Christianity is entering into the long and varied history of human religions. Vatican II speaks a few words on the rays of grace and revelation in other religions. How is Christianity the center of a process of religions that is itself lengthy, diverse, and containing grace? How does Jesus incarnate a world of grace, and how do other religions reflect the kingdom of God? How do Christians understand Christ as Messiah and Word for Hinduism? Catholicism, when healthy, takes the long view, expecting the world to change slowly: It has learned that cultures become Christian slowly. A sudden confession of faith is not the same as a lifetime of practice; the construction of one television sender or chapel in Malawi does not begin an Afro-Christian civilization. The processions of the church in time proclaim the presence of the Spirit touching all people. The medieval historian Chenu, who was at work on conciliar documents, said in one of his conferences: "God entered history and since then has never left it."

A Supernatural Cosmos

I encountered the Baroque in Rome and would meet it even more forcefully a few weeks later in Munich. Rome was a great Baroque city because it was reconstructed and decorated by the art and theology of the Catholic reform and renewal after 1570 and 1620. Despite the loss of England, northern Germany, and Scandinavia to Protestantism, there was a new experience of Catholic universality and historical continuity. New

mystics and charitable movements expressed a religious enthu-
siasm, a drive toward the most sublime prayer and the most
heroic evangelization to mark a vitalized self-consciousness of
Catholicism in the sixteenth and seventeenth centuries. The
Baroque cascades of the human and the divine fashioned
Catholicism for four centuries, up until now.

Baroque theologies resulted from a new interplay of personality and grace in men and women, in Ignatius Loyola,
Philip Neri, and Teresa of Avila. A self-analytical spirit is
linked to the analyses pursued in science and mathematics
after Galileo and Descartes. Christ is experienced in a new
way, particularly in his humanity and wide redemptive love.
The human being experiences a new freedom and active
capabilities for grace and finds God more powerful and transcendent. Emotion is prominent in the spiritual life, and the
Christian life unfolds in the extraordinary, in conversions,
visions, stigmata, ecstasies, asceticism. Grace becomes a
power within my life, a force that will aid me as an individual
to avoid my temptations and to follow God's will for me. My
spiritual life has a distinct format. Autobiographies by Teresa
and Ignatius like the methods and exercises of one's personal
Christian life are dialogues with converting grace.

In the Baroque, dramatic grace represented by light touches
men and women who are heroically active: Baroque art is theatrical. Architecture produces spaces for human performances. The
architecture and ritual of a church are places of human grace as
the presence of God; paintings on the ceilings and walls show
the church celebrating holidays in music and conversation. Art
historians have called Baroque and rococo churches "God's
home," "God's theater," even "God's ballroom." What appears to
us antiquated in the ultrarealistic crucifixions or in the imitation
marble frame for a saint dressed in precious stones was for the
Baroque the latest style, sketching out worlds for God's grace.

Church organization also became Baroque. Just as architecture and painting arranged a multitude of figures around a

dynamic point of focus, more new religious orders, more offices within the Vatican, more dioceses on newly found continents were organized around the administration of Rome. If in the Middle Ages ecclesial life had become a pyramid not unlike the facades and towers of its cathedrals, in the Baroque the Holy See arranged through organization, law, and metaphysics all the churches and church institutions around a single point, itself. The church offered a single catechism, a new liturgy, one language for worship, one metaphysics for study in a church administered by one bureaucracy.

The religious ethos of the following centuries composed variations on the Baroque. There were distortions—some bishops and nuns turned the happy Baroque world into a place of suffering or into a heaven apart from history. In silent prayer or desperate novenas grace became transitory forces from God to the believer. Little by little the church drifted off, disconnected from the world around it. Outside was a hostile, secular world waiting for supernatural Christianity to expire. To understand, to renew earlier times, and to go beyond its poorer appearances in this century—that was the work of Vatican II. The celebratory or the unhappy Baroque of the nineteenth century—these worlds Vatican II was leaving.

St. Peter's is the embodiment of Baroque art and theology. More than a church, it is an event, a living gallery, an organism. Outside in the piazza the fountains and obelisk attract you; the arms of Bernini's columns invite, encircle you, draw you forward and slightly upward toward the facade. Bernini, a lifelong disciple of Jesuit spirituality, said that the embrace in stone of the colonnade would welcome Catholics, invite Protestants back to the church, and call new populations of Asia and Africa to the center of Christianity. He brought a climax to the Baroque by combining painting, sculpture, and architecture into a whole, observing once that architecture was music frozen in stone. When his Jesuit confessor asked him if he was afraid of death, Bernini replied with the same inspired hauteur, "Fortunately,

Father, the God to whom I will give an account is so great that he does not take into account petty things."

In the late afternoons, the Council leaves St. Peter's to the tourists. There is a coolness in the basilica`s marble halls. The great size leads one to think of the past and the people who have been here, all the artists and theologians, princes of state and cardinals. Despite their plans and worries, few are remembered; most might never have existed. If they lived for glory on earth and in the church, they have none now.

The light rolls around the balcony of St. Peter's dome and showers softly fall down upon the baldachino, whose bronze columns twist upward to the orb and the cross they support. The afternoon sun sinks in the west. From that direction light comes through Bernini's *Gloria,* a white, alabaster dove set in yellow and gold glass. Beneath the window's image of the Holy Spirit is the chair of Peter encased in bronze, a chair, unfortunately, not from the first but the fourth century. Enthroned around the chair is tradition represented by four learned doctors of the church whose robes are caught up in some breeze, a Baroque storm of movement accompanying the Spirit's entry. God moves inward toward us in this architecture of grace as light. The glass and the bronze angels and the sculptured saints proclaim in varied figures human belief in the presence of God, in incarnation past and present, in the sacramental life that is Roman Catholicism.

St. Peter's is an enormous multimedia proclamation aimed against the Protestant Reformation. Contrary to the Reformation's theology of a remote and transcendent sovereignty in heaven, God is in the church and its liturgy, in the individual soul, and in the life of grace in the world. Bernini's painted glass and grand sculptures announce the arrival of the Spirit, expressing in a kind of propaganda a theology of grace and church over against the austerity of Luther and Calvin who had preached God's transcendence and wrath.

Crowds of people walking through and gazing at the grandeur of the basilica press on to the center where the four vast corridors of this basilica meet. More tourists circle along a balcony beneath the dome of Michelangelo. Above the baldachino, where a cross surmounts the papal crown, angels look down on our suffering. The bronze cross above the central altar located at the crossing of the halls of the church is not there to express defeat, horror, or self-denial but to recall the life that freely led to it and the resurrection that followed. No answer to suffering exists except the existential one of Jesus' life and resurrection, which gives life and meaning in the future to each individual. Bernini will not let us sink too deeply into the pain of history, and so cherubs fondle the crown and the cross and hold them out toward us, insisting that they have some relationship to us below. The message within the basilica declares that there is more in history than time passing, more than days leading to death.

One afternoon in St. Peter's, I was sitting near the canopy above the papal altar, the baldachino. Off to the left, a group of small boys and girls came on stage holding a homemade sign, almost swamped by adult groups. Later, high up above me on the balcony, I saw them again walking around the edge of the dome in single file. Now back on the ground floor of St. Peter's they head for the exit and I can decipher the black, hand-lettered sign—*Caldano.* An Italian guard tells me that Caldano is a small town in southern Italy and adds a discreet gesture to indicate that it is of no significance. Their leader is a priest in black cassock and broad-brimmed, Roman clerical hat. He is about 60, red-haired and red-cheeked, not much over five feet tall. Determined, busy, worried, the priest has a big responsibility. Caldano residents do not go to Rome every day, especially at the age of 12. Urging the sign-bearer to hold it up higher, the priest brings stragglers back to the line with a look or with an invocation of the Mother of God. They have seen a lot this day, visited the crypt of the popes where Peter's dust (and perhaps keys) mingle with the dirt of second-century Rome, looked at the marble tombs of the grandiose, walked up to the cupola built by geniuses with pulley and rope alone, and looked out on Rome from the high roof. But now the children, their sign, and the pastor are leaving St. Peter's.

The sinking sun in the west is hidden by the basilica, and soft light shines within through the alabaster dove. Time to give up the mental struggle with tragedy and history. The guards are gently urging the polyglot groups to leave the building. The marble and mosaics catch the last light as one day out of a long history comes to its end. Outside, the fountains still sparkle in the twilight.

The Lessons of Rome

Fashion designers, politicians, terrorists, church bureaucrats, respectable sinners, and scandalous saints—each has a view of Rome. British and American essays on Rome from Henry James to today's expatriates keep Rome at a distance. Aloof from the smells and from the faith, uncomfortable with garlic, sex, candles, and kneeling, they prefer a safer religion, one of art. At the other extreme churchmen, too, have misunderstood Rome, using it to defraud or to dominate believers, finding forged documents to claim that Roman emperors gave the city to the popes, establishing indulgences as automatic claims on divine mercy. Vatican officials, professing to love faith's teaching but frightened of its depth and variety, let ambition distract them from tradition and confuse power with the charism of teaching. The church is expert in avoiding history. Does it become tired of such a long survival, of so many experiences? Of all the pain and failure it has seen?

People rush to confront, to own, or to dominate the city, to preserve or to sack it—and the city flees. In the movie *Fellini's Roma,* beneath the stygian traffic jams archaeologists are examining some ancient frescoes just discovered by workmen who were excavating for the new subway. The air moving in with the arrival of human beings causes the frescoes to fade—and soon they are gone. So old and so fragile is the Eternal City. Its being must be sought in the foam of fountains, in birds on the branches of pines. The composer Ottorino Respighi heard in the pines and fountains of Rome the music of time. He wrote tone poems in which the timbres of an orchestra's instruments gave his impressions of Rome. The Eternal City came alive in the waters of the Trevi Fountain sparkling blue-white at midday or in the jets of the Villa Medici at sunset; the pines on the Colle Janiculo or along the Via Appia Antica sounded a past alive in the present. Fountains and pines give glimpses into the mystery of Rome. For me, Rome's lesson was learning to see, to see time, to meet suffering and glory.

Is Rome the Eternal City? Rome is the opposite of the eternal: It is a palimpsest of the past. In the Tiber, there is an island, the Isola Tiberina connected to Trastevere by the Ponte Sesto whose blocks of rock are original, if reassembled, from the third century B.C. A magnificent temple to Esculapius, the god of healing, dominated the island in those centuries. In the ninth century, piety and weapons got hold of the body of the Apostle Bartholomew bringing it to Rome, and a basilica with fine Roman columns was built, as was eventually a hospital. Today, one of Rome's main clusters of clinics occupies most of the space, although of course there is room for a coffee bar and a trattoria. So healing has no difficulty surviving millennia, and saints and gods watch over science.

The Council was giving a lesson in history and time. In the 1960s, the unimaginable happened—the Latin language, that is, its late hobbled usages in the Western Catholic Church, was coming to an end. Simultaneous translation had entered the basilica of St. Peter's to end the pretensions of a universal language. Parts of the Latin rite were placed in the vernacular early by the Council, and Latin would quickly disappear from all the liturgy and thereby from Catholicism. The church was becoming extra-European, worldwide. What had Latin to do with Yoruba in Nigeria or with Koreans? The peoples and religions of the world were hardly waiting for their faith and hope to be translated out of Latin. Could one continue to announce that the word of God had revealed itself on earth through a dead language he never spoke? The conciliar event was to be worldwide, with Latin a first casualty. The aging experts in the official Latin of the Vatican looked down and watched African and Asian bishops moving in and out of the Porta Santa Anna on their way to conciliar business with the See of Rome, conversing in strange tongues.

Latin letters in the calligraphy of imperial Rome stretch along a fallen marble block or above the entrance to the Pantheon. The Western church long administered itself through the language of the Caesars. Surviving invasions and adjusting to new nations, Latin in the West preserved Roman and Christian ideas and imperatives for Gothic kings and Viennese emperors. The person who knows ecclesiastical Latin, despite its changes from Gregory the Great to Urban V, can understand a decree from a thousand years ago, not only the words but the thought forms.

By the time I was 21, I had an education in Latin grammar almost as extensive as that received by holders of doctorates in the classics. To be a priest was to know quite a bit of Latin; to be a Dominican priest was to know more. My classmates and I could speak scholastic Latin, although hesitantly as a piecemeal and memorized product. Since some of my classmates, however, lacked a facility with languages, they had to give up their studies for the priesthood and could not become parish priests in America or missionaries in Africa because they were unable to translate Ambrose's homilies or Aquinas's commentaries. Many of those who stayed were not really fluent in the liturgical and philosophical texts we read each day, and so both the prayer and the study of the future priest were remote, lifeless.

For centuries, a mentality of sharply etched dogmas has been served by a language with clarity—too much clarity. It had been

clear for a few centuries that church life conducted in Latin gave
to the clergy an implicit permission to be impersonal. Latin was
not just a foreign language—it was a dead language. For a millennium it had had only an artificial existence. The words used in
ordinary life were unknown. The *codices, canones, libri,
rescripta,* or *acta* of the church set up barriers to the Spirit. If
Latin once meant transcendence and serenity, it had for a long
time brought abstraction and isolation from the gospel. Comparing German and French with Latin, I could see the limits of the
Roman language: too sharp a style of expression; a lack of dialogue; a difficulty in expressing time, process or history; a sim-
plicity that did not tolerate ambiguity. Latin helped but also
hindered an engagement with cultures, and its thought forms
did not much influence French life in the seventeenth century,
German art in the nineteenth, or American society in the twentieth. I had found that praying in German was preferable to
Latin, despite my long contact with the latter in liturgy and
school. The Latin words had no connection with life, and it was
not easy to pray in a complicated language that was not your
own. One did not feel *dolor* at the dentist or watch an *arbor*
change colors in autumn. There could be an aura surrounding
public prayer in a Latin liturgy, but it was a vague mystical ethos
of the unknown. Did this cessation of Latin imply that the history of the church was ending. Or was it beginning?

The lessons of Rome. Rome is still somehow imperial and
pagan, still papal and Baroque. The city is not a museum. Its
pasts are trying to teach us. The great periods of ecclesial and
theological life are not saying the same thing. Catholicism errs
when it claims recent documents and objects are unique and
eternal. The maniple, the buskins, the bugia, a dated code of
canon law, an old catechism, helpful in 1940, are being moved
to a sacristy storeroom. When Pope John called the Council, a
thousand clerics were going about their Roman work, teaching
and administering within a mentality that fought off history,
even as they moved about this city of multiple cultural ages.

This bureaucracy from 1850 to Vatican II drew together disciplined lives and devout prayers but achieved modest successes and great failures. Being above your own society and time brings arrogance, laziness, and a compulsive attention to the insignificant. The church tends emotionally gripping centers of primal cult like the catacombs of St. Callixtus or the church of Santa Caecilia in Trastevere, but it mistakes one period for another, mixes the twelfth century with the fourth century, confuses the past for the present, and the present for eternity. The church can be afraid of history: In changing times, it can lose faith in the Spirit and repress the gift of incarnating itself again and again. In the years from 1860 to 1960, defending the neo-Gothic and attacking the modern, it thought Baroque art came from the early church and distilled once medieval theologies and philosophies into a perennial orthodoxy. Curiously, this shallow timelessness was cultivated precisely at a time when humanity came to appreciate history.

How hard it is for God's inspiration to lead the powerful to give up power, to separate empire from apostolic faith, city-state from papacy, bureaucracy from the body of Christ. This is the ultimate lesson of Rome: the acceptance of history as the renunciation of dominance and as the place of incarnation.

Martyrs and Ordinary People

"The holy city, the holy city." Rome, I thought, has rarely been a holy city. Too much violence, too much sin, too much intrigue.

From whatever point you approach the church of San Clemente you must walk down to it. The front steps descend under an arch into a courtyard that was the formal entrance to a basilica in the fourth or fifth century. Through the side entrance, you walk into the dim light of the church past a fresco in which a blond and youthful St. Christopher carries the child Jesus. Steps lead down because for more than a thousand years Romans have built on the rubble of their past. When fire or age—in this case it was invading Normans—destroyed buildings, holes were filled with earlier rubble, and old walls were used to support the next structure, and consequently the church now used each day for worship and filled with tourists is from the late eleventh century.

San Clemente is a mine shaft of history. There are three levels of church here, each built on top of the other. Today's basilica from the eleventh century has some furnishings from the earlier church, marble lecterns and the holder for the Easter candle. Behind the altar is the bishop's chair surrounded by marble seats placed for his co-workers, the presbyters, the elders of the early community; this is a remnant of the basilica built in the fourth century by authority-conscious Pope Siricius to honor the early leader of the church of Rome, Clement. Above the seats is a large mosaic of the Cross of Christ depicted as the tree of life for the cosmos.

The second church of the third to the eleventh centuries has been partly reconstructed from its columns and walls and holds frescoes of persons and their stories. Paintings support the tradition that Methodius, apostle to the Slavs and creator of their alphabet, was buried here at the end of the ninth century.

Finally, below both these levels are the streets of Rome as they were at the time of Trajan and earlier of Augustus. A number of rooms may be a small part of the house of a patrician family, the Flavians, for we are close to the Coliseum built by the same family. It was in some insignificant room that Christians met with Clement, although no such place is designated by a later house church. The Emperor Vespasian founded out of old Italian stock a brief dynasty for the Flavians. He began building a vast amphitheater that would bear the family name. After his son, Titus, had ruthlessly ended the Jewish revolt in A.D. 70, Jewish captives were sent to Rome to work on what came to be popularly called the Coliseum. It was dedicated in

A.D. 80 and could hold 55,000 people. Suetonius records the sanguinary dedication: "None of Titus' predecessors ever exhibited such generosity. At the time of the dedication of the Flavian Amphitheater he provided a most lavish display of gladiators...and a wild-beast hunt in which 5000 animals of different kinds were despatched in a single day."[7]

On the lower floor we hear the rush of rivers, flowing rapidly down toward the Coliseum. Perhaps they were part of the great sewer system of Rome or brought cool water to the homes and gardens of the rich. Or, frighteningly, perhaps this was the water necessary to clean the gore of the games that went on for days at the nearby Coliseum. To their amazement, excavators found in the lowest level of San Clemente the center of a mystery religion, and so opposite the meeting place of Christians was their competition: a school, a meeting room, and a baptistery for the cult of Mithra. Popular with soldiers, a man-god, Mithra, perhaps an astrological figure, won redemption for himself and others. The community was led by a *pater,* a father. For new members, there were a catechumenate and initiation ending in rites that strengthened the neophytes' courage and fidelity. The Mithraic believer descended into a kind of sunken baptistery, where, above him (women had their own mystery religions), a young bull's throat was cut, washing the devotee in the blood. So in a time of frequent suicide and public immorality when pagan gods and goddesses had long been dead, Romans calmed their fears at bloody spectacles or through myth and liturgy.

Before Nero had them executed, perhaps Peter or Paul visited a community of poor laborers, slaves, Jews, or speakers of Greek at their eucharistic meal somewhere in these buildings. Who was the Clement of this church? *Clemens* was a frequent name among the Flavians. A trusted major domo or a slave freed after long and valued service, he became the overseer of this Roman *ecclesia,* and one of his letters has survived, one written to Christians in Corinth; it combines a Jewish view of salvation history with faith in Christ and a sense of the authority given to the Roman church. Ninety years later, Tertullian in Africa and Irenaeus in Gaul wrote that Clement had known Peter and Paul. Clement, the Roman church leader, was martyred in a work camp for exiles in the Crimea, but the end of his life is so encrusted with legends that it is difficult to learn much about him or about what it was like to be a leader of the church in Rome.

The Coliseum recalls the violence on display there, the despair of its victims, captives from Jewish or German wars, some not yet 20. Their lives ended with the ultimate meaninglessness, cruelly killed as a form of amusement for other men and women. Although Christians were rarely executed in the Coliseum, to the Christian slaves and laborers in the first century hurrying to some side room in the Flavian buildings on a Saturday evening for Christian Eucharist, the moonlit Coliseum empty of spectators appeared like an open tomb, a vast mouth of death. And to the Romans, the nonviolence and patience the Christians preached and practiced must have seemed absurd. "You are God's chosen race, his saints; he loves you and you should be clothed in sincere compassion, in kindness and humility, gentleness and patience. Bear with one another; forgive each other as soon as a quarrel begins. The Lord has forgiven you, now you must do the same." Paul described Christians belonging to the house churches of Rome as men and women viewed by the Empire as the world refuse. "God has put us apostles at the end of his parade, with the men sentenced to death; it is true—we have been put on show in front of the whole universe, angels as well as men. We are fools for the sake of Christ....When we are cursed, we answer with a blessing; when we are hounded, we put up with it; we are insulted and we answer politely. We are treated as the offal of the world, still to this day, the scum of the earth" (1 Cor 4: 9–14). The dignity of all children of God before the demons of human violence is redeemed realistically, not by some decree of God but by resurrection, the continuance of personal history into a new future.

Inside San Clemente, there are inscriptions from Roman burial tombs deep beneath the streets. The sunlight does not penetrate to where the scattered dust of the ancient dead await the power of the resurrection. A single marble lid now covers the tombs of two boys who lived in different centuries—death and time made them brothers. One was pagan, one Christian. Pagan parents, in a time of violence and evil, lost their son. One inscription reads:

"Marcus Aurelius Sabinus also called 'the little rover.' A most beloved child whose way of life outshone by far the young men of his own rank and age."

And, a more anonymous, Christian inscription:

"To Surus, resting in peace.

Erected by his brother, Euticianus."

Lines go on to mention how the young boy who raked the sand of the Coliseum and was much liked by those who worked in the amphitheater accidentally fell into the path of a lion that killed him. Senseless.

Is there a God? Modern philosophers and theologians have spent a great deal of time wondering about the existence of God. Science finds the universe, no matter how vast the galaxies or how complex the genetic code, not needing a beginner, a mind. Often motivated by the extent and mindlessness of suffering in the world, atheism or agnosticism has long been the privileged intellectual stance of Europe and America. Can God exist over against our wretched history? Who gave permission for such a history? The challenge to every faith is not whether there is a supreme cause but whether God loves us. What does the God of love have to do with so much suffering? In *The Brothers Karamazov,* the atheist brother argues against belief in God with the horrible image of the Tartars using children for target practice. Thomas Aquinas offered as his first objection in the *Summa theologiae* his broad consideration of the entirety of Christianity, an objection to the existence of God drawn from the power of evil: "*Videtur quod*

Deus non sit. Invenitur malum in mundo." "It would seem that God does not exist, for evil is found in the world." Jesus did not blame God for human evils such as floods and birth defects, although he did point to an atmosphere of human sin that furthered evils. Walking into his own suffering, he lived amid poverty, injustice, betrayal and ended tortured and executed. His response to the problem of evil is resurrection, his and ours. Even if that is theoretically unsatisfying, life and meaning beyond sufferings compose a human and, in the resurrection, a real response, probably the only answer we can grasp here on Earth.

And the church? Sadly, the church is at times an instrument of suffering. Too intensely devoted to its own power, it pursues a zeal born of a reluctance to learn. It persecutes others. How many insightful Catholics have observed that one suffers not only with but from the church?

In the Council, the bishops are admitting that the bureaucracy of the Roman church does not always have the answers to the complex issues of humanity. Centuries of avoiding new and difficult issues must yield to a consideration of what gospel freedom, ecclesial participation, and human rights mean.

Six hundred years ago, Meister Eckhart was falsely condemned by the pope; 300 years ago, the imaginative Giordano Bruno was burned at the stake in Rome; 30 years ago, Yves Congar was exiled from France. Before the Council, from 1830 to 1960 the Roman church, despite its various traditions of how the divine acts through the lives of men and women, was a frightened caretaker of institutions, some of which resembled prisons or asylums. Through the centuries, few theologians and popular speakers have taught evil or injurious ideas, and in a modern age of media-supported trends it is not clear how lastingly influential the sensational can be. Too often the negative judgment concerning a theologian, a Thomas Aquinas or a Herman Schell, comes too rapidly. Vatican officials impinge on human rights and disdain the individual made in the image of

God. Who injures the church more, self-willed creators of curious and wrong religious theories or vindictive guardians of ecclesiastical privilege and ossification? It is said that after he became pope, John XXIII took out the Vatican's file on his career, read its suspicions about his seminary professorship, and then wrote in ink, "I was never a modernist." Nowhere is bureaucracy more embarrassing than in religion. We instinctively feel that the essence of all bureaucracies is to abuse people, to move the snuffer toward the candle, to extinguish the Spirit rather than to offer a brighter light for a cold world.

The Spirit of the Risen Jesus, however, does not let the church constrict its life. The heroic, the mystical, the creative appear again and again. Movements for reformation have been brewing among theologians and charismatic leaders, even if from 1850 to Vatican II they encountered repression. "Do not extinguish the Spirit," Paul wrote to the Thessalonians, and Karl Rahner quoted those words in a first essay on the possibilities of the Council that John XXIII had just called. For that assembly, the Spirit had prepared an extraordinary number of men and women, some of whom I passed on the Roman streets.

I was sitting along the Tiber, and perhaps not far away Congar was giving a conference. What was decisive about the Council, he concluded, was that it had reentered history and so again both papacy and people could speak of things new and hope-filled, could listen to the Holy Spirit and the Spirit's future.

Churches with their art and the people praying in them console me. In the basilicas, the figures on the front-wall mosaics are more than art. Their iconic faces—apostles, Christ, saints, angels, rulers—carefully fashioned piece by piece 15 centuries ago, do not passively accept my gaze but return it. The dark eyes in the mosaics, like olives offset by gold, stare back. I am addressed:

We, too, were once men and women, alive but mortal.
Our creator-artists, of whom we are the only remnant,

were flesh and blood, talented and uncertain. We all lived briefly, long ago. We were hungry, fearful, in love, lonely.

Our eyes...! You find our eyes large, eyes dilated by surprise or narrowed in anger. They are large because of what they have seen. We have seen more violence and smelled more filth than you will. But we were much like you. We doubted, struggled, gave up, survived, accepted, hoped.

Now like him who went ahead through death to future life, we are to you dead, but we are living. What you see in our faces—Roman, Syrian, Egyptian, Greek—though only a mosaic, is elsewhere a reality, human and divine. Contemplate and be encouraged!

●

What is history? What built Trajan's column and the much earlier temples of the forum? It is a necessary force? It is destructive toward humans and their projects? Is it blind? Is it God? History is not the Holy Spirit, although the Spirit strives in the mystery of apparent weakness to work among people in each age.

Another morning of visiting faith in art has passed and I am hurrying, in my clothes from the thirteenth century, back to the main meal of the day at 1 P.M. In the streets I see cars with bishops and secretaries driving from St. Peter's after one more morning of the Council.

What is ending? The poor imitations of the medieval, the legendary devotions, the passive boredom of being a Catholic? A Renaissance and Baroque system of centralized power with simplistic axioms and an angry censoriousness? Christianity as solely European, as solely of the nineteenth century? Forms of the church in which I had grown up are being set aside, but they were only images and symbols of some European age, often not so old as people thought and little related to the preaching of Peter and Paul in Rome.

What is beginning? The universal church is beginning, and Rome will have to find a form of authority with the church and not above it, an authority of communion that respects other bishops, churches, and ministers, an authority encouraging the freedom of other churches, rites, spiritualities, and ministries.

My first days in Rome had planted in my spirit an insight and a conviction. Art from the past through stone forms and painted colors showed times with influential ideas, thought forms of creative change, beautiful and distinct. The present moment was born of various pasts still seeking to fashion new futures. I had been given a preparation for what I would find during the years ahead in the churches and classrooms, in the museums and streets of Munich.

---

1. "Summi Pontificis Pauli VI Allocutio..." (Sept. 29, 1963), in *Acta Apostolicae Sedis* (Rome: Typis Polyglottis Vaticanis, 1963), pp. 895ff.

2. Cited in Yves Congar, *Report from Rome II: On the Second Session of the Vatican Council* (London: Chapman, 1964), p. 74.

3. *Ibid.*, p. 25.

4. *Ibid.*, p. 32.

5. *Ibid.*, p. 103

6. *Ibid.*, pp. 52ff.

7. Suetonus, "Titus," *De Vita Caesarum* 6.

CHAPTER FOUR

• • • • • • • • • •

Into the Modern World

Before entering the Dominicans in 1955, I visited Montreal and New York City for a few days. Otherwise, I had never been beyond Wisconsin (including the Upper Peninsula of Michigan), Iowa, and Illinois. There, the United States was a tranquil, timeless nature. Rivers and woods, lakes and hills framed spaces that held no Greek temples or Florentine piazzas. In the autumn of 1963, my world suddenly altered—its geography expanded outward from the Upper Midwest to Europe, briefly to Rome, and then to Germany. I was sent to Munich for further studies.

Schicksal

By accident or providence, I came to study in Munich because, as I mentioned, Munich and not Tübingen had a Dominican priory. I arrived in Munich on a rainy night in October 1963. My flight from Rome had gone first to Zurich and then on to the München-Riem airport. North of the Alps, at each turn toward the east, the sky became more dark with rain. On the plane a woman offered me a ride into the city, but when her husband and children unexpectedly showed up at the gate, I was left to shift for myself. My luggage did not arrive: The tickets indicated that the Rome airport had sent it not to Monaco (Munich) in Bavaria but to Monaco where Princess Grace resided. That Sunday night a bus took the few passengers to the main train station, and at the *Hauptbahnhof* I found a taxi to take me to the Dominican priory. In the rain the driver could not find the address, a small door behind, not to the side of, an enormous Baroque church. He dropped me off in the dimly lit Salvatorplatz and I saw a button with the name *Dominikaner* above it. A voice on the intercom grasped who I was and let me in. The Dominicans were at their Sunday evening recreation and welcomed me warmly into a room redolent of cigar smoke and beer. They explained, as they had earlier in a letter, that their small, temporarily reconstructed priory had no vacant rooms and that I would stay in a nearby *pension* run by sisters, although I would eat here at St. Kajetan's and be a member of the community. Anxious to put together a first sentence from a few words I remembered from college German, I exclaimed, *"Ich weiss. Ich schlaffe mit den Schwestern,"* "I know. I'll be sleeping with the sisters." I had yet to learn the meaning of *bei,* "at."

Several floors up above the priory I spent my first night. My bed with its heavy comforter and tilted pillow, located somewhere in one of the two Baroque towers holding large clocks that struck every half hour, seemed to be a good beginning for living in Germany. As a boy, I remembered seeing movies that showed Haydn or Schubert in the poverty of their youth sleeping in cold attics, dependent on the charity of church schools, and with few prospects. Outside the rain poured down.

I began four years of living in Europe, a time during which I did not return to America. How fortunate that this voyage of youth was not fixed within the army or dedicated to some area of science or technology but was, instead, a journey into realms of religion, philosophy, and art whose teachers and creations would soon surround me. Ignorant of art history and never having visited an art museum, nourished by no wine and by only insipid American cheese, my midwestern blandness, nonetheless, was ready to turn into an avid receptivity. Very much Aristotle's empty writing pad, a "tabula rasa," I was ready to become the searching self of Schelling and Hegel, to live by the forms of the worlds soon to be encountered. While I knew only a little, I knew how little I knew, and I expected to be taught. I was not embarrassed or shocked to find that the world was larger than Wisconsin. Like a diver surfacing, as I left the Dominican priories for Europe, I had the feeling of emerging into life after a long seclusion. But first I faced a future for which I had little information and few skills—and I did not know German.

I did not know then whether Munich had a population of 14,000 or 1,400,000 and was fully ignorant of its multiple histories and vital role in postwar Germany. The next day, in mid-October, was cold as I headed out into the busy streets of the city center. I had to purchase a map, get my trunk with its coat and sweaters from customs, and move into my pension. My room was in a four-story house on *Unterer Anger* (Lower Anger Street), run by teaching nuns known in Germany as the School Sisters of the Poor but in America as the School Sisters of Notre Dame. Their motherhouse, where they had been founded a century and a half earlier, lay across St. Jakobsplatz. My room held a comfortable bed, a wooden desk, and a large wardrobe; there was a bleak view of some inner courtyard. Twice a day large china pitchers and bowls were filled with water. For heat, there was a coal-burning stove next to which were a metal box of paper and kindling wood and a supply of coal briquettes. I learned once winter came that on particularly cold nights the stove reached its maximum heat at two in the morning, casting a stifling heat and red glow into the room, while by six the fire was always out. Presiding over this austere but welcoming and orderly house of students was Sister Gerwina. A spirited, wise, and engaging person of deep faith who had passed through years of Nazi horror with strength and humor, she greeted my confused efforts to begin to live in Germany with bewilderment and kindness–for instance, I pronounced "auto" as if I was saying "Otto," and so it was unclear whether I was talking about a car or a person.

Each day for the next nine months I walked through the center of Munich, the *Marienplatz,* to the Dominicans–to Mass, meals, recreation–and usually on up the Ludwigstrasse to the university.

The German language was everywhere–in the streets and stores, newspapers, signs in streetcars warning of something, words on the radio describing with complexity the arrival of rain due to a *Tief,* a meteorological "low"–guttural, long, and complicated words. Little of the vocabulary had remained from my college German. All the previous summer I had been trying to memorize a list of 500 theological terms, but without success. In Munich, from that list, only one word still stuck in my mind: *Schicksal,* "destiny."

The first word I learned in Munich was *Löffelchen,* "little spoon," because during the Mass in Bavaria a little spoon mixes some water into the chalice of wine. That first morning, as I went about buying the necessary *Schirm* (umbrella) and *Mappe* (brief case), the language surrounded me, implying my ignorance and aloneness. Why was *Ausfahrt* an exit but *Ausschuss* a committee and *Ausschank* a beer stand? What kind of mind thought in such a way that verbs appeared at the end of a dependent clause in decreasing order of their importance? The outcome of every German sentence seemed momentous–but also, until the last moment, in doubt.

I liked German and sympathized with its complexity, doubtless because I had studied Greek and Latin for many years. German, however, was just one of my difficulties; I was plunged into a babble of languages. Classes used German but also some Latin and Greek, while French was the language of many of the theologians of Vatican II. Latin in its German pronunciation was still the language of the Dominican priory's daily hours of prayer. Nonetheless, German was going to replace my second language, the medieval Latin by which I learned neoscholastic theology and philosophy.

Then, too, there was the vocabulary of modern philosophy that was utilized in contemporary theology. *Wesen, Begriff,* and *Bild* ("essence," "concept," and "image") were not words as much as mental intersections around which theological houses and philosophical schools were built. With an effort intensified (and assisted) by loneliness, I was learning two languages: German with its complex grammar and the abstract terminology of modernity.

Yet, what was modern? What made the eighteenth and the nineteenth centuries distinct? How was the twentieth century different from both? Did the modern world begin with Schiller and Beethoven around 1795 or with Marx, Freud, and World War I? Regardless, Munich witnessed much. The Baroque church of St. Kajetan's stood opposite a palace with two theaters: in one, Mozart's operas had been performed, and in a second, Wagner had attended his premieres. The *Platz* in front of the church had witnessed Hitler's failed putsch in 1923. In Eisenhower's America, there had been no real past: The present and future were one, a sunny sameness. In Europe, however, the twentieth century was a collection of four or five different, turbulent periods. So not only the present but the various pasts were waiting to instruct me. Nevertheless, of the famous citizens of Munich whom I might take as teachers, Mann and Romano Guardini were known to me only superficially, and Friedrich Schelling, Joseph Görres, Rainer Maria Rilke, and others were unknown to me. Curiously, I was much more ignorant of figures who had lived only 30 years earlier than of the sixteenth-century disciples of Thomas Aquinas such as Cardinal Cajetan or Domingo Bañez, whose theological texts I had been taught in Illinois and Iowa.

I had no time to learn about the past, even the recent past: I was here to learn about Protestantism and modernity, to grasp something of what was happening now in the Catholic Church. Catholicism was finally pondering modernity without hostility, admitting that condemnations and repressive measures could not be a way of life, and restoring periods before and after the Middle Ages. For almost a century and a half the church existed between energetic theologians exploring modern themes and papal censures of all that went beyond the Baroque. Certainly, Catholics had been spared the precipitous and destructive enthusiasms of a century of liberal Protestantism that was just beginning to weaken Protestant churches. Now, Catholicism had accepted that it could no longer pretend to live apart from its own times. In Rome, aided by French and German theologians, some of whom had been condemned in the 1950s, it was pursuing new initiatives for contemporary life. Liturgy, theology, historical research, existential and personalist expressions of grace, biblical studies drew from the themes of the self emerging within areas of culture, freedom, and history.

Thus my struggle to learn German was joined to the need to learn contemporary philosophy and theology. The beginner needs a basic orientation, and I found it in a book with the title *Fragen der Theologie Heute (Today's Theological Questions)*. It gave overviews of various areas of Christianity: Heinrich Fries on myth and revelation, J. R. Geiselmann on tradition, Otto Karrer on apostolic succession, Karl Rahner on nature and grace, Thomas Sartory on ecumenism, Edward Schillebeeckx on the sacraments, Hans Urs von Balthasar on eschatology, and Alois Grillmeier on Christology. The writers had a similar method: After surveying an issue as treated by the Bible, and by the Greek and Latin theologians of the first centuries, they alluded to the richness of the church's expressions of some area of faith in the history of culture (everything had not begun and ended in the thirteenth century) and then presented contemporary issues and ways of thinking. By translating this book phrase by phrase in my room, I learned German theological vocabulary, but, more important, I had mature scholars lead me into the present status of their disciplines. Meanwhile, Vatican II was pursuing its second session, one of open discussions on important themes, a time that Karl Rahner was describing as one in which the church irrevocably overcame its past format of intellectual monoformity and intolerance.

In Bavaria

After a few months, although I could understand little of the midday news, broadcasts to which we listened in respectful silence at the Dominican priory, I was able to read an article on *Sakrament* or *Tradition* and recognize some ideas and terms in a professor's lectures on biblical exegesis or Luther's thought. I could follow classroom lectures as long as the subject matter stayed within my limited religious vocabulary. Out on the streets of Munich, however, the situation was disturbingly different because I encountered another language: Munich Bavarian. Part of the linguistic family of south Germany, Austria, and Switzerland, Bavarian in the Munich style was used in a beer hall or hockey stadium, in warnings of parents to their children or in the shouts of construction workers. *Bairisch* fudged on declining the article, omitted the imperfect, and had a broad pronunciation. Friendly clerks adjusted their language to their clients, noticing who might speak German as it is written and whose demeanor indicated a person for whom dialect would be more suitable. I needed not just to be able to pile up dependent clauses and reflexive verbs but also to grasp *Gemma, Gelt, G'wesn, G'Kapt.* Bavarians liked to talk: Restaurants and beer halls, filled with people at almost every hour, were noisy with talk. As the months and then years passed, this language would become increasingly the one surrounding me—in the streets, in hilarious Alpine comedies on television, and in Richard Strauss's *Der Rosenkavalier.* This was the language of humor, of a good time, the grammar of

daily life and sorrow. If an official in the post office or a wait-
ress in a beer hall stared at me with bored incomprehension,
nevertheless, as the months passed, I understood more. I was
on my way.

There was—I had to be told this often—really no Germany.
The Federal Republic was a recent creation, and former prin-
cipalities and duchies refashioned into states retained their
proper realms of language, food, and customs. One needed
to know not so much the map of Europe as the geography of
Bavaria: Oberbayern, Upper Bavaria was south; Lower
Bavaria was neither south nor north but east. If the Pfalz was
east of the Rhine near France, the Niederpfalz was north of
Munich near Czechoslovakia and East Germany ("the so-
called DDR"). To the east of Upper Bavaria was Lower Austria. Franconia alone was quite diverse: *"Man muss Gott für
alles danken: für d' ober- mittel- und nieder-Franken."*
("One should thank God for all things: for upper, middle, and
lower Franconia.")

The German language remained complex, even if newspapers, television reports, and the *Münchnerish* of the streets
made it a little familiar. Words had families. *Weihen*—I learned
it was an old Germanic word—meant to make holy or sacred.
My ordination had been a *Priesterweihe,* and there were
higher and lower clerical orders of ministry and liturgy, *Weihen.* An auxiliary bishop was one who did not administer a
diocese but blessed things, a *Weihbischof.* At certain times
houses and animals were blessed, and Beethoven had composed an overture, *Weihe des Hauses,* "The Blessing of a
House." There was also the interesting verb *eingeweiht,* to be
initiated into something such as the mysteries of a religion or a
scientific system. And there was the outstanding beer of the
Munich area originally brewed at a Benedictine monastery,
Weihenstephan, dedicated to St. Stephan.

I was fortunate in having read almost no German philosophers or theologians in English, and so I learned their ideas in

German. Moreover, since for me every German page was difficult, their writings were no more difficult than other books. In fact, apart from their love of accumulating of clauses, their style was not academic or abstract but original and forceful. Martin Heidegger had not created *Dasein*, "existence," and Karl Rahner had not discovered *Mitteilung*, "sharing": Those words were all around. Just as there was a benefit in seeing the place where history happened, so it was valuable to read theology or novels not only in the original but amid a community expressing itself in that way. Through this often concrete language—your contemporary was your "comrade-in-time"—I entered a world.

The silence of the beginner, the childish attempts to speak something in a new way—I needed a guide, a minister of help. At the Dominican priory, a brother showed me how language worked in daily life. Benno was his religious name. Baptized Hermann, he had grown up on a farm near a lake in the Black Forest. Not being the oldest who was heir to the farm, he became a butcher, then entered the Dominicans, and was now in charge of the general administration and maintenance of an enormous church. He was responsible for everything, from setting up every liturgical service to washing the vast floor space and seeing that electrical wiring problems, exacerbated by the destruction from the war, were fixed. Methodical, tireless, responsible, he had to take care of a public monument in uncertain repair that was every day a place of religious pilgrimage and prayer.

Benno spoke with a Black Forest accent but to me it was not all that different from Bavarian, and it only became unintelligible to me when he was excited. He led me into the world of the German on the streets of Munich and into his circle of friends, ranging from a retired plasterer to elderly ladies of the former Bavarian nobility. I learned about people's experiences as widows or prisoners of war. Later I was invited to privileged gatherings, on a Monday noon or a Friday evening after the day's work was done, to a special table, a *Stammtisch*. There, an assembly of Munich originals gathered to hear Benno's jokes, for he was an accomplished storyteller with a small book that contained key lines for 350 jokes. Once, an elderly gentleman turned to me and said spiritedly, "Brother Benno represents what is best in Catholicism: humor, love of life, kindliness."

In the large sacristy of St. Kajetan's, I asked Benno questions about German. I had the impression that he was not optimistic about my chances at the university and rightly so—I could not say much and what I said was mixed up. One morning I had arrived late for Mass with the excuse that my watch had "exploded," and the Sunday before I had returned from the train station mentioning how picturesque it was when the conductor "blew the train over." For a few days, I took to speaking of ordinary people's "consorts" instead of their husbands and wives, and I must have appeared deranged when I used the word for the "eye" of a needle when I meant the organ of seeing (they are not homonyms in German). What I read in the faces of the Dominicans was unnerving, a skepticism about me as a doctoral student in Germany.

Alone

There was a side to Germans I found intimidating: a quest for order and routine joined in some to a latent sadness or slight anger. At the same time, I misread people going about their daily routines because I misunderstood attitudes different from midwestern America. Everyone worked in one or another hierarchy, and there seemed to be few appeals upward or generosities downward.

I had many customs to absorb: not to put your hands in your pockets (a rude sign of taking things casually); never leave a door open; don't go out without your umbrella; don't carry any object outside a sack or a briefcase. In those first days in Germany, a new, unexpected introversion began to take hold of me. I had just spent eight years in the Dominican monastic houses of study and formation with almost a hundred friars living close to one another. Now I was alone in a foreign country, living there not as a tourist but as a resident. A tourist retains his personality, her own civilization and looks for a few weeks out into strange things from a confidently protected self. Unprotected and searching, I was neither a native nor a tourist but a foreigner needing to become a a quasi-native. Certainly not knowing the language brought a special isolation. It was difficult to deal with postal rates and impossible to respond to questions about the *Bürgerrechtsveränderung des Grundgesetzes* ("the American civil rights amendment") then being debated. For one who is alone, with whom few speak, there are minimal distractions; living in Europe for years certainly honed my faculties of observation, but it was a painful intensification. Did loneliness heighten seeing? I think so. Because I could not speak, I saw more. Silence amplified what I experienced and would remember.

My aloneness explains why I liked spy stories. It was the fiction of the times: novels by John Le Carré and the exploits of James Bond made into movies were popular in Munich (on the screen, Bond spoke German). Spies were real in Europe: One had been killed by the KGB in the center of Munich in 1962. Was I not a spy? Didn't I live alone, a foreigner, in a linguistic solitude that set me apart from the crowds of people hurrying home in the cold evenings? They didn't notice me. I had no links to them. I barely existed. I, too, was here to learn new things, to learn to think in a new way. During those years, I was not a charming or eccentric foreigner but a student behind whose muteness lay absence and ignorance. Being alone was itself a school.

If there was loneliness, there was also pleasure in my existence. I was on my own, outside of years of monastic isolation; I was beginning to live by and for myself. Who had I become by my mid-twenties and what had I not become? How many paths were not chosen and now blocked off? My own self was a mystery—the cloister had silenced some of its questions and decisions.

My education now beginning lay, however, not in repeating classroom exercises but in exploring worlds. I had no interest or need of being critical in the sense of American academia: Being critical was a bad beginning and too presumptuous a conclusion. I was too ignorant for critique and had too much to learn. In Germany, *Kritik* presumed mature historical knowledge. Later, there might be time to judge, to dismiss, but now I needed to survey fields of theology, to gauge historical periods, to learn about the art, music, and modern philosophy touching religion and church. My apprenticeship involved learning a language and learning cultural languages that had shaped ideas and societies. I was ignorant of the world and of its history. My Aristotelian education had prepared me for Dante's final vision but not for the journey to it, not for anything terrestrial or historical, and so my inner eye and spirit were awakened, drawn out into seeing the new and the old. The inner person partly decides what out of all that is heard and read would be retained. What would I keep in the spiritual cavern of memory for the future?

Generally, I did not avert to the difficulties or the benefits of my situation because I was not accustomed to think about myself. All my philosophical education had been about abstract beings and natures; the writings of mystics and spiritual directors spoke of the individual but only in the realm of prayer and meditation. In the Catholic Church the individual did not refer often to his existence. I did sense that it would not be easy to gain a doctorate in a foreign country, not easy to make friends. A subtle, probing anxiety rumbled inside me. For some time I did not escape the feeling that I was in a kind of prison. Only the bus from the train station to the airport after graduation would set me free.

Cold Streets

In November, when classes had begun, the university streets were often damp from late autumn rain or cold after light snow. By late December, the cold in Munich kept the snow on the sidewalks and in the parks, although on some days the blue sky and the white Alps were visible. At night the towers and churches above the streets, illustrations from a book of Grimm's fairy tales, looked down on me walking back to my room with its coal-burning stove.

Munich was entering its own future, a mixture of modern prosperity and history reclaimed. The birth of the Federal Republic within which lay the free state of Bavaria was a burst of restorative energy. Laboriously bombed-out palaces and churches were being reconstructed out of rubble. Searchlights permitted skilled crews in three shifts working around the clock to rebuild from old plans and photographs a state ministry or a department store. Since I could not read much of the German newspapers and current politics was the least of my interests, it did not register that a few weeks after my arrival in Munich Ludwig Erhard was chosen as chancellor. Konrad Adenauer, a Rhineland Catholic, had directed the restoration of Germany, guiding its new democracy and even establishing some degree of reconciliation and companionship with France by meetings with Charles de Gaulle. Adenauer's resignation led to Erhard, architect of the economic miracle, becoming the second head of Germany since the war. He was a professor and a practical businessman, a Bavarian Protestant. His years would bring further recovery and prosperity to Germany.

What connected all the parts of the city were the blue-and-cream streetcars conveying people where they wanted to go. The painter Wassily Kandinsky singled out as his favorite Munich impression *die blaue Trambahn,* which, he said, moved through the streets like an embodied spirit. In *Doctor Faustus,* Thomas Mann described how cold, blue electric sparks shot out from those trams. I was part of the mixed population crowding the streets and the streetcars, going to and from a long workday—apprentices from shops and factories, widows whose lives Hitler's madness had ruined, thousands of immigrant Germans from other parts of Europe, and the growing corps of foreign workers, Italians, Turks, Croats, and Portuguese. There were also 30,000 American soldiers in Munich and 70,000 more in Bavaria. Then, in summers came the first waves of American tourists. Munich was becoming again a picturesque capital, a cosmopolitan crossroads, a big city with a heart.

I don't remember owning a guide book: I learned by reading the placards on buildings stating their periods and architects. Along Munich's streets where Turks were carefully fixing stone blocks into sand, I walked past the many movie theaters, past the grandiose *Justizpalast* (its stones were black from bombing raids), where war criminals were still being tried, past people sitting in restaurants. My daily beat led north from my pension past the neo-Gothic *Rathaus* and the famous *Glockenspiel* in the central Marienplatz to St. Kajetan's church opposite the royal palaces. There, after Mass and a breakfast of rolls and honey, strong coffee, and cheese and tomatoes, I walked up the Ludwigstrasse past the palaces and ministries to the university.

By walking through Munich, by attending lectures and concerts in churches and concert halls, I grasped more or less unconsciously some characteristics of cultural epochs—Beethoven was not a contemporary of Wagner; Picasso came after Monet. Although I was interested in contemporary theology and philosophy, I absorbed forms and ideas from the recent centuries that Americans had presumed were too distant to be influential. Munich was a multilayered urban center reaching from 1160 to 1960, and its monuments and museums, churches and cafes had not suddenly come into existence but had lived through different periods. Nor did a culture usually just disappear: It underwent further metamorphoses. Regensburg still had its wall constructed on the Danube by

Marcus Aurelius and Munich had its inn visited by Mozart. Old Bavarian churches and the special religious names of the Dominicans with whom I lived led me far back to the evangelization of the Franks and Bavarians by Magnus and Pirmin or to the Ottonian dynasty of Burchhard and Theophane. I took a train to a Benedictine abbey near the Czech border to attend an ecumenical meeting. The rows of pine trees swayed by the wind or the nave of the church unlit except for candles were corridors back into cultures, into centuries of black monks in central Europe, working and praying. Silently, I was being taught about how time penetrated human life.

December moved into January. For me, the foreigner, time stood still although of course it never slowed or paused. In the center of Munich the church bells announced seasons and feast days, tossing sounds from tower to tower at the times of the Masses (one would be accompanied by Mozart, another by Palestrina). On January 6, Epiphany, children dressed like the three kings appeared on the streets. Priests blessed homes and marked the initials of the three kings' names and the date on the doorposts. This feast of gifts to Jesus also began carnival season *(Fasching),* leading to Lent. On the final festival days, "Roses Monday" and *"Fasching* Tuesday," just before Lent, there were parades. Soon one was looking forward to March's feast of St. Joseph and the weeks of strong beer brewed to dampen the austerity of Lent.

Some walls of churches and palaces in the heart of Munich still showed their past destruction. The bombings I had watched in newsreels during Saturday afternoons in movie theaters in Des Moines had left tenacious ruins. The feast of All Saints on November 1 was overshadowed by the following feast, All Souls—so many dead in two wars. Munich writers occasionally wrote poems in dialect, and I never forgot one of them composed for All Souls' Day:

The thousands and thousands of people at the Forest
    Cemetery
on All Saints' Day are in a hundred years all gone;
they themselves lie dumb in the green ground.

The blond little boy there who now sprinkles holy water
on his grandfather is long dead.

Perhaps when the sun, at some later time
hangs just as gray in heaven,
then a little boy like him will stand on the same gravestone
while above our Father in heaven is talking with his
    grandfather.

We stood much closer to 1945 than I then realized. The time
of the SS, the huge rallies, and the Gestapo was only eighteen
years earlier, although to me in my twenties it all seemed as distant as Napoleon. But of the Nazis there was little to be seen. A
postwar law prohibited any indication of key places or monuments from the Third Reich. Across the street from the building where I was studying early Christian theology was its twin
structure (now a music school) in which Hitler and Chamber-
lain had signed the Munich agreement. Nearby had been the
"Brown House," the headquarters of the Nazi Party, and further on the residence of the papal nuncio where Eugenio
Pacelli, later Pius XII, had nourished his love of German culture and papal power, passions that would tragically over-
power his religious sense. Bavaria had been a source and
headquarters of the Nazi Party. Munich was associated in the
United States with Nazism, but that state voted less for Hitler
than other parts of Germany. Already in 1923, Thomas Mann
had bemoaned that happy Munich, a center of pluralism, of
European literary and artistic spirit, a milieu of inculturated
Jewish families, was embracing Germany's false destiny symbolized by the swastika.[1]

The two world wars, however, were distant to me. My eyes
were fixed on the future even as I walked past smoke-stained

buildings, went to school with students orphaned by the war, and saw displaced persons living in dilapidated buildings at Dachau. Self-government began in 1949, and Germany had joined the North Atlantic Treaty Organization by 1955. This was uninteresting history. Sometimes when the weather was particularly gray and cold, my imagination pictured life in nearby Dachau, the first concentration camp for Hitler's political prisoners and for the clergy. Living near its mysterious threat, who would have had the courage to stand without hope against a bloody machinery of total control? Hitler seemed from a distant past, and no less so when I saw pictures of the Odeonsplatz (upon which the Dominican church opened) set up in the 1930s as the great Nazi shrine. Spotlights, swastika flags, huge pots of fire, and SS guards honored the place where Hitler had attempted to seize Bavaria in 1923 and where he was arrested and sent to prison, occupying his time by writing *Mein Kampf.*

Nonetheless, Hitler was not a magician of romantic myths but a modern populist, a genius of technology rampant in armies of planes, tanks, and submarines. His uniforms and torchlight rallies built up a collective ritual. Strange that this time of horror 17 years earlier seemed so remote to me because it involved events from the years of my boyhood. What I found in Germany and in Europe was a memory and a remnant of universal suffering and deprivation, a continent where almost everyone had known terror, hunger, and inhumanity. No one around me spoke of those years better left forgotten.

American liberation had brought Germany not colonization but democracy, not poverty but affluence. Technology brought modern comforts and vacations to people whose history had been one of class subservience. If, as I soon learned, a Bavarian nostalgia for historical traditions and festivals existed, there was also a reluctant appreciation of much that was *typisch amerikanisch.* The United States was for Europeans a land filled with hardy and clever individuals who had political independence and enterprise. Nonetheless, in terms of Catholicism and culture America was without significance, and I was here to learn what was modern and new theologically. What was modern? What had Hegel created? What had Pius IX condemned? Religion in Munich was modern but also Romanesque; theologies were many and varied. The Baroque church was embattled and marginalized long before Hitler came to power and before two world wars brought crises of secularism. Could the church survive not modernist disinterest or fascist persecution but renewal?

Universität

Famous for its philosophers and scientists, Munich's university—the official name was Ludwig-Maximilian University—was also being rebuilt. The "Uni," important in German culture after its establishment in 1826, found its popularity increasing as more and more students came south. Fountains and parks in summer, skiing trips and concerts in winter drew them to spend in Bavaria their "free semester," one they could use to attend any German university other than their own. Munich also was attracting a new, if small clientele, as after 1962 the spirit and thought of Vatican II brought foreign students to study with the theological faculty. During my first semester, there were three English-speaking students, but 18 months later there were 50, mostly Americans. The Roman schools of the religious orders rapidly lost their monopoly on doctoral education and failed to draw those seeking new theologies for a new church. The German system of higher education differed from English and American universities as well as from French, Spanish, and Italian schools. The university never reminded me of its American counterparts with their frequent exams, term papers, credits, classroom discussion, textbooks; in Schwabing, the Greenwich Village of Munich artists, I overheard in a pizzeria a student just returned from a year at the

Ludwig-Maximilian University in Munich as it appeared in 1966

University of Michigan explaining what a textbook was. *Time* magazine called German universities "the very best system of higher education—for the nineteenth century!" If there was little trace of an American university's organization or of its community, on the other hand, its traditions of research and historical understanding and heritage from Immanuel Kant to Max Planck were unexcelled. German tuition was around $40 a semester to which were added fees of a few marks for each course taken.

The entrance procedures were difficult for someone who knew only a little German. There was no personal assistance for foreign students, no information on how the university worked, and little initial contact with faculty or students. I learned how to register that first October by copying down complicated German instructions posted in the portico of the main building and by translating them back in my room with a dictionary. A most important word was *melden* and its cousin, *anmelden,* which embraced "registering," "pre-registering," "reporting," "apply-ing" and stating important steps to be taken prior to entering classes. At the beginning of each semester a *Vorlesungsverze-ichnis* appeared, a book that held the official list of professors and courses, with days and times but no descriptions. Theology, "the queen of the sciences," came first. Philosophy included other disciplines such as history, and many pages further, veteri-nary medicine was listed (thus cattle diseases were joined in a quasi-system to Egyptian archaeology). The university, like the state library, post office, or the train station, was filled with employees upon whom various forms of position bestowed identity. The students, docile, serious, and industrious, were fre-quently children from fatherless homes, impoverished by war. They just wanted to make a life for themselves in the new econ-omy. Aided by conversations with students and secretaries, I was able to register. Nonetheless, I never really grasped clearly what the educational system intended.

In each faculty there was one professor to teach courses in the various specialized areas—for instance, New Testament or liturgy within theology—with the result that the few theology professors were overworked by teaching at undergraduate and graduate levels (some were further burdened by composing and critiquing the documents being prepared for Vatican II). Courses were lectures, and the lectures in philosophy and the-ology set forth professorial ideas not infrequently drawn from the manuscript of a book soon to be published. Professors did not give much direction. They did not lead discussions, answer questions, or refer students to books and articles. A professor held the highest title and position in Germany (Ludwig Ehrhard, the chancellor of the Federal Republic was referred to first as "professor") and was highly paid and well-staffed. That staff, his *Hilfskräfte,* "helping forces," monitored a specialized library and worked with students; some were busy writing a second dissertation to qualify them as potential university teachers. Preoccupied professors, helpful enough if you could reach them, moving in haste and protected by their assistants, made rare appearances. Administration secretaries, powerful figures, were fairly inaccessible to me because of my ignorance of both the language and the educational procedure. At every corner, notices and signs gave some further set of rules—for an unlikely fire drill in a building of marble and stone, for umbrellas, for checking coats. I felt I had entered a past time, both romantic and formal, something from a novel or an operetta.

The professors, however, were models in research, representatives of the German tradition so admirable in searching out the historical context of a central idea or person, of a church or war. A student's understanding was developed by becoming acquainted with the best sources and by a thorough compilation of pertinent prior writings. The German professorial approach did not so much bolster a thesis as unfold an idea. The goal of intellectual life was not just data or logic but projects, themes, and systems. History offered varied topics, and so Platonic and Aristotelian metaphysics, the documents of popes in the past century, the artistic program for one church could hardly give the sole viewpoint on Christianity. Clearly, there were different views of Christ.

The professors knew their specializations well but also had a broad education and could discuss Aquinas, the New Testament, or Hegel. Most were open and did not insist that their ideas were unique. Even canon lawyers held a new approach by referring to the authority of Jesus, the sacramentality of the church, and society.

And so I pursued doctoral studies in a language I little knew, in philosophies I did not understand, and in a pedagogy I did not grasp. I barely passed the German exam required for foreigners to register at the university; I was helped by some odd words I had picked up from the Dominicans: *Flügel* for grand piano, *Kelch* for chalice, *Pforte* for gate. I was a new boy at school picking up words in the schoolyard. As I left for class in the gray mornings, the Dominican brother-porter sympathetically would observe: "Back to school again..." or, more seriously and very German, *"Der Kampf um die Wissenschaft geht weiter"* ("The struggle for science goes on.").

An absence of exams, broad requirements at the doctoral level, teachers at a distance, and writing a dissertation before the comprehensive examinations put the foreign student into a state of anxiety. In retrospect, I see that I never really went to graduate school, never moved to a campus, never had fellow students, never discussed anything with new teachers. No longer reading or listening in my own language, I was transported into colorful epochs with their own schools of culture and religion, was shown how intellectual life, far from being the fabrication of antiquarian curiosities or trendy jargon, was an exploration of consciousness, an archaeology of cultures.

Like many in those years, grandchildren of Vatican I but destined to be adopted and set free by Vatican II, I went to graduate school twice: once in a cloistered seminary, a second time in a modern university. How would they relate to one another? Regardless, theology was never again about scholastic axioms or obscure texts: It was about thought forms mirroring a culture, about ideas from the Bible or the early church that were always seminal, about facing changes in society and developing them in the church.

The Splendor of the Baroque

In America I had been told that Munich was "a European Milwaukee." It was not. It was also not a medieval town or a city of the 1920s. It was a city of several eras: The curved lines of facades and statues set forth the Baroque, while sober blocks of classical and romanesque architecture indicated the nineteenth century. Since I knew nothing about the past, I could not perceive the styles of Zucalli or Cuvilliés, of Gärtner or Klenze, or note the eras of Minister Montgelas or the Prince-Regent Luitpold. At first, I saw Munich simply as a European city full of curious old buildings, important to me because its church and university were fashioning Vatican II.

Walking through Munich over many months, however, taught me not to expect the Middle Ages on every corner. There was the cathedral and a few rooms of medieval castles but little more from that time. What struck the newly arrived American was the dominance of the Baroque, and like most Americans I was annoyed, even shocked, by that swirling drama of color. I said Mass daily in a great Baroque church, visited others such as St. Anna and St. Peter decorated by rococo genius, and walked past palaces whose masters had fashioned architectural history. I had been transported from American open plains and modern skyscrapers into a world of palaces, abbeys, and churches more or less celebrating the Baroque. In the Bavarian capital, that age had encompassed the music of Orlando di Lasso and the architecture and arts of the Asam and Zimmerman brothers. If those churches were not museums (of which there were more than 30 in Munich), they were, however, theological as well as liturgical spaces.

The churches had been built for hearing lengthy, prepared sermons and for listening to Masses by Mozart or Haydn (at first, the preaching sounded to me like lectures, while the singers sounded like opera). The many statues illustrated men and women active under divine impulse as here the action of God appeared in plaster and artificial marble. In the corners, kindly St. Barbara and heroic St. Sebastian looked down. The saints not only interceded but entertained; off to the side there might be a saint's skeleton dressed like a centurion or a mechanical toy of the magi visiting the crib. The ecstatic figures in adjoining chapels, the grand complex of the Triune God at the end of the sanctuary, the paintings on the ceilings— they also were giving theological lessons.

But how could one pray in these places? Munich's churches were cold in winter; a few electric heaters in the front of the nave fought bravely against the winds from the Alps rushing in through the rear doors. I was not alone in my negative impressions of the Baroque and rococo: Jakob Burckhardt had referred to Bernini's statute of Teresa of Avila in ecstasy as "the outrageous degradation of the supernatural." The shooting galleries of saints, the crowds of angelic babes, the hypostatic unions of artificial marble and real gold—what did these niches of art have to do with existentialism or biblical criticism? Nothing. I thought this was just another outmoded form of a Catholic past, unhealthy, past pieties connected to neoscholasticism, too vivid and too shallow.

During my first spring, on a Sunday evening I gained a slight understanding of that world as a cultural moment. I had gone to hear a performance of a Mozart Mass at a Eucharist in honor of Mary. The church that evening was brightly illumined, something rare in Germany of the 1960s. As the orchestra and singers completed the *Gloria,* I realized that the music, the architecture, and the Baroque liturgy (still the Roman rite from Trent to Vatican II) belonged together. Different media, similar style. The ecstasy of the saints in paintings stimulated joyful music; the lines of the fugal *Cum sancto spiritu* led the eye from angelic wing to martyr's sword and down to the cruets and thurible and on to the acolytes in their red cassocks. The liturgy and devotions of Catholicism in recent centuries joined to corresponding architecture and arts made up that Catholic ethos from 1580 to 1780. In the Mozart vocals and the twisting white and gold pillars, the reverent drama surrounding the Eucharist formed a coherent world, a world in diverse arts, a world that had been widely effective. American churches presented many imitations of the Baroque, but they were cluttered, aesthetically poor, clean but not well preserved. And, too, Catholic piety from 1830 to 1960 had often emphasized sin, suffering, guilt, and God's anger over against the happy, sensual, ecstatic, transcendent Baroque.

Painters such as Kandinsky and Oskar Kokoschka wrote of how
Baroque culture stayed alive, of how the visual arts had their
counterparts in Haydn, Mozart, Beethoven, and Schubert, of how
a mystic vein was found in Bernini and El Greco.

From where did this Baroque world come? And why? After
the shock of the Protestant Reformation and inspired by saints
such as Ignatius Loyola and Francis Xavier, Philip Neri and
Teresa of Avila, the Catholic Church underwent its own
reform. Faith destined churches to be places of the luminous
presence of God, spaces decorated to point to the festive and
triumphant church in heaven populated by holy people of all
centuries. This Catholic renewal centered on the individual
Christian, on methods of prayer, and on new services to faith
and church. Art did not just affirm what the Protestants
attacked—the Virgin, the saints, church authority, images,
sacraments, works and prayers for the dead—but gave a sacramental theater for the varied realms of Baroque life joining the
human and the divine. Passing through several stages, it
reached the rococo's even more elaborate theological art of
grace in the human personality, in mystics and martyrs.

At St. Kajetan I was plunged into the Baroque enterprise.
Because she had conceived an heir, the wife of the elector built a
huge church in the mid-seventeenth century, and to serve it she
brought to Munich the Theatine Order. Like the Jesuits and the
Capuchins, the Theatines were a major force in the Counter-
Reformation and remained so until the late eighteenth century.
St. Kajetan was modeled after their large church in Rome, San
Andrea della Valle. At St. Kajetan's, I walked out from the sacristy
to say a public or private Mass into an enormous white cave in
which there were large windows, many columns, artificial marble curtains and large statues of biblical figures, angels, and
saints. Voices and music could fill this soaring white and gold
space, but pots of flowers, candles, priests, and visitors were
somewhat lost in the grandeur of the space. In winter, the tem-
perature in the church sank, and an electrically heated cone was

placed over the cruets of water and wine to keep ice from form-
ing. I sometimes sat in a confessional from the eighteenth century, a wooden carriage bearing forgiveness, hearing confessions
with a cap on my head and an electric blanket on my lap. Sunny
days sent shafts of light down to illumine the people moving
about a theater of grace.

Not a parish but a great chapel for the royal court, the *Theatin-
erkirche,* when the Theatines could no longer care for it (by 1800
they had all but died out), passed into the care of diocesan priests
installed as royal canons. In the mid-1800s the church historian
Ignaz von Döllinger was their superior. As a boy, he had played in
his father's study while that professor at the University of
Würzburg conversed with the young philosopher Friedrich
Schelling. Living through almost all of the nineteenth century,
the younger Döllinger was a Catholic pioneer of historical
research; he criticized the exaggerations of the papacy and
refused to accept the dogma of infallibility at Vatican I. While the
reluctant archbishop of Munich was forced by Rome to excom-
municate him, the Bavarian court never removed him from his
benefices and offices. The church of the royal palace passed to
the care of the Dominicans around the time of World War II.

Not many blocks away was an earlier outpost of the Counter-
Reformation, an architectural descendent of the pioneering
church in Rome: the Gesu. The Jesuit Church of St. Michael in
Munich offered a prominent altar and a commanding pulpit
placed well into the nave of the large hall. In that setting, beneath
a large painting of the prince of angels hurling down the prince
of devils, good struggled with evil as Catholic sacraments sur-
mounted Protestant Puritanism. By 1615, only 65 years after their
foundation, there were 13,000 Jesuits in 500 houses. The Society
of Jesus largely determined how Catholics would consider God,
life, nature, and church for several centuries. Jesuit architecture
served Jesuit ministry. The choir was removed because the
Jesuits established religious life without a monastic, communal
liturgy of Lauds and Compline, and because personal private

devotions as well as sacramental faith were the goal. The interior architecture of their churches pointed to a new prominence for preaching as well as to smaller eucharistic assemblies at side altars dedicated to a recent saint.

The Baroque church is a theater of dramatic interplays of grace and personality: conversions, lives of heroic virtue, mystical experiences. Theologians in the sixteenth and seventeenth centuries argued over how divine grace touched human freedom. Their ideas directed painting and architecture where light suggested grace. Art became theology, the human and the transcendent in stone and plaster, the spiritual through sensuality. Even the churches that were Gothic and romanesque, such as St. Peter's, were, inside, Baroque. If medieval architectural lines and chapels were still discernible, in Bavaria the Baroque influence had already arrived.

The Dominicans at St. Kajetan explained something of this world to me, but I did not grasp easily its cultural and religious origins or the differences between St. Kajetan's conservative Roman Baroque and the exuberance of rococo abbey churches out in the Bavarian countryside. I learned slowly.

I could not connect the Baroque to Vatican II. I did not then understand the role of the nineteenth century in the Catholic Church, that period from 1830 to 1960, an age of restoration and condemnation, of neoscholasticism and new religious orders. For American Catholics, the nineteenth century looked at from 1962 had been a period of immigrant exuberance and clerical control, of institutional expansion but educational limits. Textbooks, devotions, and church institutions prior to 1960 in the United States offered mainly thin versions of the Baroque. The solemn High Masses and Eucharist devotions of my childhood that one imagined came out of an ancient sacrality were of the nineteenth century, the grandchildren of the Baroque. Unfortunately, it did not occur to me to read about that historical style, just as I did not, at first, learn about the background of the large buildings along the Ludwigsstrasse, from the romantic and modern periods of the nineteenth century. I had been set free from the past. Why return to it? Whatever the recent two or three centuries had been did not concern me. They had exercised their power too long. I was struggling to get beyond the recent century, beyond the courts of Pius X and Pius XII, now ending. New worlds were being born. Let the dead bury the dead.

Slowly, I would come to see the past as education, even as liberation. The Baroque was itself a powerful dynamic of Christian incarnation and sacramentality, and if the Baroque and the medieval and the patristic were past, could the modern be trusted? Could the church combine the Baroque and the modern or did it need to find something beyond both? In frescoed domes the Baroque depicted angels and saints in a heavenly life above, while the Council meeting in Rome was emphasizing the presence of God in individuals and their history, engaging a future that lay not so much above but ahead.

A Bavarian Florence

I expected to find a Germany of medieval castles, of the existentialism of the movie *Cabaret* and Kurt Weill's "Mack the Knife," of the Protestant theologies of Tillich and Bultmannn, but, instead, I found a Baroque town and a nineteenth century city. Munich had achieved a greatness in the nineteenth century under Ludwig I, the duke of Bavaria created king by Napoleon. That scion of the durable Wittelsbach family that ruled almost seven centuries served with Napoleon and then traveled through Italy collecting Renaissance paintings and classical sculpture for what he called "a Bavarian Florence." From 1826 to 1848, Munich drew scientists, philosophers, artists, and historians, and Metternich praised the city in 1837 as a showplace for the arts and sciences. The devout Ludwig had conceived his capital as a realization of renewed Catholicism, a

Catholic cultural center reflecting the classical, the medieval, the Renaissance, and the modern.

Ludwig himself was a product not just of Napoleon but also of a follower of modern ideas applied to the church, Johann Michael Sailer, professor and then bishop of Regensburg. Around 1800, when the crown prince attended the university then situated in Landshut, Sailer served as his tutor and spiritual father. An early pastoral theologian and developer of religious education, he gave the young man a sense of history, a belief in the reality of truth, and a poetic feeling for the dignity of the Catholic ethos, drawing Ludwig's attention not only to the classicism of Greece and Rome but to the Middle Ages. As king after 1825, Ludwig built a state library along a new boulevard and a home for orphans and the blind. Further down the Ludwigstrasse was the university, including the ducal Georgianum, a regional Bavarian seminary. Hellenic colonnades sheltered the arrival of the professors of romantic idealism or the new science of chemistry. Beyond, the street led to a concluding triumphal arch. On a second broad street moving west in a perpendicular line, Ludwig constructed museums in a Greek style. Thus architects representing both Graeco-Roman classicism and neomedieval styles worked next to each other on new museums, academies, and churches. To French ambassadors the king remarked, "Creative art is now to be found not in Rome but in Munich."

Ludwig I resolved also to restore the monastic life swept away by the secularization of 30 years before. The king turned to the Benedictines for they incarnated the ideal union of religion, learning, and art, restoring first the originally Carolingian monastery of Metten and then building in Munich a new abbey, St. Bonifaz, in 1835. By 1851, there were houses of 43 different religious orders, new or old in Bavaria. In the 1960s, a number of Benedictines from American abbeys had come to Munich to study, and from them I learned that St. Bonifaz had been a center of ministry to

American immigrants and contributed to the foundation of the remarkable series of abbeys in the United States.

At St. Kajetan, the royal Wittelsbachs and an Iowa boy met. The church of the royal court still had links in the 1960s to the royal family which, I was told, had graciously abdicated in 1918 and then had been generously rewarded by their Bavarian subjects. The princes and princesses owned investments, homes, and lands and had at their disposal the use of palaces such as the Nymphenburg, a Bavarian Versailles, when they reserved it in advance. The family numbered among its lineage the protector of William of Ockham in the fourteenth century and, in the eighteenth century, a ruler who neglected to hire Mozart. Occasionally in the 1960s, they attended Mass at St. Kajetan's, the former royal church. A few times a year as I was vesting for the solemn Mass to be accompanied by the choir singing the works of Orlando di Lasso, court composer in Munich, I was told that the Wittelsbachs were there. They had their own box, their loge above the sanctuary on one side, and they could enter this glassed-in balcony by a private entrance and staircase. To indicate the royal presence to the people a candle was lit. The German Dominicans acknowledged them at the beginning of the liturgy by bowing toward them, but I was reluctant to do this lest I lose my American citizenship. The electoral and royal court also had survived in the way things survive in the Catholic Church. The Legion of Mary, a pious auxiliary popular in the century before World War II, had a chapter at this former court church. Because the church had been royal, the chapter of the legion must be royal: Thus, by its ordinances, only ladies from the Bavarian nobility could be admitted as members. Since the nobility had more or less officially ended with World War I, "the noble Dames" were aging. Nonetheless, they were reluctant to change their rules for admission and faced a certain end with dignity.

Day after day I walked through two worlds, one of the Baroque and one of modernity. The Baroque had been beautiful, but what role could it play in Chicago? Bruckner's interminable developments and Mann's lengthy essays came from a modernity that had lost its contemporaneity. I was in no danger of becoming an introspective subjectivist: perhaps a romantic, a cultural enthusiast, a casualty of optimism, but not a critical relativist. In the 1950s, books, plays, and movies from a further stage of modernity presented existence as lonely, tortured, caught up in the moment, in the anxiety of betrayal and ambiguity, while in the 1960s different themes of community and history and liturgy were in the air. The renewal of the Catholic Church at Vatican II was very much a reintroduction of ideas and worship from church life in the early centuries. I learned early on that in theology, philosophy, and art the present needed the past, the many pasts creating the present. Human life, cultural life was not about memorizing things but about seeing. You lived and studied in order to meet revelations; languages, paintings, and books still held insight—and there was always more insight, more life ahead.

In the School of Music

German philosophers of the nineteenth century were enthusiastic about science and philosophy, but the climax of life they placed in religion and art. As Schelling's philosophical poetry described it, art burns in a holy of holies as an eternal and original flame in which nature and history illumine each other. Art gives insight. It leads men and women into the structure of reality, the dynamics of spirit. Art is not a pretty thing but a realization in paint or stone of the life of spirit. Philosophers compared the Absolute and its revelations in nature and art to a playwright involved with the actors in composing a play in which both the human and the divine unfolds. Art gives access to understanding. German Catholic theologians from 1920 to 1960 had been joining faith to art, commenting on the poems of Hölderlin or Rilke, and fashioning the liturgical movement of restoration and renewal. In Munich, after 1950, there were churches built in modern architectural styles, and there were churches where some Baroque or medieval remnants from the war had been retained in combination with the modern, unadorned walls around preserved gold and red and blue statues.

Art and music as much as philosophy and theology were to expand my world. When I left the Midwest for Europe I had never been in an art museum, had heard one concert by a symphony orchestra, and had attended two operas performed by a touring company of the Metropolitan Opera. Now, numerous concerts and operas were advertised in advance on kiosks with seats costing a little less or a little more than a dollar: Bach's B Minor Mass, the symphonies and concertos of Brahms and Beethoven, the operas of Verdi, Mozart, and Richard Strauss.

Munich lived amid music: from yodelers in lederhosen at the *Platzl* to a string quartet in the Cuvilliés Theater where Mozart's *Idomeneo* had been premiered. Thousands of theater and concert seats were available each evening. I attended a performance of *Tristan und Isolde* and not long afterward heard for the first time modern atonality in the violent opera *Wozzek*. Popular music on the radio station of the American armed forces with the noontime "Luncheon in München" and the afternoon "Bouncing in Bavaria."

From the Dominicans at St. Kajetan I learned something about the musical history of Munich and came into contact with composers unknown to me—Orlando di Lasso, Anton Bruckner, Max Reger, and Carl Orff. On Sundays and feast days, there were three great offerings of church music in the center of the city: At the Jesuits' St. Michael you heard Haydn, Mozart, and Schubert; at St. Kajetan the polyphony of Palestrina, Vitoria, and the Munich court composer, di Lasso; at the cathedral the range was catholic, from Schubert to Stravinsky.

I often celebrated the High Mass at St. Kajetan's, a rite unfolding amid layers of polyphony from the sixteenth and seventeenth centuries. Announced by bells and the choir's Introit, the

congregation stood as the solemn musical and liturgical production began. The celebrant, wearing vestments from the seventeenth century, faced a thousand people. The unaccompanied
choir kept unseen by a curtain sang from behind the sanctuary;
its director, the organist, and the priest were linked to each
other through mirrors. I was alone—there could be no hesitation
or mistakes—in this Latin Mass except for the altar boys who
could be budged only by addressing them in the recondite second person, informal plural of German. The choir sang a cap-
pella in a church with rich acoustics. Chords from the large
organ appeared as the Mass began and then again at the end of
the distribution of communion. Those sounds after communion
were a prelude, however, for when Mass was completed, the
organist played a great work by Bach or Max Reger.

The Bach chorales I had heard at services in the Lutheran
seminary in America were German and Protestant, but in
Munich some of them were sung during evening Masses. A
number of distinguished musical groups performed Bach
throughout the year. Each week on Sunday evening one of the
cantatas was performed at a Lutheran church. During Advent,
ensembles performed the Brandenburg Concertos and in the
days surrounding December 25 and January 1, the Christmas
oratorios. I had grown up playing the piano and so could play
an organ as long as only infrequent sounds from the pedals
were required. Sometimes on winter Sundays I took the place
of the church's organist at the evening Mass and struggled to
shift the accompaniment for the hymns from the great organ to
the pipes of the smaller, distant "people's organ." I worked at
not getting lost in the five keyboards and at avoiding the pedals.

Occasionally, I read that Anton Bruckner was the equal of
Johannes Brahms, which puzzled me since before my arrival in
Munich I had never heard of Bruckner. His symphonies were frequently performed in Munich: the silent beginnings, the repetition of emotional build-ups, the long soaring melodies, the
orchestral color of Wagner's operas. The music of the devout

Austrian organist seemed to be an aesthetic religion for the late
nineteenth century, leading its hearers into mysticism and transcendence. These symphonies, however, like German philosophical systems, were long and dense, and I liked better the
humor, the pulsing melody, and lush harmonies of Munich's
own composer Richard Strauss, son of a horn player at the opera
and son-in-law of the distinguished brewery family Pschorr.
Thus, just by living in the middle of Munich, I was introduced to
polyphony, the Vienna classics, and late Romanticism.

If great works of art are not identical with their *Zeitgeist,*
some still contain its patterns. Slowly, I came to see similar patterns at work in monastic spirituality and Romanesque painting, in a statue and a fugue, in a play or philosophy. Art, at
times, served religion; philosophy and theology were verbal
expressions of what could be seen and touched in sculpture or
opera. Couldn't you reach out and touch time and meaning on
the surface of stone?

A Medieval Temptation

I was a Thomist in a capital of idealism, a neoscholastic of
1960 in a city of Baroque churches, a midwesterner in Europe,
a student and a priest in a changing church. Had I left my past
behind? Was my Dominican education centered in Thomas
Aquinas to be a casualty of the Council in Rome?

A mixture of Aristotelian and Thomist terms and ideas had
been dominant in the Catholic Church. Three times in the
last 400 years Catholic popes and intellectuals had urged a
reexpression of Greek and medieval ways of thinking upon
the church, indeed upon the entire world, as the best expression of thought and faith. Seven centuries passed from Albert
the Great and Thomas Aquinas up to us. Undaunted by the
Renaissance or Reformation, the scholastic river flowed on,
touching Pico della Mirandola, Cardinal Cajetan, and, in

Spain, Francisco de Vitoria, who expounded human rights for the Americas. If neoscholasticism warded off moral relativism and the denial of revelation in history, nonetheless, the popes for a century after 1848, from Gregory XVI to Pius XII, discouraged dialogue with modernity or creative theology. Did not human freedom claim too much independence from God and human subjectivity claim to be the source of all religion? Dare one speak of Christ or labor unions in non-Aristotelian terms? Roman authority locked up history and reality in a machinery of laws and axioms and deluded itself into thinking that church life and parish forms of 1660 to 1960 were medieval or patristic. It pretended that monarchies would soon return, taught that vaccination was against the natural law, and insisted that all the peoples of the human race in their conceptuality and language thought the same way. Although it combated both, neoscholasticism was itself a kind of idealism or positivism, even a fundamentalism or a mathematical logic.

The Germans, however, understood that the recent neoscholastic revival from 1860 to 1960 was not the same as the writings of Aquinas and that some of his ideas had an affinity with what later times called modern. For Aquinas, too, the human subject forms life, while grace and revelation come not as psychological jolts but as a deep, interior principle of personality. Nevertheless, a gap existed between studies in medieval theology in Europe—the volumes of the Grabmann Institute at the university, the scholars in Paris, a century of research into medieval thinkers in the Low Countries—and the thin libraries in the United States, where both ignorance of foreign languages and fear of contamination with ideas kept the collections impoverished.

The library of Munich's university had been seriously damaged during bombing raids, and so space for reading and research and many of the books were inaccessible because of rebuilding. The Bavarian State Library, one whose several million volumes ranged from illuminated manuscripts to

international acquisitions, was in service, although sometimes the request for a book came back with "destroyed by
fire," which meant destroyed in a bombing raid. Although for
most of my work the seminar-libraries of the university were
adequate, sometimes I came to the state library. Its collection
of reference works, old and new, was a teacher because the
countless volumes of lexicons held articles summarizing historical research on topics ranging from the Muratorian frag-
ment to the bishop's crozier.

The windows of the reading room looked out onto courtyards of government buildings. One late afternoon in December, I was browsing through the area that held the current
issues of close to a thousand periodicals. In the section on
philosophy and theology, I came across *The Thomist,* a journal published by the Dominicans in Washington, D.C. While
at times it offered more than a reconsideration of Aristotle's
or Aquinas's metaphysics, generally it stayed with an analysis
usually written by a Dominican of some minute neoscholastic issue. This periodical was always found in Dominican
houses—not many Catholic journals in the United States
existed before 1965, and the Jesuits' *Theological Studies* was
viewed as quite liberal—although its metaphysical articles
were rarely read. The journal's familiarity seemed foreign
here in this European library, but how simple and easy were
its offerings: English, Aristotelian, logical, confined, and to
me at sea in so many unknown worlds it held out a certain
safety. Had it appeared on this evening to suggest to me to
return, to give up? What a relief it would be to stay with the
mode of thought I had learned over the years. Why not
quickly write up a dissertation treating a problem whose
answer I already knew? Why step out into the flood of history, which had already swept away meatless Fridays and
clerical clothes? I should give up becoming something different, ignore new movements, and return to where the pieces
of the intellectual puzzles were few, all on the board, and in

place. How enjoyable Germany would be if I just became a
tourist for a while and then went back to America happy to
preserve the one, lengthy education I had already been
given. That temptation took on strength as I walked out into
the night to St. Kajetan for dinner, late and alone. But I had
gone too far: I had seen in Europe, and even in the United
States, a little of different ways of thinking and believing; had
glimpsed brighter vistas filled with people nourished by
something other than definitions and rules; and sensed that
the seminary and parish of the past were tedious and destined for decline. An Ecumenical Council was taking place.
Everything would change, and nothing could change back to
how it had been before. The only way for me lay ahead: three
or more years, an eternity.

Im Lokal

After eight years of eating in a midwestern monastic refectory whatever was placed before me, I moved into the world of
German cooking. The German Dominicans had limited
resources, and the evening meal of bread, cheese, rice, and
apples could be sparse, but there were more than enough meals
of pork, dumplings (the excellent and omnipresent *Knödel*),
creamed vegetables, and salad laden with cabbage and radishes.
Unlike most Bavarian religious houses, sparkling mineral water
and not beer was the daily beverage, but we did have beer for
the simple meals on the evenings before Sundays and feast days
and for times when the cook was absent. On Sundays and
important feasts we had wine at the midday meal; afterward, in
the recreation room, there was some cake of fruit and chocolate soaked in rum, strong coffee, and sometimes brandy. This
was different from Iowa, where every citizen's consumption of
wine and liquor was still being rationed by the state, and from

the Dominican seminary where for eight years beer was rare and other drinks nonexistent.

Munich was filled with restaurants: In the countless *Gastätten* a meal could be had for under a dollar. In the winter, a large or small *Stube* or *Klause* welcomed you with warmth and cigarette smoke and the smell of roasted pork; you opened the door and walked in through a small antechamber formed by heavy drapes keeping out the cold. Numerous *Konditoreien* showed their creations of chocolate and marzipan in the windows.

Cities have smells: In the center of Munich there was the smell of grease from sausages frying and of coal smoke from small and large ovens; there was the smell of the street, of coffee, of rolls and breads. The smells flowed into a mix that was at first strange and then comforting. There were neighborhood or traditional reasons for choosing this or that place—your *Lokal*—for your snack of *Wurst* and *Brezen,* sausage and a large pretzel with mustard and dark beer. Often the choice was made on the basis of the brewery whose beers were served there. One favorite was *Zum Spöckmeier* at the "Corner of the Roses" in whose entrance was hung a marble plaque listing the owners since the late 1400s. The tables were of dark wood with red and white checked tablecloths, and during the evening, perhaps to accompany a dessert of the Emperor's Pudding, a zitherist played at least once the song from the movie *The Third Man.*

A spirituality of beer was not unrelated to thinking about faith and church. The breweries had been begun by the religious orders: The Benedictines at Andechs were still at work, teaching and brewing, while the Paulinians were long extinct. Above a restaurant's stairs, Baroque statues of saints blessed the patrons. This was a Catholic sacramentality of food, drink, and friends and also of humor and of enjoying God's gift of life. Along with the saints, the seasons, and the feast days, eating and drinking also marked time. History could not be halted, but it could be enjoyed and slowed down (then, too, you could get lost in amber and dark beers, pretending that time had not moved on bringing new challenges). The restaurants and beer halls were filled with people's lives, breathing an air of rest, of conviviality.

●

The windows of the university bookstores displayed more and more magazines and books reporting on what was happening in Rome: changes in church forms, theological views of being human joined to being Christian, an unexpected openness to other religions, a sympathy with society's suffering and hope. A flood of theological books, popular or scholarly, poured forth. There was always more to read.

The days passed. Themes of theology, architectural styles, tunes from churches or concert halls, philosophical worldviews—these were the musical voices of a fugue, separate and yet echoing each other in my life. They sang above the somber sustained baseline of work, lack of money, uncertainty, and loneliness. The music of time sped along into a future uncertain but real. My optimistic expectations clashing with my anxieties composed their own modern pieces whose tonalities searched for a resolution. Something sustained me and kept me in that world, alien and wonderful. In the winter nights, as snow began to fall, I headed back to my room from a class or the library or from some concert where a theme from Bach or Richard Strauss had been planted in my ears and mind. In the winding streets, my spirit was led outward and upward, beyond the towers and gabled roofs, toward some better future, some living ideal, some friendly force.

---

1. Thomas Mann cited in Jürgen Kolbe, *Heller Zauber: Thomas Mann in München* (Berlin: Siedler, 1987), p. 409.

CHAPTER FIVE

● ● ● ● ● ● ● ● ● ●

Journey toward Summer

The university's winter semester covered the months from November to March, and so in March 1964 my first semester in Munich was ending. I was intent on ecumenism. Ecumenism was new; it was openness; it was churches listening and talking. The Council in Rome was busy composing the first Roman Catholic document accepting ecumenism. So I went on a theological journey through the world of northern Europe to learn about Christians and churches in dialogue.

An Ecumenical Journey

On Passion Sunday, I took an early train to Switzerland, leaving behind Bavaria with its rain and cold. With little money and quite dependent upon the hospitality of church institutions, particularly Dominican houses, I reached Zurich that afternoon; it, too, was enclosed in a mix of fog now intermittently turning to light snow. I did not know then about the city's connections with Richard Wagner and Thomas Mann, but through the pioneering work of Victor White, an English Dominican who wrote on C. G. Jung and religion, I knew that Jung's center was in the Swiss city. The thrill of touching ancient stones swelled up in me again and drew me from one Romanesque church to another. At the cathedral there was a sign stating that Charlemagne had stayed nearby, but the interior was bare and the Gothic windows empty of color, unadorned space for the austere theology and worship of Zwingli.

My journey that March and April would take me to Switzerland, France, England, Belgium, northern Germany, and Denmark. It was a journey around Europe to learn about theologians and theological centers, a journey to new ideas, into change tangible in meetings and people. After Zurich, I visited the Ecumenical Institute of the World Council of Churches at Bossey, outside of Geneva, up along Lac Léman. Then I took the train to Lyons to see what an ecumenical center, the Centre S. Irénée, looked like. I spent Holy Week at the Dominican priory designed by Le Corbusier outside of Lyons, visited the Protestant monastery of Taizé, and made a retreat at Citeaux. After a visit to Oxford, I attended an ecumenical meeting at the Belgian Benedictine center of Chevetogne and traveled on by train and boat to Copenhagen to visit Kristen Skydsgaard. Then, with a new semester about to begin in Munich, I took an overnight train south and back to Bavaria.

A kind of theological pilgrim seeking the future, looking to glimpse new worlds sprung from the fire of a modern Pentecost, I sought Pope John's "bringing up to date" in priest-workers and catechists, in teachers and scholars. The long trip introduced me also to a deep and sometimes painful solitude, but traveling and solitude can bring insight and a longing to share later what is being experienced.

Travel meant not only being alone but being poor. We students in Europe in the conciliar years had little beyond the money we received from our diocese or religious order for tuition and austere living arrangements. Were there enough francs or marks to afford a beer or a coffee after a lecture on a gloomy winter afternoon? Our standard of living in Europe was different from that of a bishop or provincial who visited his student at a European university because he tended to stay in an Americanized hotel and frequent expensive restaurants. One provincial took a cab from a Paris railroad station to Nijmegen in the Netherlands rather than face the uncertainty and trouble of changing train stations. Even if financially limited, we thought ourselves fortunate to be studying theology in Europe, to be on our own, to be learning early on the ideas changing the church and the world. Just as some of the million Americans in the military were said to live "on the economy" in Europe, so I lived on the economy of European monastic life, and for the foreigner in the cloister there were no alternatives to the evenings of lukewarm lentil soup, salad, and bread, of silence and cold.

Bossey, a small town near Geneva, was the site of the intellectual center of the World Council of Churches. A villa with recent modern additions, it had a multilingual library whose books in many languages were resources for some work on my dissertation on Paul Tillich. (A year or so later I would return for an ecumenical conference where the participants would spend the June evenings in theological discussions, eating strawberries and drinking local white wine in a restaurant's rose garden.) I started up again the journal begun in Rome. It notes that in 1964, at Bossey, I met Lutheran missionaries at work in Brazil who found Catholicism there quite pagan and listened to a Dutch Catholic bishop arguing for the presence of grace and the real presence in the Protestant liturgies of the Lord's Supper. I noted that in European countries Protestantism had only one major form, and so ecumenism was easier but more tense. I also jotted down what I then characterized as a "creative idea." An American theology school or seminary might educate "nonseminarians" in theology and ecumenism.

Someone on the staff at Bossey overheard me speaking my high school French—it was no worse than my new German— and asked if I would celebrate Mass that Sunday, Palm Sunday, in one of the parishes nearby. That would save the parish priest a trip to one of his mission-parishes. I was happy to do it. The Mass was still in Latin—but would I be able to read the epistle and gospel in French? Sure. That morning, Holy Week began, and someone came to pick me up. When I arrived in the sacristy and looked at the missal a chill of panic was added to the cold of the church. For Palm Sunday, of course, the gospel was the entire narrative of Christ's passion. At the Mass, I foolishly embarked upon that long biblical narrative in French (there were no lay readers yet). My reading plowed through odd forms of verbs. Adults look baffled, children laughed, as on and on my mispronounced narrative careened. A certain silence existed in the car ride back to Bossey; some had not been amused.

More than Germany with its scholarship, France brought me into contact with creative ideas and practical applications. I took a train to Lyons where the French Dominicans had founded an early ecumenical center named after the patron of the city, Saint Irenaeus. The Centre Saint Irénée was directed by a pioneer of ecumenical contacts, Réné Beaupère. He organized groups to discuss the Bible and informal meetings of Protestants and Catholics who presented their ideas of church and faith. This did not dilute their Calvinist or Catholic traditions but strengthened them, and soon Christians found more and more in common. Ecumenism among the laity—that was a new idea for an American. The friars welcomed me in their detached Gallic way, curious but satisfied that finally an American had arrived in their midst to learn about theology and the renewal of the church. While I could speak some French, confused by the rapid outpouring of unpronounced letters I could understand almost nothing. I could say that I was from the Chicago area and was studying in Munich, but they had to repeat their questions. Eventually, they grew tired of this situation where I appeared to be hard of hearing or rather dense. I was suffering from a block. My brain had shut out other languages. There was one section for English and a second for all other languages. German, which I knew poorly, was the only other language that now came out.

I first had access to the French Dominicans in college through books with dramatic pictures and literary texts published to attract vocations. Paul Claudel's poetry or Henri Lacordaire's thoughts on preaching were opposite pictures of Dominicans in woolen habits playing volleyball or two friars holding tall candlesticks heading a Compline procession in a vast Gothic church. Dominican life in the French-speaking world combined the maximum in medieval romanticism with the latest overtures in ministry and theology (both aspects were missing in the United States). The Order in France had a long history. The priory of Saint Jacques in Paris lasted from the 1240s to the French Revolution and was reestablished in the 1840s on a second site. Evidently Dominican life could be marked by an intense *engagement* with the currents of the times and not just by a flight into timeless logic, for the French were priests working in factories, scholars producing a modern translation of the Bible, and editors of popular editions of Thomas Aquinas. They published beautifully illustrated magazines for parishes, composed studies on Alexandria at the time of Origen, and interpreted Rouault or Picasso.

The membership of the Dominican Province in Paris was extraordinary: Yves Congar (pioneer of ecumenism), M.-D. Chenu (the authority on the medieval context of Aquinas's *Summa theologiae*), Pierre Benoît (biblical scholar), M. E. Boismard (expert on the Gospel of John), Roland De Vaux (one of the leading experts on the biblical history of Israel and the man to whom the Dead Sea Scrolls were first brought), Marie Alain Couturier (pioneer of the dialogue between liturgy and modern art), P. R. Régamey (early writer on peace), Georges Anawati (an Egyptian convert and expert on medieval Islamic science), Raymond Bruckberger (author of the libretto for Poulenc's opera *Dialogues of the Carmelites*), and others. Unfortunately, American Dominicans avoided contact with these important figures. Why? In the eyes of the Vatican, the French Dominicans were irresponsible troublemakers, and their activities had been justifiably curtailed. Surprisingly, out of nowhere an article with pictures of Dominicans, "Adventures of the Freewheeling Priests," had appeared in 1956 in *The Saturday Evening Post,* and in 1961 a book titled *Voices of France,* describing the vitality of the French church, was published in the United States. For American Catholics, however, modern art in churches, dialogue with Protestants, new liturgical music, participation by people in the Mass were inconceivable. My American Dominican teachers and superiors knew little of the French church except for A.-G. Sertillanges's book on the intellectual life published in English in the 1940s or M. J. Lagrange's struggles to found the École Biblique amid Roman condemnations decades earlier. Yet the writings of Thomas Merton and journals such as *Commonweal, Cross Currents,* and *Jubilee* presented French ideas and approaches.

I don't believe I had read anything of Yves Congar until around 1960 when Vatican II was announced and ecumenism reached Iowa. At 26, Congar saw his vocation to renew the Roman Catholic Church by research in theological history on the limits and dynamics of church institutions. Through that history, he would renew the Catholic Church and work for unity among all Christian churches. A half dozen years later, in 1937, the French Dominican had published a theological program for the church. It included acceptance of the mutability of ecclesial forms, the pursuit of church unity and renewal, and deeper views of papacy and tradition. History was not an enemy of the church. It ran through the narratives of the Hebrew and Christian scriptures and bestowed on the church forms past and present so that the church would be both the same and different for various ages and cultures.

Was not the reduction of faith to laws and abstractions a neurosis and Rome's hostility to anything new a scandal? Congar had to be content with small beginnings gained through hard work; his efforts as ecumenist and ecclesiologist developed through encounters with small groups. Even the years he spent in German camps during World War II made their contribution: He learned German well and met Protestant pastors. Through his teaching and scholarly research into the institutions of the church in the Middle Ages, the Roman Catholic world came to alter its view of tradition from being a collection of papal and patristic texts to existing as the church's collective person, living and diverse, past and present. History became a treasure and an inspiration, and contacts with Eastern Orthodoxy and intimations of lay ministry a reality. The future toward which Congar walked in the shadows of faith and hope turned out to be greater than he planned or imagined.

Lyons was rainy and cold during my days there. As in Rome, faded placards in the churches described their history, and the musty Romanesque naves into which dark blue light flowed down from the windows again transported me back through the centuries. The boy who, in 1947, had poured over illustrations in the *Book of Knowledge* walked into their medieval reality. A battle, a pope, a council held me spellbound; in a church consecrated by Pope Pascal who had come to France for the event in 1107, bearded or young faces sculpted on the old columns almost a millennium before showed a touching individuality.

Irenaeus, bishop of the Gallic church, was among the first Christian systematic theologians, and he wrote that he had learned about Christianity from a direct disciple of John the Evangelist. He had confronted Pope Victor in Rome in 190 over the pluralism in the East and the West concerning the date for the celebration of Easter. I knew then only a little of his broad theology that placed the life, death, and resurrection of Jesus Christ at the center of not only the biblical history of salvation but of all human history. Grace was not just a remedy for some long past sin of Adam and Eve, for a devastating series of violent evils. Rather, God was a God whose help and illumination centered, looking ahead or backward, on the risen Christ dispelled the darkness of sin through a process of education for all men and women.

How could Irenaeus's faith be so strong? He had become bishop when the previous bishop was martyred in a persecution. How did he become so well educated as to write a creative religious philosophy? Was he ever with the educated throng attending plays? What a surprise it would have been to those who lived sumptuously in Roman Lugdunum to have learned that Irenaeus would be widely known and remembered in many subsequent centuries. How could he argue that the slaves and poor of the eucharistic communities in this city were the center of history, insist that Jesus lived on as the center of all time for all peoples beyond the power of Rome and of Plato? Other Christians also ended up in prisons, measuring their faith in the newness of salvation history after Christ over against the cold emptiness of an amphitheater where death awaited them. Whatever they thought or prized, it was not a religious myth or a symbol. The poor and the condemned have no time for myths. Cold cells like gray weather need a hope and a faith more promising and realistic than academic theories.

I could see from the Roman ruins a nearby hill: Fourvière (the name came from the Roman *forum vetus,* "the old forum"). In recent centuries, this had been a center of French Jesuit intellectual life. The scholarship and discipline of the *pères* had prepared for Vatican II and were now assisting at its birth. Henri de Lubac, chaplain to the University of Lyons, had written in the 1950s on the inadequate theology of grace dominant in Roman Catholicism, where grace was only a transitory religious force and a man or woman was a neutral selecting agent of passing actions, good or evil. Devotions to a God locked in the Vatican or a tabernacle were expanding outward, into theologies of God present in the ministries of the church

or on a quest for justice in society. Baroque theologies of
actual grace were now being replaced by considerations of
how all people were inwardly loved by God in a changing history of salvation. From here, de Lubac had written letters to
China to the Jesuit paleontologist Pierre Teilhard de Chardin.
He composed books defending Teilhard's theory (not unlike
that of Irenaeus) of how the universal theme of evolution
touched the history of God's grace, of how Jesus brought a
sphere of love for human society, about how all leads over long
spans of time to the return of Christ. He had also known Jules
Monchanin, a diocesan priest of Lyons, and had corresponded
with him after he went to India to ponder and pursue contacts
between Christian and Hindu theologies of plurality in the
deity. India, Monchanin wrote back to France, is filled with
countless numbers of seekers of God and has received from the
Almighty an uncommon gift, an unquenchable thirst for whatever is spiritual. He established a monastery in the Indian style,
an ashram where western contemplative activity joined to the
asceticism of a Hindu Sanyassi would seek some harmony
between the Christian Trinity and the Hindu absolute. Reading
Teilhard de Chardin and Justin Martyr (a contemporary of Irenaeus), Monchanin (now called Parama Arubianandam)
reflected on how India, "the new Greece," had over time
received the seeds of God's word, the word incarnate in Jesus.
In 1950, a Benedictine monk from Brittany, Henri Le Saux
(Abhishiktananda), joined him in the ashram. Carrying this
transcultural monasticism further was the British Benedictine
Bede Griffiths who worked to convince the English-speaking
world of the depth of Indian religion and to show the Hindu
world that in Christ myth and history had met. His autobiography, *The Golden Thread*, was popular among American
Catholics in the 1950s, an existential witness to the possibility
of grace and religious experience in Asian religions. Thus, out
of Lyons, Irenaeus' perspective on the long history of human

religion maturing through Christ was finding an undreamed of length and breadth 18 centuries later.

Holy Week with Le Corbusier

In the Roman ruins, I met two German students who said that one of their hopes in visiting Lyons was to see La Tourette; a priory about 20 miles away. It has been designed by the modern architect Le Corbusier for the Dominicans, and I was headed there for Holy Week. I told them that they were welcome to come along when I went there on Wednesday, and I would ask if they could have an inside tour. For the holy days, I was joining a Dominican from my Province who was in France collecting the latest ideas on liturgy, religious education, and the theology of living among the poor. At work in Bolivia, he was already publishing books and articles in English and Spanish on the church in Latin America as it put into practice the new theology.

Each day the rain poured down on the narrow streets as the Lyonnais did their shopping for approaching Easter. After meeting my confrère at Centre Saint Irénée, we hurried to the train station. Like many American expatriots I met in that first year in Europe, he was slow to accept the idea that the church in the United States was changing, that it even could change. How could the ecclesiastical monolith so fixed in the authoritarianism and theological vacuousness that he had known during his seminary studies in the late 1950s accept anything new? Some missionaries who left America in those years stayed in foreign and demanding apostolates because of the rigidity and emptiness of the church in their homeland. For expatriate Americans and for Europeans, the church in the United States had a negative image. Why was American Catholicism so backward? Why were American bishops so empty of ideas? Why was the church so indifferent to liturgy?

The Dominican priory at La Tourette, France, designed by Le Corbusier

In France and Germany, bishops were educated and pastors subscribed to the best theological journals; the society and university respected church and theology and knew something of its history and its struggles.

Together with the Germans we set off on a commuter train for Holy Week, Holy Thursday to Easter, within the walls of avant-garde architecture. La Tourette, completed less than five years before in 1959, was a gathering of forms similar to Le Corbusier's mystical chapel of Ronchamps set also on a hill among plains and woods. As we walked up the road toward the priory, we saw ahead heavy cement walls soaring in a white lightness. Inside and out, along the walls of prestressed concrete ran red, blue, and green painted containers for water, electricity, and gas. In the large library, refectory, and common room, windows looked onto the countryside. Each friar had a small room, with a balcony, while a promenade on the roof surrounded by a low wall directed one's gaze into the sky. The variety of curved shapes spoke of the transcendent, while the concrete blocks in primary colors spoke of modernity. Austerity and mysticism, symmetry and subjectivity—the building was searching out, expressing its moment in history.

We had come there to see the presence of the old and the arrival of the new. In a showcase of ultramodern architecture, Holy Week would be celebrated in a liturgy that was mainly medieval but incipiently contemporary. The rites came from the 1250s, but they were complemented a little by the French vitalization of liturgy from the 1950s. Seventy young men were living here, studying for the priesthood. Dominicans at the liturgy wear white robes and black cloaks from the thirteenth century. I had not brought my cloak, my *cappa,* with me and was loaned the last remaining one in the priory. It had an antique cut, and I looked like a diminutive figure from a Renaissance fresco.

The Holy Week liturgies combining Latin Gregorian chant with some new antiphonal singing were well done; they had a drama and a depth not present in the rushed efforts of the American church, where from Trent until the late 1950s the great paschal liturgies had been done early in the morning with only a dozen parishioners attending in the dark unintelligible words and rites. Composing popular, religious musical phrases, the Jesuit Joseph Gelineau was revitalizing antiphonal song, the singing of refrains by the congregation after solo verses, or by one side singing alternately with the other side of the choir (its beginnings lay a millennium and a half before with St. Ambrose in Milan). I felt after experiencing French reading and contemporary music that God could enter the lives of individuals through the liturgy, and they could respond. One moving piece repeated a line from a psalm, *"Car éternel est son amour,"* "For his love is everlasting." It was the first time I had heard any church music that resembled the musical world of this century. Singing and praying even in a foreign language such as French were more personal and emotional than anything in Latin. Gelineau psalms, a little French in the liturgy, preaching on biblical rather than neoscholastic themes (the drama of *foi, Chrétiens engagés, histoire du salut*) told me that this vast concrete ship, this house

and church whose architecture pointed upward and ahead, on a
hill near Lyons, was moving away from the Council of Trent.

La Tourette was impressive in many ways—it was also cold. I
slept at night in my sweater beneath my Dominican tunic, and
my pillow rested on the radiator, but in vain. Meals of decreasing
substance and liturgies of increasing length carried us through
Holy Thursday, Good Friday, and Holy Saturday. On Saturday, in
anticipation of celebrating the Easter Vigil and its theology of
baptism, I searched for a shower, but those I found had little
water, and as I walked up from floor to floor the water was pro-
gressively colder. Then came Easter with its feast of French cuisine: At noon, I ate great amounts of soup, bread, and cold ham,
not realizing that five more courses were to follow.

From Taizé to Citeaux, and an Ecumenical Meeting in Belgium

On Easter Monday, we two American Dominicans left Le
Corbusier's La Tourette for Taizé to see the famous center of
Protestant monasticism and ecumenism, only a few years old
but much beloved by European youth and by Paul VI. To this
place of European pilgrimage crowds of people came to attend
lectures, sermons, and the monastic services in a large, partly
open, modern hall. During those Easter days, a thousand people were at morning or evening prayer, attending a monastic
office uniting Protestant texts, Catholic forms, and new music.
My journal noted, "I have passed into another time zone with
Protestant monks playing host to Catholics, chalices given by
the pope to Reformed theologians, crowds of young people...but also a lack of experience in monasticism." I listened to
discussions about Dominican nuns and Lutheran deaconesses,
mysticism and Calvinism, and about the office of Protestant
bishops. A mile or so away from Taizé, I saw a few stones left
from the twelfth century, the ruins of Cluny where in the

twelfth century the center of a vast monastic and economic empire had flourished. Beige blocks set in the midst of early spring flowers sketched the huge dimensions of the abbey and its church, but they gave little indication of what had been an enormous abbatial church, from which flowed out to Europe first monastic reform and then monastic empire.

After only two days at Taizé, however, a Dutch *frère* in charge of guests told me impatiently that I had to leave at once, within the hour. My bed was needed: A large group was arriving. I was directed to the local railroad station near Cluny, where I could find a train to take me to the north of Burgundy where I was headed. As if to atone for his abruptness, he mentioned that there were two other Americans who also had to vacate their rooms; they were eating lunch now—and they had a car. I went to the guest refectory and met two friendly Methodists, Wayne and Tim.

The two American were Texans. I had never been in the South and had never talked with southern Protestants. In fact, I had hardly ever spoken to Methodists, although Iowa had been very much under their aegis. Wayne was a young university pastor, and Tim was a student. With a VW bug they had embarked upon the European tour typical of Americans in the 1960s. Staying in youth hostels and eating little, they had driven from Germany to Greece and back to Western Europe. If they were the first southern Protestants I had met, I was the first Catholic priest with whom they had spoken. In a new ecumenical atmosphere, we talked about our lives as well as the forms and curiosities of our churches. They asked me about the intricacy and eccentricity of Catholicism in different countries of Europe and about Greek Orthodoxy. I knew something of Cluny's empire and Citeaux's reform (there had been reforms before the Reformation), as well as the monastic side of Protestant Taizé. In my journal I copied down some ideas they mentioned: "Their views on Taizé, on its inexperience and monastic enthusiasm were like mine.

But they were also bothered by the lack of church work by the monastic brothers. Methodism is at a crossroads, they said, because the frontier is gone, and because it can too easily be identified with the American lifestyle. All Protestant churches in America have been formed by Methodism." They were headed north to Paris, and I was headed north also: to Citeaux, the original monastery of the Cistercians, the Trappists, the monastery of Bernard of Clairvaux. I wanted to see the birthplace of the Trappists and to walk around the monastery that was the geographical source of Thomas Merton's spirituality, and the medieval parent of Iowa's New Melleray. They offered at once a lift to Citeaux, which led to an unusual 24 hours, and to a new kind of ecumenism—the ecumenism of the vineyards.

We headed down the road—the luxuries of being in a car, of controlling your destiny for a few hours, of speaking English—and soon turned onto a main highway. After a few miles, there was a prominent sign proclaiming this road to be "the royal route of the vines." We were in Burgundy's "gold coast," moving through its wine regions, and signs appeared offering wine tastings for about a dime. Town after town, domain after domain begged us to stop and sample the Burgundies of the late 1950s and early 1960s. Fortunately, my companions were not inhibited by Methodist extrabiblical customs, that is by Protestant *adiaphora* (a serious Lutheran word I had picked up at Wartburg meaning things of secondary religious import). We pulled over to a small medieval tower for a few vintages and then stopped at a second. This introductory, and, as it would prove, preliminary *dégustation* escalated after we entered Beaune, the commercial capital of Burgundian wines. In the city's *caves,* custodians ladled out from large casks flowing red gold for our sampling; our entrance ticket costing less than half a dollar included all the *crus* we could sample. An aged attendant explained what we held in our glasses and urged us, whose tongues had seldom tasted more than Coke and American beer, to compare the various reds, wines already "unavailable in New York." Even the magnificent medieval hospital had its *cave*.

We emerged from the dark cellars onto the streets of Beaune as the April twilight began. The day was coming to an end, far from Paris; we had not even reached monastic Citeaux only about 50 miles from Cluny. We decided to stay in Beaune. For some time, my Methodist companions had slept only in youth hostels, more or less clean, unheated dormitories along the road from Athens to Lyons, and I had been living in various monastic institutions with cold rooms and colder water. We decided to stay one night in a hotel, a cheap hotel, but a hotel, nonetheless, whose beds would have mattresses and whose faucets would have hot water. Then, for the first time in weeks, we would go to a restaurant, have a steak and, perhaps, even sample some more great wines. We found a hotel a little away from the center of Beaune, agreed that we could afford the three dollars it would cost each of us, and checked in. The young son of the owner, who served as porter, was intrigued by the new arrivals, three Americans. He showed us to our room, demonstrated that there was indeed hot water, but then he stayed around, asking questions and doing a good job of deciphering our French. He asked each of us what we did and summed up the results: "Methodist Pastor, Dominican priest, and a student." He added: "Perfect—if only the student is a Communist!"

The next day, the sons of the Reformation, filled with the desire to see more monasticism, drove me through the flat, brown fields edged with streams and sparse woods to Citeaux. In 1111, young Bernard of Clairvaux and his companions had ridden out from Dijon to enter Citeaux and fashion the strict Cistercian reform of the Benedictine rule. The Cistercians' descendants were the strict and vital Trappists. I found Citeaux to be a group of nondescript buildings from a 150 years ago with a few ruined cloisters from the twelfth and thirteenth centuries.

Later, I watched my ecumenical companions drive down the road leading north to the main highway and to Paris. When one is young, the idea never breaks through that departures bring irrevocable separation. I would never see them again, but my memory kept a flood of impressions of the hope and excitement that came with discovery and friendship over 24 hours. They and I were a kind of personalization of changing Christianity in America—but I had forgotten to record their last names in my journal.

I spent a week at Citeaux. The sun came out as I read in the ruins of the medieval cloister St. Bernard's sermons and Jean Daniélou's books on early Christianity. Coincidentally, Jacques Loew, a founder of the priest-worker movement, was there making a retreat with some of his co-workers from the docks of Marseilles, and I joined this well-known Dominican for Mass after the predawn office.

At La Tourette, a French Dominican had told me of an ecumenical meeting and said he would arrange for me to attend it. When it was time to leave Citeaux, I caught a ride to the railroad station with an American Trappist abbot, changed trains in Paris and Brussels, and found my way to the Benedictine monastery of Chevetogne in Belgium. Chevetogne had been founded by the Benedictine Lambert Beauduin in 1939 as a further house of the monastery of Amay, which itself was begun only in 1925. Chevetogne was a center of liturgical renewal and a pioneer in ecumenism, and that conjunction of liturgy and ecumenism furthered the community's mission of dialogue with the churches of Eastern Christianity. The journal *Irenikon* was well known for articles on Eastern theologies of the sacraments, on bishops existing in a college, and on the Russian understanding of communion, *sobernost.* I did not know that this community had also been influential in starting *Lumen Vitae,* the institute of pastoral liturgy in Brussels where more and more Americans were studying. Beauduin, who had died a few years earlier at 81, conceived of the Benedictines mediating between East and West and in this he had been encouraged by Pius XI. His theological opinions, however, because they had richer sources than the neomedieval philosophies of seminaries, and his concrete plans for church life, because they advocated more than a silent, passive parish, were controversial. He had written to a Belgian bishop in 1957: "The power of the pope becomes more and more absolute, personal, centralizing. It is uncontrolled, to the point that the episcopacy is effaced and reduced to the role of pontifical civil servants. The laity are fully neglected and ignored. Such a state of affairs is absolutely contrary to the power established by Christ....The church has her faults, her history, but there should always remain the ideal." In the 1930s Beauduin was silenced, exiled from the very monastery he had founded. Before his death, however, he was rehabilitated by John XXIII and asked to prepare for Vatican II, an assembly he would not live to see. His co-worker for decades was our host, Olivier Rousseau, who explained to us how Beauduin had anticipated the great themes unfolding in the autumns of the 1960s in Rome: liturgy, ecumenism, ecclesiology.

The April days passed suspended between winter and spring in a gray mist. The woods around the monastic buildings, unfortunately not medieval but built according to this century's imagination of the Middle Ages, were brown. The monastery was cold and I slept close to a portable electric heater. The ecumenical meeting had been called by two groups, ILAFOR and CCQOE (I never understood the acronyms), and consisted mainly of Catholics and Anglicans with some Orthodox and Old Catholics. The latter included Donald Allchin of Oxford University; Dom R. Petitpierre, abbot of Nashdom ("If we, the monastery, that is, entered into communion with Rome tomorrow, we would need to change only one word in the liturgy. Which, do you think? The name of the local bishop!"); Roger Greenacre, chaplain of St. George parish in Paris; and W. H. Dunphy from Margaret Hall School, Versailles, Kentucky, chairman of the Ecumenical Committee of the American Church Union. There were two orthodox scholars from France, three Old Catholics, one Lutheran, and one Reformed. Among the Catholics were the great historian Roger Aubert, the important Jesuit theologian Georges Dejaifve, a Dominican ecclesiologist who was the protégé of Congar, Bernard Dupuy, and Frans Thijssen, a Dutch pioneer of ecumenism and founder of the Catholic Ecumenical Council in Europe.

Much of the discussion was on episcopacy and papacy. To the Orthodox, biblical and patristic images were vivid and dominant, and they pictured in their minds a historical but limited Apostle Peter with a circumscribed ministry in the church. They did not employ as did liberal Protestants a priori principles to dismiss all authority and all concrete historical church forms, nor did they, as did Roman Catholics, turn ecclesial figures into ahistorical forces. Protestants and Catholics discussed whether anything succeeded the apostles, because, for the Reformation Christianity left after a century or even less a privileged time of Jesus and St. Paul and became an organization caught up in rites and offices. All agreed that the local church had again become the center of activity and reflection. I heard for the first time of the important Slavic thinkers such as Nicholas Berdaiev and of Russian émigré orthodox theologians living in Paris, and of their connections to Schelling and German philosophy. The history of Christianity in its churches even over the past 150 years was more complex than American Catholic diocesan chanceries or Protestant divinity schools imagined.

Of course, I found the European theologies of the church being discussed completely new. They began with biblical themes and forms from the early church but also took into account social and psychological life in the twentieth century. My years of reading Latin works on ecclesiology had found only one work, composed in French by a Swiss theologian, that was more than a deductive system of papal rights and a pyramid of jurisdictions—Charles Journet's original system combined the writings of mystics and recent thinkers with new and controversial issues about the universal church. America, however, knew little of the theologies the Council was pursuing—views of the church by J. A. Möhler, Romano Guardini, and Congar and the theologies of Louvain and Tübingen where ecclesiology was more than a codex of canonical and scholastic definitions. Most theology through the centuries had not seen the church as a legal institution, but as a community or a sacrament. "The age of the church"—so Otto Dibelius and others had named the twentieth century. Now, an understanding of the church revealing the potential of its life past and present was emerging to liberate people in the church to be agents of the future.

Foi *and the Avant-garde: French Catholicism*

On my trip to Lyons, La Tourette, and Chevetogne I was in search of a spirit, one whose reputation had touched gingerly the United States: the esprit of French Catholicism. Vatican II was building on the dynamic of French Catholicism after World War II. That church accepted in 1946 the need for an extensive pastoral renewal: The situation had reached a depth where France could be called a missionary country. The years after World War II were a time of excitement, intellectual creativity, and energy as an extraordinary ferment brought forth the liturgical movement, adult religious education, church music, a return to the Bible and to the Fathers of the Church, ecumenism, and dialogue with social issues. Moreover, pastoral renewal joined theology to praxis even as it drew forth a knowledge of history. Liturgy and baptismal life came from the writings of Paul or from Cyril of Jerusalem four centuries later. The approaches of French Catholicism became mentor and model to those seeking renewal and life for Western Christianity. Chenu had written as early as 1931 of the sad situation where Catholic reactionaries wanted nothing but a catechism and a seminary textbook of religious truths, little shields for resisting anything modern. "Those who enclose themselves in a scholastic Thomism hardened by generations of textbooks and manuals, and marginalized by the intrusion of a massive dose of Baroque scholasticism feel obliged to produce summary condemnations of most issues, condemnations furthered by an ignorance of the very positions being discussed. This would certainly not be the way for the disciples of Thomas Aquinas."[1] The richness of history would empower church life. Around the same time as the French theologians developed new directions in Paris, Maurice Merleau-Ponty wrote from the perspective of modern philosophy: "Since we are all hemmed in by history, it is up to us to understand that whatever truth we may have has been gotten not in spite of but through our historical inheritance. Superficially considered, our inheritance destroys all truths; considered radically it founds a new idea of truth. As long as I cling to the ideal of an absolute spectator of knowledge with no point of view, I can see my situation as nothing but a source of error. But if I have once recognized that through it I am grafted onto every action and all knowledge which can have knowledge for me, my situation is reversed to me as the point of origin of all truth."[2] History brought incarnation: If history deprived medieval thought of any claim to be uniquely important, at the same time it gave that theology a vitality as the understanding of historical origins did for theologies from every age.

Religion is not a collection of odd rituals and clothes but a free, adult participation in a mysterious presence. A new theology of God's revelation and grace rejected the previous barriers dividing independent and secular structures of the world from the realm of God's grace, lines bestowing the sacred upon the clergy and the profane upon the Christian laity. The activity of the divine appears in the commonplace and complexity of human lives. In social movements and currents of agnosticism, in films and in the novels of Mauriac and Bernanos (or Flannery O'Connor and Graham Greene), grace is not supernatural electricity available for moral jolts but intimacy with the loving Other. Moreover, for the French and German theologians of Vatican II God's personal love met individuals within the church and outside it.

The new directions in French Catholicism after 1946 were the liturgical movement, modern art in churches, historical and biblical theologies, and ecumenism East and West. By 1950, in the eyes of Rome the situation had reached a crisis and had become an intolerable challenge. The object of some notoriety was one experiment aimed at drawing the church into contact with ordinary life: the priest-workers. Some priests and nuns began to work in factories to seek out contacts with the alienated workers. Emmanuel Suhard, cardinal archbishop of Paris, had initiated after World War II a new program of evangelization for "the eldest daughter of the church." He wrote in 1946: "When I go out into the factory areas, my heart is torn apart with sorrow....A wall separates the church from the masses." The clergy, constrained in Nazi labor camps or sharing the life of the working class, looked differently at how grace addressed society, about how liturgy might change politics. By 1951, there were about a hundred priest-workers. Chenu showed how earlier religious orders had anticipated this movement and how work, the world of matter, and the tumult of daily life were not alien to the incarnation of the word in Jesus and his world. Real evangelization, he thought, does not simply expand institutional offices but brings forth a new way of thinking, of explaining religion. Were not the dramatic changes occurring in economics, politics, and church life in the twentieth century similar to those that had occurred in the thirteenth century?

But Pius XII and Cardinal Pizzardo, director of the Holy Office (formerly the "Inquisition"), were adamantly opposed to the new theology and the new pastoral practices aimed at winning back the working class to the church like the priest-worker movement. How could priests and nuns work in factories, when being a priest and a nun was tied essentially to a lifestyle whose Latin Breviary and religious habit or soutane were incompatible with the factory's assembly line, whose status excluded any kind of ordinary work. Perhaps they were motivated by the fear of Communism in Europe at the time—some priest-workers were said to be more or less in the party, for in the autumn of 1953 they took measures to stop not only the apostles of the factories, but to silence a spectrum of theologians, pastoral planners, historians, and religious educators allied with the new approaches. Pizzardo wrote to the general headquarters of the Order: "You know well the new ideas and tendencies, not only exaggerated but even erroneous, which are developing in the realms of theology, canon law and society and which find a rather large resonance in certain Orders....This deplorable state of affairs cannot help but preoccupy the Holy See when it considers that the religious orders are forces upon which the church can and must depend in a special way in its struggle against the enemies of truth."[3] There were, the letter continued, "so-called theologians" who "with brilliant phrases and generalizations" were teaching falsehood. The Vatican official commanded the master general to visit the *studia,* the seminaries of the Order in France and to search out the suspicious ideas of teachers and students. In February 1954, the master general of the Dominicans, Emmanuel Suarez, arrived at the priory on Rue Faubourg Saint-Honoré (the headquarters of the Paris province) to hold a formal meeting with the provincial and his council (Chenu was a member), the superiors of houses with priest-workers, and the director of studies for the young Dominicans at Le Saulchoir. After the prayer, *Veni Sancte Spiritus,* the master general indicated to the 20 or so men that the Vatican was accusing the Order of fostering in France a cluster of dangerous innovations; there were rumors of closing the three provinces' novitiates and seminaries (an action that would have resulted in the dismissal of over a hundred young men) and of forbidding anyone to enter the Dominicans in France (which at that time numbered 1,000 members, about an eighth of the Order).

"We must give some satisfaction to the Holy See, signs of obedience and of discipline," Suarez said, "and then after a while all this will be forgotten." Chenu, Congar, and Henri Féret had to stop teaching at the both the Saulchoir and at the Institut Catholique, and they were sent into exile, as was the director of the large, innovative publishing house, Cerf. The priest-workers were to examine their apostolate, take seriously the Roman positions, and think of becoming a larger but clerical movement. Finally, on the spot Suarez removed the provincial from office and appointed a replacement, an unprecedented action for Dominicans, all of whose superiors had been elected since its founding in the thirteenth century.

Chenu was no stranger to controversy. His book on the Dominican school of Le Saulchoir and its new style of theology, historical and yet engaged in contemporary issues, had been placed on the *Index* of forbidden books in 1942, and he had been at that time dismissed as the director of the school. An adviser when the priest-worker movement began, he was removed from the provincial council, forbidden to teach in Paris, and sent to Rouen. For him history was inescapable, central, and blessed by the incarnation of God in Jesus. What happened in a corner of Judaea lasts, undertakes new enterprises, follows a kind of law or realm of incarnation in the divine life at work in the centuries, touching each man and woman. Congar, too, knew that the Holy Office had objections against his writings on ecumenism, the laity, the vitality of tradition, and reform in the church and sought to keep from being published his ideas of the church as an organism with different points of activity and charisms. The brilliant and tireless theologian would have to leave teaching, stop publishing, and submit any writings to Roman censorship. Congar, not known for a reluctance to speak his mind, exclaimed: "This is absurd! Simply inconceivable!" But the Dominican superior general responded that the difficulties with the Vatican all had a French origin.

It was not only the activities of seminary teachers or priests in factories that Rome wanted terminated in 1954. Artists and theologians of art were disdained. Was not a church with windows or mosaics in the style of modern art as dangerous as priests attending union meetings? The Dominicans and others had even produced in the years just before 1950 an example of modern art in a liturgical setting: the church at Assy where the works of Rouault, Léger, and Chagall looked out upon the Mass. At first, the controversial issue was whether non-Christian artists (agnostics and Communists) should decorate a church, but then a more serious issue came to the fore: nonrepresentational art. Reactionary French writers and Vatican officials saw in abstract or expressionist lines and colors only distortions of simple reality, while angular, grimacing, and nonhuman figures composed not a picture but a profanation. The entrance of modern art into the church surely had to be a plot, although reactionaries disagreed over whether the plot was directed by Communists, Protestants, or Masonic Jews. The Vatican, echoing a talk by Pius XII, condemned in 1952 the use of modern art in churches. Any theology and praxis that accepted existential and cultural forms to express the gospel and tried to meet people in their actual lives threatened a church authority that lived resolutely in Baroque and medieval worlds.

The Dominicans mostly stood by their persecuted members. A year or two after his exile began, the community in Strasbourg elected Congar as prior, an office over which Rome had no direct supervision. At Rouen, Chenu was treated by the prior and brothers of the Dominican community as though he had retained the offices of which he had been stripped. He had already written his great introduction to the world and thinking of Thomas Aquinas, and he turned now to the twelfth century, keeping time to write on the issues of work and war.

The condemned theologians of the 1950s were rehabilitated by Pope John XXIII a decade later when he personally
insisted that they be enlisted to serve on the commissions
preparing for Vatican II. When Congar came to Rome to work
at Vatican II, Cardinal Ottaviani expressed such anger toward
him and his work that he wondered to himself if he would
ever be more than a disdained, dangerous outsider in the
Catholic Church. People asked why he, treated in such an
unjust and childishly demeaning way, remained within the
church during what he called the "years of patience." He
observed that if he had left the church, his theology would
have been a curiosity, and his work for renewal would have
ceased. By staying, he retained the hope that the church
would change and improve a little, that some Christians
would think in a way both new and more traditional. Congar
said of the renewal of the 1950s that, despite being marked
by authority's cruel suppression, it was the best of times.
During the years of Vatican II, Congar, once silenced in
France, became a voice to the world.

●

France was more exciting than Germany. The concrete
applications of scripture and past theologies to new pastoral
situations were to be found in many churches, schools, and
centers, in many priests, nuns, and laity at work with the
young, with artists, or with the sick and the imprisoned. In the
spring evenings on my ecumenical voyage, on the grounds of
some old monastery or in the streets of a European city after a
day of rain, I sensed time poised on the edge of the world.
Someone was watching, waiting to lead people beyond a hasty
Mass in Latin to sacrament and song celebrated by clergy and
laity together. Change was tangible. It moved through people
attached to *cadres* or *équipes,* through young priests for
whom constant activity and the excitement of being in the

avant-garde contrasted with an evangelical poverty distinguished by old gray pants and sweaters, and by coffee and cigarettes. How far all this was from the American clergy with their immutable routines, long cars, expensive black suits, and gold but tasteless cufflinks, and their networks of promotion.

My ecumenical voyage led through a church of the future. Studying theology in the 1960s meant entering into the contemporary European world. However, I remained an outsider. I felt adrift amid so many creative people, so many books and journals, so many languages. After the rains of Geneva and Lyons, the wines of Beaune, the cold of Oxford and the hospitality of Copenhagen, I returned to Munich for my second term, the summer semester beginning in May 1964. I was still a beginner.

---

1. Chenu, "Le Sens et les leçons d'une crise religieuse," in *La Vie Intellectuelle* 13 (1931), p. 380.

2. Merleau-Ponty, *Signs* (Evanston: University of Northwestern Press, 1964), p. 109.

3. François Leprieur, *Quand Rome condamne* (Paris: Cerf, 1989), p. 45.

CHAPTER SIX

• • • • • • • • • • •

Pathways

From October to March when I began my ecumenical tour, I had spoken English for only a few days. Returning to Bavaria in May, I found that my German verbs and nouns had not been asleep but had deepened their presence. My internal language school even away from Germany had stayed in session as my subconscious worked on vocabulary and grammar. As my second semester began, I could understand with some ease the lectures because they employed the same theological vocabulary from week to week. I could take part in some ordinary conversation, even if my tongue, like an untrained horse before a stream, shied away from verbs waiting to be assembled. Of course, talking to children and animals with their forms of "you"—*du* and its difficult plural, *ihr*—was beyond me.

Summer at the University of Ludwig and Maximilian

The windows of the university buildings were open. Outside, the fountains of the colonnades sprayed water, their music alluding to concerts of Haydn and Mendelssohn advertised on the nearby kiosks. Students parked their bikes and visited or read under the white-blue sky of Bavaria. The professors, nobility with their courts of *Assistenten, Hilfskräfte,* and *Doktoranten,* moved to and from seminar libraries and offices about which Hegel had observed, "Our universities and our schools are our churches."[1]

An academic storm suddenly arose, drawing me into it, or rather, a situation I had had to face earlier appeared again. My first semester at the university had brought about an intrigue that belonged in the nightmare of a foreign student. Although my interests in America had been in ecumenism and ecclesiology, my Dominican superiors had hastily decided as I left the United States that I should pursue a career in New Testament studies. Their decision meant that after the German doctorate, which in my first semester seemed so difficult, I would move on to yet more years of study in Jerusalem and, subsequently, to special exams in Rome. The professor of New Testament studies at Munich had the reputation of being unpredictable, touchy, difficult. A German Dominican just finishing a dissertation of about 1,200 pages took me aside and advised me against pursuing a doctorate with that professor: "Look around; he has no students; they never finish. If he met you in the English Garden, he would ask you what you were doing here, neglecting research for taking a walk." Through a few letters back to Chicago, I was able to convince my superiors to let me return to my real area of interest, the field that included ecumenism, ecclesiology, revelation, grace, and the history of theology, the field German academia called *Fundamentaltheologie.* Armed with a letter from my superiors and using the beginner's ineptitude in German to my advantage, I told the professor in New Testament studies—I had found him imperious toward Germans but kindly toward foreigners—that, sadly, I had to withdraw from his direction.

This shift meant that I could study with the Jesuit Karl Rahner. The increasingly famous theologian was in the process of assuming at Munich a professorship in the philosophy of religion. Eventually, he would be viewed as Catholicism's great modern systematic theologian in this century and the most influential theologian after Vatican II. His goal was to explain what was most basic in Christianity, the ways in which God's grace is active in each person and in historical periods—to explain it to people living today by interpreting Jesus' preaching of the kingdom of God through idealist, historical, and existential prisms. Nevertheless, after my successful move away from scripture to fundamental theology, I found myself, as the summer semester was beginning, in a second awkward situation. I learned from students in the seminars that I faced further difficulties in my search for a *Doktor-Vater*. Professors were then considering whether the newly arrived Rahner could direct doctoral studies in theology. His position, Romano Guardini's chair of the philosophy of religion and of Christian world-view, was not in theology but in philosophy. Evidently, some professors in theology were envious of his reputation and viewed the Jesuit as an outsider. I decided not to wait for several months to learn the outcome of this academic struggle. As it turned out, the students had surmised correctly: Rahner would not be able to direct candidates for the doctorate in theology. So in ten months the ship of my intellectual life had twice almost crashed on the reefs of German academic policy.

I found a welcome from Heinrich Fries, professor for fundamental theology, ecumenist, and theological offspring of the great Tübingen tradition. During an initial interview in which some flimsy constructions of grammar teetered and then collapsed, I expressed my desire to write a dissertation on Paul Tillich. I chose Tillich because I already knew something about him, his later writings were in English, and I could show Fries the page proofs of the collection of Catholic essays on Tillich that I had edited, along with Tillich's afterword responding to the various chapters. In the 1960s, the Germans were intrigued by Tillich but knew little of the development of his theology after his immigration to New York in 1934 to escape the consequences of his politico-religious views. Fries suggested that I might compare Tillich with Thomas Aquinas. As a Dominican, I was presumed to know Aquinas, and it was then an ecumenical trend to compare the medieval theologian with Protestants. I was never convinced of the value of that dual enterprise, and the dissertation (a compilation more than a study because I had so little knowledge of modern philosophy and theology) emerged as mainly on Tillich, with its comparisons to Aquinas never well integrated into the project. Nonetheless, Fries was warm and welcoming.

June, too, was welcoming with its sun and flowers, strawberries and the much prized asparagus. The summer semester moved brightly through weeks decorated by feast days: Ascension Thursday, Pentecost and Pentecost Monday, Corpus Christi. I had passed eight months in my pension, had learned some German, had seen something of Europe, and had survived two academic intrigues. In the mornings, fountains around the city, built in 1650 or 1850, splashed under the sun while during the long northern summer evenings, concerts of Mozart and Schubert held outdoors in palace courtyards accompanied a happier time.

American Stadtpfarrkaplan

In the summer of 1964, toward the end of my first year in Munich, I found a new place to live: a home, a position, and a job all in one. I had gone to the chancery of the Archdiocese of Munich-Freising and within an hour was assigned to a parish in the western part of the city. I became a *Stadtpfarrkaplan,* an assistant priest in a parish. The homes of the parishioners lay to the south of the railroad lines going west through Laim to Passing, and not too far north were the gardens of the Nymphenburg Palace, once the palatial summer residence of the Electors

The author in the courtyard of St. Ulrich's parish in Munich in 1966

of Bavaria. I moved out of the kind but austere care of Sister Gerwina, out of my garret room and into quarters of two rooms and a balcony looking out over the neighborhood, where people were fast asleep by 9:30 P.M. and on their way to work by 7:30 A.M. I lived in a rectory and helped in a parish, St. Ulrich in Laim. Already in the eleventh century, a village church existed there outside of medieval Munich on the road to Augsburg; the side chapel of the church was from the years around 1450 and held traces of a Gothic style from a century earlier.

The diocese gave me room and board and 100 marks (about $25) a month in exchange for saying Mass each day and helping out on Sunday. Sundays were long days with Masses in the morning and the evening as well as confessions. I would usually take the early confessions, help out with communions at other Masses, and say a morning and an evening Mass. Each weekend one priest preached at all the Masses—but the pastor and the full-time, German assistant preached two or three weekends to my one. I had to write out my sermons and have passages grammatically enhanced. Caught between a lack of much experience shared with the people sitting in front of me at Mass, and threatened by a collapse of my prepared compositions when a sentence went on too long, my sermons were surely stilted. I tried, however, to begin each one with some current event, and so my evangelical rhetoric drew for its opening lines on the sophisticated style of the morning paper, the *Süddeutsche Zeitung.*

Immediately after my arrival I heard confessions. There were many at Christmas and Easter, and some on weekends. The American Benedictine who had shown me how to apply for a parish position helped me prepare for that sacramental intersection of counseling and moral theology. I had to expand my vocabulary: "Rhythm" as birth control was *periodische sexuellen enthaltsamkeit.* Lots of sins and so lots of words to learn. Unfortunately, on the Saturday evening when I entered the confessional for the first time my second penitent was a challenge. She knelt down but hesitated, paused for quite a while, and then mentioned that this was difficult for her. I tried to guide her to what she wished to confess. Again she mentioned something that was difficult. As I was urging her to express what had brought her to seek the sacrament of penance, she fainted and fell out through the door of the confessional on to the stone floor of the church. Several parishioners, certainly shocked at this early effect of my ministry, carried her into the sacristy. *"Es geht mir schlecht,"* I had just learned, does not mean, "This is difficult for me," but rather, "I don't feel well."

In the parish house lived the pastor, titled the *Stadtpfarrer* (the "city pastor"), an assistant, the pastor's aged sister, and a housekeeper. The parish house was large and quiet. The pastor was a tall distinguished *Herr* with white-blond hair, a prominent nose, and difficulties with his eyes. He was energetic, approachable, and affable but seemed to me to be very old. Born more than 70 years earlier in the town on the Austrian boarder where "Silent Night" had been written by its parish priest, he had served in World War I, had been captured after being wounded by the British, and had spent some time in England in a hospital. That experience of the wide world unnerved him and he never again left Bavaria. He had been ordained to the diaconate by Cardinal Pacelli, then nuncio to Bavaria and later Pope Pius XII. The money given to him by friends and relatives on the Sunday after his ordination to the priesthood, he told me, because of the rate of inflation in the 1920s, just paid on the next Monday for his commemorative holy cards.

Although he loved to follow on television the incipient exploration of space, the *Stadtpfarrer* dressed in a frock coat. The administration of the parish and the rectory house mirrored an earlier time. With 10,000 parishioners, there were many weddings and funerals and no lack of people at Mass. The personal, friendly outreach of an American parish even before Vatican II or the vitality of one being altered by the Council was yet to come. A Catholic German parish was partly a branch of a ministry of the government, and the parishioners prized order and service. Paradoxically, the pastor enjoyed reading the latest theological journals. He was conversant not only with the theology of Karl Rahner but knew something of Paul Tillich, a level of theological education not to be found in the United States even among seminary professors. This was the opposite of the United States where Catholic priests read little but were more involved with people. The parish helpers, particularly a nun who was a member of a religious order founded for parish work, were open and progressive, unfailingly kind and helpful to the many parishioners. One day, while making daily rounds on her bicycle, parish sister Kunnegunde was accidentally hit by an *amerikanischer Fussball*. Two Mormon missionaries from Utah were playing catch, and the sister rode into the path of their ball and was knocked off her bike. The Latter Day Saints solicitously paid for her medical and therapeutic treatments.

Although at first the pastor was skeptical about having an American as his helper, I think he found informality and openness of some value. I was always around and had no family or other obligations to distract me. The parish house had a television set and together we often watched the news reports. Each Friday we followed unfailingly the weekly detective program that during those years was a popular series, *Auf der Flucht,* "The Fugitive." The work of the weekend concluded with Sunday dinner, which was Bavarian fare at an elegant level: a broth soup with noodles or small meatballs, pork, potatoes, and a creamed vegetable accompanied by beer, and then a cake for dessert served with a bottle of the pastor's Sauterne purchased eight years before from France.

In the parish house and in the sacristy one heard the Bavarian dialect. Everything took on a diminutive form, the imperfect tense disappeared, and the genders of nouns were not so important. So, as the months passed, while I entered more deeply into German life, my academic German found little practice. As I took the streetcar to my seminars, I had to withdraw from two linguistic worlds: my English and my apprentice Bavarian.

I never got to know many people in the parish. They seemed remote and preoccupied, and apparently an American student-priest held no interest for them. The only people I met were those who came to me because of some serious problem having to do with family life, with the problems of adolescents. They seemed to think I might be of help because I was younger.

Sometimes the pastor would ask me to bring the sacraments of the dying—confession, holy communion, and extreme unction—to former Nazis. They had been minor figures in the party, for instance, the director of public schools. The pastor had seen them force young people out of the church and send teenagers off to fronts from which they never returned. He admitted that he found it difficult to forgive them, and so I went out in the cold nights to the spartan rooms of further casualities of Hitler. As a young priest, the pastor had given talks in factories during the 1920s and 1930s. Ten or more years later, in 1944, a man came up to him amid the rubble of bombed-out Munich and said that he had heard him give a talk years before in which he had stressed that both Communists and Nazis were evil, but that a Nazi dictatorship would be worse than a Communist one because the Nazis lacked any humane motivation. "At that time, Herr Pastor, I thought you were wrong, but now I see you were right." The pastor leaned across the table toward me, fixed me with his weakening eyes, and said: *"Eine späte Einsicht,"* "a tardy insight."

Semesters passed. In my room or in the woods near the Nymphenburg, I read the volumes of Karl Rahner's *Schriften* as they kept appearing. At times, I moved away from courses on philosophical theology to other areas, taking valuable seminars on early theologies from Egypt, Ethiopia, and Syria and studying philosophy. I was well into writing my dissertation and attended mainly doctoral seminars where we listened in overheated rooms to papers read by intense doctoral candidates overwhelmed by (and now overwhelming us with) bibliographical data. I needed to make myself visible during at least one semester in each of the eight theological areas, for those professors would examine me both in writing and orally during the comprehensive exams.

Existence

In my first months in Europe I had learned a great deal of theology. Much of it involved remedial reading. For instance, I had learned how history and personality gave new meaning to traditional topics such as the role of Christ among the world religions or the teaching office of the papacy; I had learned that faith was not just an intellectual collection of religious phrases but a meeting with the Spirit of Jesus. Theology "pointed" (*Hinweis* was an important word) to the task *(Aufgabe)* of finding the real underlying sense *(Sinn)* or contemporary meaning *(Bedeutung)* of something being realized *(Verwirklicht)* in an existential *(existentiell)* way. As the summer began I was ready to learn something new. My subconscious had been taking stock of all that I did not know and of all I wanted to know. Deep in its ocean, somewhere near its center, suggestions and searches were asserting themselves, silent messengers addressing me. I had spent the first semester taking courses in the New Testament and reading the history of modern biblical exegesis from David Friedrich Strauss to Rudolf Bultmann. During the second summer semester, I turned to the other catalyst of theology—philosophy.

Philosophy lay at the heart of theology, and I was learning that philosophy was not timeless logic but was, as Hegel put it, "the spirit of the times expressed in words." My Dominican education had left me ignorant of the philosophies of the nineteenth and twentieth centuries. Holding that there was only one, timeless world-view, my neoscholastic textbooks had nothing good to say about thought after Ockham or Descartes, of groups that were *sceptici* and purveyors of "a science falsely so-called." Apart from reading Tillich, I was a novice in reflection on the human subject from Kant to Nietzsche. To study modern philosophy was to leave behind Aristotle and Aquinas, John of St. Thomas in the seventeenth century, and Reginald Garrigou-Lagrange in the early twentieth. Indeed, to study modern philosophy, and, equally important, to see it at work in art and science was to be a refugee from the church's recent mindset and to walk through foreign lands where, I had been often told, land mines of atheism and relativism might explode.

Day after day, going to the university I crossed the Schellingstrasse, a south boundary of the university area leading to the Romanesque portal of the university church. Who was

Schelling? I had barely heard of this philosopher of Munich's golden age in the 1830s who had concluded: "That which in time is most properly temporal is the future."[2] Friedrich Wilhelm Joseph Schelling, a Swabian Protestant, was a precocious developer of modern thought; his theories of psychology, science, and art applied the analyses of Kant and Fichte to the new sciences of electricity and magnetism. Contrary to what I had learned in the seminary, idealism did not assert that nothing outside the mind existed but, instead, explored the structures and activities of consciousness, human and divine, showing how cultural and intellectual forms gave us much of our world. By 1800, at the age of 25, Schelling grasped and stated the great theme of the new century: "Consciousness has a history." The self, each intellect and spirit of men and women in every age, has its own history and is part of the stories of the age, creating and changing science, art, and religion.

Schelling was also the philosopher of Romanticism—but what was that? Much more than soaring emotions or heroic figures alone in forests, Romanticism was the individual, receptive and creative, the free person endowed with intuition as well as reason, human spirit struggling with great forces. What gave mystery and power to Romanticism (Schelling's first systems appeared at the time Beethoven composed his musical system, the *Eroica* Symphony) was its conviction that it could understand the spirit of time and of every time and its conclusion that life flowed from the ages of the self, of the world, and of God. The deity itself, including us and the universe, is struggling to act out its process of self-unfolding. When the university was being established in Munich in 1826, at a session of the Bavarian king's advisors a minister exclaimed, "Schelling must come—to give the university brilliance, movement." The young king agreed and said later that he valued the recruitment of Schelling to the university "as much as a victory in battle." Schelling, for his part, congratulated German society and the Catholic Church for their interest in him.

An eyewitness described Schelling's opening lecture in the new university at Munich in November 1827. "At 6:00 P.M., on a winter evening, the crowd assembles in the chosen hall....A carriage comes, and Schelling accompanied by two of his best students enters. Ahead of him is a servant, with two lamps in his hands. He withdraws as soon as the sublime teacher has mounted the *Katheder*. The doors are closed and the lecture begins."[3] Schelling, after praising the youth of Bavaria as impressionable and receptive to his ideas, lectured on his "Christian and positive philosophy." It depicted the life of the Absolute realized in the human spirit and in world history; through tension and process, the Second Person of the Trinity pursues its odyssey, out into creation and then further into religion. Schelling lectured not only on Descartes and Kant but on the religious systems of Egypt, India, and Greece, on the divine powers active in each mythical system. God is on a journey to becoming God—this is the meaning of the Trinity. Schelling, however, failed to bring his system to a conclusion. What came at the end was, however, surprisingly religious, an ecclesiological dialectic where the Petrine church, Roman Catholicism, and the Pauline church of Protestantism find their fulfilling resolution in the Johannine church, a church of love. Was the Johannine church to be found in the churches of Eastern Orthodoxy? Nationalist thinkers in Russia and Poland, the Slavophiles, believed so and drew Schelling's thought into their messianic nationalism.

I was at work on my dissertation on Paul Tillich's theology of God, and I knew that he had written two dissertations on Schelling, one in philosophy and one in theology. A hundred fifty years before, Catholic intellectuals, too, had been inspired by Schelling's writings to work for some harmonization of theology with modern philosophy. From 1800 to 1850, Johann Sebastian Drey and Johann Adam Möhler in Tübingen, the laymen Franz von Baader and Joseph Görres in Munich, and Friedrich Schlegel and Anton Günther in Vienna

developed theological systems incorporating his pattern of
the ideal realized in the real, of the divine and spiritual in the
material, what was in fact incarnation and sacrament. Apparently, German Catholicism had a colorful history beyond the
seminary textbooks of neo-Aristotelianism. In 1965, a minor
Schelling renaissance was under way, and it was largely pursued by Catholics because Romanticism attracted them.

But contemporary, really modern philosophy—wasn't that
"existentialism"? Existentialist ideas were found in paperback collections of writings by Søren Kierkegaard, Jean-Paul
Sartre, Martin Heidegger, or Martin Buber. They were subjective, agitated, slightly depressed, momentary, ambiguous,
finite. Didn't existentialist philosophies lurk behind the
films of Jean-Luc Godard and Ingmar Bergman and behind
modern art? Existentialism had given to theologians such as
Tillich and to exegetes like Bultmann not only fashionable
terminologies but insights. Their writings, nonetheless, gave
the impression that existentialist theology was a philosophical and psychological substitute for the content of Christianity, a view of revelation as no more than human decisiveness
or a vague faith in something transcendent. Existentialist
theology resembled an abstract painting where a lonely line
or a block of color against an empty canvas was the bearer of
a slight religious meaning. And yet, Luther was said to be the
first existentialist and Karl Barth had once drawn from this
approach. Heidegger was its creator—or was that Sartre?
What was existentialism? A philosophy, a theology, a
nihilism?

A young professor was offering a course on the philosophy
of Karl Jaspers. The teacher had written popular books on existentialism but also one on liturgy, and one comparing Jesus to
Socrates. His lectures began by giving a competent introduction to existentialist philosophers with dates, books, and
themes. After sketching the differences among Sartre, Buber,
and Heidegger, he concentrated on Jaspers.

Jaspers came to philosophy through the study of psychiatry—his early books on medicine were still in print—and taught most of his life at Heidelberg. I found his book on "the three founders of philosophizing" (Plato, Augustine, and Kant) to be dry. In the *Existenzphilosophie* of 1937, which I bought in its new paperback edition, Jaspers viewed the philosophy of *Existenz* as a rediscovery of an ancient philosophical tradition. "The task of philosophy, a long forgotten task, is to uncover reality in its origins and to grasp it through the way in which I, thinking, live with myself, live in my inner activity."[4] No longer is philosophy a science; it is not a *Wissenschaft;* its status as a university area of study has become dubious, and people have lost interest in philosophy and turned to the natural sciences. "Science has taught the impossibility of finding what one had sought from philosophy in the past. Still whoever had sought in science the ground of life and the direction of activities, whoever had sought Being itself must have been disappointed. We need to find the path back to philosophy."[5] In the twentieth century, the theories of relativity and quantum mechanics, atonal music, and expressionistic theater challenge philosophy to go beyond logic and ontology, to reach beyond just knowing about things, beyond modes of speech and categories of thinking, to reach reality. "Existence is one of the words for reality. Kierkegaard had said that all that is real for me is so only through the fact that I myself am. We are not simply there but our existence is entrusted to us as a place and our body is given to us as a realization for this origin."[6] For people living in the 1930s or in the 1960s, in an age of monoformity, threatened by mass movements and mechanization, the response is not to find a better form of faceless social control or to promulgate some pathetic psychology drawn from the past. There is a real philosophy lying deeper, an interpretation of one's existence.

Jasper's philosophy was sober and clear but it did not strike me as being overwhelmingly personal. His existentialist questions "Who am I?" or "Am I happy?" seemed to me to be general and abstract. I had had years in a monastery to think about God's silent presence in my personality—medieval monasticism, too, could produce a world that was subjective and introspective. Nor did I find existentialism with its obvious roots in the history of metaphysics and psychology to be a dangerous, anchorless ideology that seduced readers into libertinism and irrationality. Jaspers introduced me to words such as *Denkform,* the way or style of a time's thinking, a thought form, a German term expressing the influential forms in science, religion, and art, a "model" or "world-view." Cultural forms brought and formed an age, and philosophy was not so much new conclusions, new data, new axioms as it was new perspectives. Time brings a succession of worlds of meaning; a stream or an apple stayed the same and yet appeared in different ways in the paintings of Botticelli or Cézanne. The spirit of the times flowed from and mirrored our own world-view.

The course at the university dealt also with Jaspers's recent book on religion and Christianity, his widely noticed *Philosophie der Offenbarung.* That philosophy of revelation, however, was intent not just on explaining but on taking over the gospel: Jaspers's process of emptying biblical history was like that pursued by liberal Protestant exegetes. He explained religious doctrine through his theory of *chiffres.* A person, a place, a thing where revelation became existentially vital might be a cipher: Cult and church were secondary. Revelation itself has become a *chiffre,* and Jesus, no longer Messiah or God-man, is one. Recognizing God is impossible but thinking about God is unavoidable. For me, Jaspers's hundreds of pages struggling to produce an austere existential faith in a contentless revelation remained empty. The reduction of Christianity to a philosophy or psychology attracted only intellectuals who had found faith's stories and sacraments untenable. If Roman Catholicism was moving into modernity, it was on a different track where the personal complemented a realist history of salvation accepted by faith.

Those ciphers were related to Tillich's symbol and Bultmann's myth, vague and mental presences of transcendence typical of contemporary interpretations of religion. Much attention was being paid to myth, which was a solution to the problem of faith and subjectivity. German thinkers understood myth in religion or fiction as an insight into life and history, an event or symbol with psychological effects, but academics could not twist the mythical into something that was real to people. Myth was a poor and inadequate word for revelation, for the impression remained that a myth never really existed. Religion about myths was pre-Christian, preincarnation, and not interesting. Better to find flesh and blood, the person and the event, the stone and the sound in religion. Catholicism for better or worse was interested in realities not words: God's grace lay behind religious things whether a dogma, a statue, or a sacrament. Catholic theologians, without setting aside the reality of church and sacrament, were also pondering anew the approach of philosophers of consciousness and history to explain how objects incarnate and serve but do not control the transcendent. Some kind of real divine presence exists as revelation, stimulates religion that is not idolatry, permits a lengthy history of world religions, and lets each person experience the divine in his or her own way. But that God was also not a generator of momentary graces or an official of church law.

I heard the German nouns and verbs used by philosophers and theologians out on the streets of Munich; it was a living language as Latin was not. German philosophical terms were applied to art and psychology. The words of theology and philosophy that British and American scholars had struggled to translate and explain were ordinary; they were found in the German newspapers, not only in book reviews but also in police reports. As the months passed, my consciousness began slowly to bypass English.

Heidegger

During the summer semester of 1964, when I booked my course on Karl Jaspers in order to learn something about philosophy after the Renaissance, I also began to study the philosophy of Martin Heidegger. He was the dominant philosophical figure of the time and of some importance for learning about theology in the twentieth century. Jaspers himself had written that "among German professors of philosophy of our time only one interested me: Heidegger. All the rest seemed to be intellectual business."[7] I knew that Tillich, Bultmann, and Rahner had been influenced by him: Bultmann and Tillich as colleagues, Rahner as student. What was original in Heidegger was human existence, a portrait of life that was metaphysical but personal, philosophical but psychological.

In a bookstore I bought Max Müller's introduction to Heidegger, and then I found out that Müller was lecturing at the university. He had been a pupil of Heidegger, and his life—I found out decades later—had been marked by the impact of Heidegger, negatively as well as positively. Müller's book was valuable; its pages of direct German rejected the notion that contemporary German philosophical language was overly complex, a conviction producing American attempts to imitate the complex styles of Heidegger or Hegel. Müller's chapters also related phenomenology and Heidegger to scholasticism. Far from appearing as a work of almost serene isolation, *Being and Time* was part of a cultural world swirling around *Existenz*. The notes I made in the yellow-jacketed book show how much I related what I read and heard to Protestant theologians or to the theologians fashioning Vatican II. Is Heidegger so original, so different from Aquinas? How do Jaspers and Heidegger relate to Tillich? Were literature, painting, religious movements gifts of a dynamic self, or of Being? Müller could take the wind out of Heidegger's sails in an inoffensive way by noting that the distinction between Being and beings was found in Aquinas and by mentioning Heidegger's unscientific exploration of etymologies and poetry. I was impressed by Müller's directness as he considered "the end of metaphysics," "phenomenology," and "system" within modern German philosophies.

I was surprised to read repeatedly that for Heidegger there is only one theme of philosophy: not the human person or existence but Being. The polemic of Heidegger against too literal, too hard, too ontic a theology and the polemic of some Catholic thinkers against an amoral existentialism were both misreadings. Heidegger's thinking had apparently never been intended as an existentialism or as a theology. The "end of metaphysics" might mean not the cessation of philosophy, but a radical critique of what neoscholasticism had made out of the history and eschatology of the New Testament. For Protestant thinkers, time and finitude were great problems; for Catholic theologians, history and grace were liberations. The event of the Council, the *Kairos* of Tillich, the historical existence of Heidegger struggled to express the same thing, an arrival in time of a way of thinking.

In the 1950s and 1960s, Heidegger seemed to have reached the high point of his reputation, and an international audience could not get enough of his meditative refrains on care and disclosure. Heidegger was a short, self-confident person. One can hear the strong, meditative, and engaging voice in lectures preserved on records. The man, the philosopher, his teaching style, and his thought had been an "event." In Marburg in the 1920s, the students referred to him as "the magician from the Black Forest." By the 1960s, his cooperation with a totalitarian government and his postwar banishment from academia were forgotten; he had cloaked his life during the Nazi period by asserting that his membership in the party was forced on him so that by serving as rector of the University in Freiburg he might preserve for that institution some academic independence. In the 1960s, intellectuals were content to accept his hermeneutics of his fall and permit him to cultivate the image of a detached thinker. In fact, he seems to have been for some years an enthusiastic Nazi who wanted the movement to save the academy from forces that were liberal, scientific, post-Wilhelmian. He expected from National Socialism a cultural renewal and a solution of social tensions, and (as with so many) a salvation of European existence before the dangers of Communism. In 1933, Engelbert Krebs, a priest and professor, and onetime friend of Heidegger's, wrote in his diary: "Heidegger gives the impression that he intends to work totally for the principle of the *'Führer-system.'*" Heidegger said that he would lead the Leader, the *Führer.* Karl Jaspers also experienced a Heidegger who enthusiastically greeted the arrival of Hitler's regime. Karl Löwith, Heidegger's first postdoctoral student, as he was beginning a Jewish exile in Rome in 1936, met his teacher there giving some lectures. Heidegger was wearing the Nazi Party symbol on his jacket, apologized for none of the actions of Hitler, and passed over the fact that Löwith, who earlier had cared for Heidegger's sons, would not be able to attend his address that evening because Jews were not permitted to enter the property of the Third Reich.

Max Müller had studied in Berlin with Romano Guardini and after some time in Munich went to Freiburg, writing a dissertation under the neoscholastic Martin Honecker with Heidegger as second reader. "When I moved to Freiburg to finish my studies," he recalled, "I knew nothing of Heidegger except for his huge reputation. A magical aura emanated from *Being and Time....*I tried to find the room on the first floor of the university in which Heidegger was giving his introductory lecture, since the philosophy seminar room with its twenty to twenty-five places did not have enough space. A small man behind me asked me: 'What are you looking for?' I said: 'I'm looking for Heidgger's lecture room.' He responded: 'I'm looking for it too. I am Heidegger.'"[8]

In the decades after the war Müller avoided discussing Heidegger and the Nazis, but after Heidegger's death he wrote: "When Heidegger came to the university, he entered a strange environment, and this would always be a conflict for him. Two forces pulled within him. On the one hand Freiburg, very famous in the field of philosophy, and on the other hand, small unprepossessing, Upper Swabian Messkirch....He had to break away from this yoke of the church but he could never really leave its tradition."[9] In the 1930s, Heidegger left the church that had long supported him with scholarships, but the ethos and traditions of Catholicism, mystical as well as metaphysical, remained present in his thought. Later in the 1980s Müller told a disturbing story. "The atmosphere in the seminar had already changed in 1935. In 1937, I was denounced because of my activity for the Catholic student group..., [and because of] the articles I had to write for the encyclopedia *Der Grosse Herder* at the time." Finishing his studies and applying for a teaching position, he learned of his denunciation from the vice-rector who exclaimed, "You are lost!" Heidegger's evaluation of him for government officials stated that his involvement in a Catholic student group indicated the wrong political views for service in a Nazi regime. He would be rejected by the government ministry for an academic career. Müller asked the philosophy professor to revise his letter of recommendation, but Heidegger refused to cross out the one sentence on politics, "I have wrapped it in a cover of justifiable good things." The young student replied, "That won't help me. The sentence is there." Then Heidegger said, "As a Catholic, you should know that one must tell the truth. So I cannot cross out the sentence....Don't hold it against me." Müller ended the interview with a pointed phrase, "It is not a question of holding it against you; it is a question of my existence."[10] Müller taught in the diocesan gymnasium until military service called him up; after the war he assumed the professorship of Honecker in Freiburg, moving to Munich in 1960.

Through Heidegger's essays on art and truth, I learned there was more to his philosophy than *Being and Time,* the book with which he was identified outside of Germany. It seemed to me that he wrote more in the world of Aquinas and Aristotle than in that of French existentialism. Even my slight education let me see that his claim to be ending philosophy or to be restoring its origins was embarrassing. English-speaking philosophers and theologians before 1963 believed they knew who Heidegger was: the creator of existentialism, an advocate of solitary self-determination, an atheist or a nihilist, a thinker attractive to the avant-garde. Germans, understanding his intellectual milieu and evocative language, knew that he remained a thinker of metaphysics in the line of Aristotle, that he was the heir of idealists and neo-Kantians, and that he was an inspirer but not a partner of Sartre. Some followers neglected his wider context and sources that included not only the history of Greek philosophies of being and philosophies of the subject after Kant, but also of theologians and medieval mystics. Actually his theme was Being, the central topic of Greek and medieval philosophy, and his thought was a geography of realms around and within men and women. His originality consisted in focusing not on things but on their milieu and on their world. Human existence was the place where being and time disclosed themselves because men and women always live in a circle of disclosure, in a luminosity of cultural revelation. His philosophy was related to Einstein's relativity and Picasso's juxtaposed faces. Truth is more than the logical adequation between the mind and an empirically perceived object: Truth is a disclosure process. Being discloses itself to humans and the objects of the world as a lighting-process coloring people, art, and science; a cultural age highlights them in a certain way through influential cultural forms. When we understand how time, continuity and change fashion us, Heidegger wrote, then we can move modestly and slowly into the realm of the holy and beyond the holy God who might await us.

Intimations for Theology

The Catholic origins of Martin Heidegger had been largely forgotten after World War II. The famous philosopher was a son of the caretaker of the parish church in the Black Forest town of Messkirch. His pastor inspired him to pursue an intellectual life, while church scholarships supported him up to his reception of the doctorate. After his years at the *Gymnasium,* intending to become a priest, he had entered the Jesuit novitiate, staying only a few weeks before switching to the diocesan seminary in Freiburg. Leaving the seminary during the years of the modernist crisis, his earlier, quite traditional views of church and dogma took a liberal swing. In 1915, he saw his work to be a creative reconciliation of neoscholasticism with the phenomenology and neo-Kantianism he found so interesting. His first position was teaching seminarians. At the end of his doctoral work, he sought without success the professorship in Christian-Catholic philosophy established by the Vatican's concordate with the German state of Baden. The Catholic chair, however, went to someone else, and soon Heidegger distanced himself from church and faith, writing in 1919: "Epistemological insights touching the theory of the historicity of our knowing have rendered for me the *system* of Catholicism problematic...."[11] Later, as we saw, during the Nazi period he persecuted Catholics: "I have experienced for years the networks and powers of these people in the greatest detail..., but one still is not adequately aware of Catholic tactics."[12] For the synthesis of *Being and Time* published in 1927, he drew from his reading of Paul, Luther, and Kierkegaard, and in the eyes of the university world he had become a Protestant. Then, after World War II, his religious orientation shifted back to a private, mystical Catholicism.

His home, Messkirch, lay between Lake Constance and the Black Forest. In 1949, to help the townspeople commemorate an anniversary of another famous son, the musician Conradin

Kreutzer, a composer contemporary with Franz Schubert, Heidegger wrote a small essay, *The Pathway.* This autobiographical meditation takes place in the countryside around Messkirch on a pathway running out from the town park through the woods. "The old linden trees in the *Schloss* garden gaze after it from behind the wall—whether at Easter when the path shines bright between rising crops and waking meadows or at Christmas when it disappears in snowdrifts behind the next hill. At the wayside crucifix it turns off to the woods." The path is rich with memories and insights for the thinker. In the woods, as a boy, he would go with his father to gather wood. The father might then work in his workshop, and the boy made toy boats of shaven bark to sail on make-believe journeys. Later, there would be more difficult, real journeys. The young philosopher used to read under a particular tree, puzzling out the meaning of philosophers, trying to decipher what they were clarifying or obscuring. "Often there lay on the bench one or another of the great thinkers' writings which youth's awkwardness attempted to decipher. When the puzzles ran together, and no way out presented itself, the pathway helped." Along the path are the smells of trees and fields and bushes; growing means to open oneself up to heaven and sink roots into earth. "The breadth of all growing things which rest along the pathway bestows world. In what remains unsaid in their speech is—as Eckhardt, the old master of letter and life, says—God, only God." The message of the pathway can be silenced by production, technology, and the noise of the media. "So man becomes distracted and path-less. The Simple seems monotonous to the distracted. The monotonous brings weariness. The annoyed find only the uniform. The Simple has fled. Its quiet power is exhausted." The philosopher's walk occurs in different seasons and different hours of the day; here it ends at night. "It shines dimly in the starlight. Behind the Schloss the tower of Saint Martin's church rises. Slowly, almost hesitatingly eleven strokes of the hour sound in the night. The old bell, on whose ropes boys' hands have been rubbed hot, shakes under the blows of the hour's hammer whose dark-droll face no one forgets. With the last stroke the stillness becomes yet more still. It reaches out even to those who have been sacrificed before time in two world wars."

I translated *The Pathway* for a newly founded Dominican periodical because I sensed that it presented the existentialism of Meister Eckhart more than that of Rudolf Bultmann. To inquire about the meaning of a word from the Swabian dialect, I wrote a letter to the author and soon received from Heidegger a kind reply, hand-typed. After mentioning an entry in an obscure dictionary of dialect vocabulary, he offered several paraphrases and concluded. "How you translate this into English, of course, can only be decided by you." The paths I walked through the English Garden—were they the pathways of thinking in Heidegger's pages? Thinking is a journey, a path without an important destination. Thinking is similar to the medieval image of contemplation as thoughts circling around the human or the divine, a pathway of insight. "We never come to thoughts. They come to us. That is the hour of dialogue, and dialogue cheers us in companionable reflection."[13] Later, Heidegger said that his writings were ways, not works, "paths of thinking for which the past is indeed past, but as what has happened it remains, nonetheless, coming toward us, waiting for those who think to walk down these paths."[14]

During the 1950s and 1960s, Heidegger had an immense influence on Protestant theology, on Paul Tillich and Rudolf Bultmann, and on their American followers such as James M. Robinson, Robert Funk, Schubert Ogden, and John Cobb and the Germans Gerhard Ebeling and Ernst Fuchs. While Tillich employed his understanding of human existence to explain the crucified Jesus and the Christian's New Being, Bultmann asserted that Heidegger expressed the message of the New Testament better than the inspired writers. An entire generation of Protestant professors was Heideggerian in language and Bultmannian in exegesis.

In the English-speaking world, however, Heidegger was somewhat misunderstood. He was a philosopher of decision and death; translations and superficial introductions in English paperbacks linked him with nihilism and atheism and presented an existentialism that was little more than popular psychology. A volume in a series on contemporary theology discussed "The Later Heidegger" and a further volume on "The New Hermeuentic" treated Heidegger's influence in post-Bultmannian biblical studies. These volumes, however, did not transcend the Protestant perspective of Christianity as being about faith and words, about existence and brittle language-events. The theologians offered human existence without Being as Truth disclosing itself in time. Curiously at that time, Japanese Buddhists (who found Eckhart, Schelling, and Heidegger of particular interest) might have had a better feeling for what his meditations on place and language meant than the Protestant exegetes who sought, by means of existence and hermeneutics, to flee the supernatural and the historical.

In 1964, a significant book on Heidegger appeared. An American Jesuit, William Richardson, gave to the English-speaking world a correct orientation to Heidegger. The thread running through this thought was indeed not existence but being. "It will become strikingly clear," Heidegger wrote in his "Foreword," "that the Being into which *Sein und Zeit* inquired cannot long remain something that the human subject posits. It is, rather, Being stamped as Presence by its time-character which concerns *Dasein*."[15] Heidegger began as one who pondered Being in Greek, medieval, and modern philosophies, and already in the 1930s he was passing beyond the existentialism of *Being and Time* and returning to the disclosure of truth-in-world. Heidegger's philosophy was not an atheism or existentialism, nor an interpretation of texts; he was not a nihilist but a disciple of medieval mystics and idealist theologians. Since the

Germans knew their own philosophical history, they, like Richardson, never fell into the illusion that Heidegger had appeared from nowhere: They understood his debt to Plato, Scotus, and Schelling.

I read with some dismay Heidegger's dismissal of technology: Machines and industries were the result of thinking reduced to calculation and the source of present and future evils. He seemed to find nothing good in trains, cars, or electrical appliances, and his global critique of the masses who enjoyed their benefits irritated me. What did he, bombed-out citizen of Freiburg and solitary inhabitant of the Black Forest, know about the value of telephones and washing machines? He even implied that Nazism had been justified by the need to combat mass society and technology and that ultimately Russia and America were the same in catering technologically to mass culture. "Many Germans have lost their homeland, leaving their towns and cities, driven from the ground of their homeland....And those who have remained in the homeland? Perhaps they are more without a home than those driven out. Each day, each hour they are condemned to the world of radio and television; each week movies take them into unusual realms of imagination where they exchange a world for something which is not world."[16] The modest amount of technology found in a refrigerator, television coverage of the Olympic Games, or in space exploration was hardly an enemy of humanity like the Third Reich. However, if technology—later, after the 1970s it was to be bedecked with violence and pornography—is understood as the amplification of all that is trivial and the reduction of intellectual life to electronic entertainment, Heidegger was prophetic. Still, it was difficult to appreciate how someone who had just been seduced by the greatest union of inhuman technology with genocidal evil could complain about people owning a hot water heater.

In the 1960s, past political orientations were buried. Heidegger's rehabilitation had been in place for a decade, but the atrocities of the historicity in which he had lived were not fully ignored by him. His religious origins surfaced again. His thinking become more and more a reflection upon the presence of Being in a manner that was not only aesthetic but mystical. This history of Being as time and truth seemed similar to the history of salvation and the history of theology; Christianity had stepped forth in Alexandria or Aachen in different forms and rites. Could Vatican II with its changing forms be illumined by this theory of historical and collective knowing, the church's life? To this Heidegger pointed.

Heidegger was not a theologian, and yet his philosophy did resemble a secular version of the biblical salvation-history. It was not surprising that he had attracted the attention of Catholic thinkers, for his dissertation had been on a medieval thinker, Duns Scotus, and his first book (never written) was to treat Meister Eckhart. Some of Heidegger's first critics were Catholics—Alfred Delp, Erich Przywara, Guardini, and Edith Stein—although they were not so interested in the psychological anthropology of the solitary individual as in Heidegger's view of the history of metaphysics as gift, revelation—in time, as a succession of cultures. To look at human subjectivity and the history of culture is to attempt to understand God's working in time and to explain it for people living today.

One semester Karl Rahner had to be away at the Council in Rome for more than his usual commitment, and he arranged for the doctoral colloquium held at his institute to be taken over by a visitor. The professor selected, flying up each week from Switzerland for afternoon sessions, was Heinrich Ott, the young successor of Karl Barth in Basel. He had made his mark by publishing a doctoral dissertation on the unlikely topic of the positive relationships between the theologies of the conservative Karl Barth and the liberal Rudolf Bultmann, based on their uses of Heidegger. He handed us purple mimeographed copies of a rare document, an unpublished manuscript by Heidegger: the unfinished section of *Being and Time,* "Time and

Being." The great work had been left incomplete—Heidegger remarked that language did not seem capable of yielding up a completion of the theme. Three things struck me about the text. First, there was the deftly written opening paragraph where Heidegger observed that contemporary art, modern poetry, and subatomic physics are no longer "immediately intelligible." Philosophy, too, without surrendering its claim to be universal and relevant to life, may not be intelligible to readers who, picking up an article or book, scan a few pages. Second, there was an intimation that being and time were interflowing modes of one reality or horizon. Finally, there was a hint of the transcendent in the shift of emphasis from being and time to what bestows both. Heidegger analyzed the ordinary German for the phrase, "there is:" *Es gibt* means literally "it gives" and not "there is." There is time; something gives time. "This giving that gives time is determined by denying and withholding nearness....We call the giving which gives true time an extending which opens and conceals." Not just a backdrop for events, a particular time permeates a facade or a sculpture. Historical time and changing forms give a new understanding of the real. Being, however, never comes completely to presence and so time leads history through culture from age to age. "The sending in the destiny of Being...a giving in which the sending source keeps itself back and, thus, withdraws from unconcealment."[17]

There was a similarity between Heidegger's view of the cultural illumination in a period by Being and how Catholic Christianity believes the Spirit is a source and empowerment of grace in the church. The internal problem for Roman Catholicism was to rediscover history and tradition. To accomplish this, Catholicism needed to be liberated from the Vatican policies and ideologies that were little more than the imitations of one or another faded past eras. In the 1960s, for Catholics the theological issue of the "development of doctrine" or the "evolution of dogma" was of particular interest. Was church teaching changeless? Did the papacy add dogmas to revelation? The event of being in time could serve as a model—aesthetic rather than logical—for the history of the church's life and the panorama of church tradition. Cultural times let the church be the same, and, equally important, let the church address living people and be different. At no time does divine reality manifest itself fully. The presence of the Spirit in the history of men and women or in the church is neither devolution nor evolution. As with epochs of art, an epoch of the church and its expression of Jesus' teaching emerges out of time. A constellation of thought forms and styles makes up a time, and for a while some aspects of the Christ-event are seen sharply and others are forgotten.

I overlooked, however, in the optimistic rush of the 1960s, what was hidden and concealed, overlooked forces that were being surpressed or repressed. A Utopia could not be constructed, and the forces of ignorance and fear—they so often seek refuge in religious things and institutions—were not disappearing forever but were withdrawing to the wings and waiting. Unwilling to accept any change, they felt left out and were pouting—perhaps the future would bring a turn to their advantage.

My worn, notated copies of the booklets of Heidegger's essays became my companions as I walked along the Isar past the buildings where professors, past and present, lived—Schelling had had his quarters there. Several times I had to summon up my courage to visit a professor in his dark lodgings to get his comments on a seminar paper. The existentialism I heard in lectures and read in the Munich parks led not to the agnostic searchers in a Bergman film or to the desperate choices of a lonely spy, but to a contemplation of history changing. The days with their long evenings sometimes ended with dark beer and chicken at a *Wienerwald*, a Bavarian chain of restaurants. But there was no lack of months when the trees were bare, when cold rain had people scurrying for shelter, when anxiety made me wonder about my years in Europe and their end. What lay ahead?

Modern Art

I was living and studying in a city of art, a city of originality in the arts, whether in 1720 or in 1920. The spirit of modernity was waiting to teach me not only in books but in the concert hall and gallery.

The activity of the subject, the force of time, the anxiety of the modern seeker—I tested them as I sat before masterpieces in the museums, before a Casper David Friedrich in the *Alte Pinakotek* and a Paul Klee in the *Haus der Kunst.* I waited to be seized by the moment, to learn, to find out what art might disclose to my existence, to see if I could notice a transcendental meeting between subject and object. What passed between me and a painted canvas, a Rubens or a Marc? The existence of the lonely human figure facing the abyss of anxiety was not only the subject of philosophy but the theme of modern plays, music, and sculpture. In high school in Wisconsin, the band where I served in the percussion section had played a few pieces by Debussy, a prelude by Shostakovich, and something by Hindemith. It was strange music, wandering through key signatures, unpredictable sounds with only a snatch of a tune. Ten years later in Munich, still an ignorant pupil, I underwent a slow education in art history, a private education in museums and churches. Bookstore windows displayed richly illustrated or profound tomes on Ottonian or Expressionist art. Tutored by pamphlets and paperback surveys, I went to exhibitions in the museums because I thought they would help me understand the century in which I was living, understand why impressions of forms and colors had replaced portraits of saints and knights. In Munich, I walked through a birthplace of modern art, of all the arts in their jagged abstract lines of paint or of sound.

Remarkable things had happened in Europe in the years around the World War I. The quantum theory of Max Planck, Freud's interpretation of dreams, and Einstein's theory of relativity emerged in the span of a few years. By 1900, Munich was the artistic capital of Germany as more and more exhibitions were sponsored by wealthy and royal patrons and by associations of thousands of artists. That autumnal time marked a late romanticism in art and a late idealism in philosophy. In tone poems such as *Death and Transfiguration,* Richard Strauss drew music into an expressionist mode where long, passionate melodies over lush harmonies indicated something coming to an end and yet continued, searching. In 1912, Arnold Schoenberg completed a song cycle, *Pierrot Lunaire,* while in the same year Thomas Mann finished *Death in Venice.* The previous year Wassily Kandinsky, Franz Marc, and Schoenberg had produced an almanac, *Der Blaue Reiter.* It called attention to the changes taking place in art through Picasso, Matisse, and Cézanne, as well as featuring votive pictures from Russian and Bavarian churches and peasant paintings. The almanac dealt not just with the visual arts but with published songs by Schoenberg (words by Maeterlinck), Alban Berg, and Anton Webern (words by Stefan George). Art, literature, and music would be a science and a revelation of the spiritual. Kandinsky described the Munich world to his wife: "There is a Schoenberg concert this evening, at which we shall all of course be meeting....Yesterday evening I went...to Jawlensky's apartment and spent the evening talking to Kandinsky and Münter who are wonderful people." Thomas Mann wrote in his novella *Gladius Dei:* "Art blossomed; art dominated; art extended its scepter adorned with roses over the city and smiled....Munich shone."[18] Ibsen and Lenin, the poets George and Rilke, and Thomas Mann lived in Munich in the 1890s. In 1929, the year Mann received the Nobel Prize, he lectured to a thousand students at the university. The city celebrated his reception of the prestigious prize with a dinner in the Rathaus. He responded emotionally about the place in which he had settled: "I love this city, precisely as a city-picture. It is the most beautiful in Germany. I love this city in its south-German popular life, in its happy serenity of feast days, in the blue color of the *Föhn* in the southern sky, in its contrasts of weather and in its refreshing unity of the conservative rural with the urban. Munich is not only the capital of Bavaria, it is a German and European capital, a center of European culture."[19]

What had arrived in art after the biblical or Florentine frescos of mother and child? What style replaced the boat tied to the dock against Venetian or Dutch backgrounds? Colors are forces, forms carry energy, lines are visible traces of invisible presence. Kandinsky, whose art was moving to the abstract, was born and educated in Russia, had imbibed Russian mysticism and studied idealist philosophy and theosophy. He was drawn to painting by an exhibition of the French Impressionists in Moscow and moved to Munich. His blues, golds, and purples transformed Bavarian towns at the foot of the Alps. Rich, often primary colors are the grammar, the language of the spiritual. Around 1912, Kandinsky broke through into nonobjective or, as it came to be called, abstract art. To the viewer his "Improvisation" and "Composition" held no objects, no scenes of a battle by Alexander or Napoleon. Still, from the painter's point of view they did have an objectivity, one without recognizable figures but an objectivity mediating some mystical reality. Kandinsky wrote: "The abstract idea is entering into art, although only yesterday it was scorned and obscured by purely material ideas....The harmony of the new art demands a more subtle construction, something that appeals less to the eye and more to the soul."[20] His apologia for those new directions, *Concerning the Spiritual in Art,* proclaimed that far from leading to nihilism, certain juxtapositions of lines and tones would lead to a spiritual depth, to a disclosure of the the ultimate.

The poems of Rilke, the chairs of the Bauhaus, the myths of Jung, Heidegger's existentials, Jaspers' *chiffres* were not unlike

Kandinsky's linear swirls or patterns of color or Schoenberg's mathematical rows of sounds. Something similar happened also in theories about religion around 1912. Rudolf Otto's travels in the East brought to Europe a new aproach, a look at the holy present in the forms of religions. That same year, Paul Tillich received his licentiate in theology with a dissertation on Schelling, and Rudolf Bultmann began explaining at Marburg the literary forms of the four gospels emptied of historical events. It was not hard to see that philosophers and theologians had some affinity with the artists: The pages of Bultmann, Tillich, and Heidegger, the lines of Klee, and the meticulous scores of Alban Berg all aspired to go beyond objects. Better to express the human and the holy in open-ended forms and symbols, which, nonetheless, sought the transcendent, the holy. A Tillichian analysis of a religious symbol was like Kandinsky's paintings or Berg's violin concerto ending with a Bach chorale, each mediating revelation in some form, were not the bars of an agnostic prison but openings to the mystery beyond—small forms disclosing the holy.

I was learning a new meaning for the word *world.* Each great or genuinely new work of art expresses its world. The colors, lines, and ideas of these worlds form a cultural milieu, a particular age, a place with its language and art, a way of thinking and feeling, a pervasive realm more fundamental than the things themselves. For Heidegger, being and time came together in bestowing what modernity calls a world, in fashioning culture. Along with the arts, philosophy and theology, too, existed in their world.

Modern philosophy of religion and liberal Protestantism offered plenty of examples of Christian revelation being reduced to modern philosophy. Faith and religion as purely mental or psychological forms was adequate for only a few. It seemed clear, however, that in the 1960s religion and revelation were breaking out of subjective prisons, academic clubs. While Catholic theologians read modern Protestant exegetes and theologians, those evangelists of subjectivity, they avoided the ideology of liberal German Christianity that began and ended with transcendental forms and held up a contentless New Testament. Nonetheless, the worlds of ideas and culture, even modernity, need not overwhelm the gospel. The Catholic mind could find subjective and historical approaches to incarnational sacramentality and service. After all, what is more historical than the events of Jesus' life, than the service by external religion to the graced presence of the Spirit in people? Having seen so many cultures and having fashioned so many rituals, Catholicism could not be sold on worshiping subjectivity, freedom, and relativism. Now in Rome a modestly modern approach had a voice in the Council's debates over its final texts: "The church then believes it can contribute much to humanizing the family of man and its history through each of its members and its community as a whole....There is a considerable and varied help that it can receive from the world in preparing the ground for the Gospel....The modern individual is in the process of developing a fuller personality and of discovering and affirming human rights. The church is entrusted with the task of opening up to humanity the mystery of God the ultimate destiny and in so doing it opens up to men and women the meaning of their own existence, the innermost truth about themselves."[21] Modernity in Catholicism would mean further disclosures of the divine in the human, the recharging of history in tradition, renewal around the world.

Changing Seasons

By the standards of America's Midwest, Munich had a lot of rain and many gray days. During a brief autumn, the weather swirling around the Alps was unpredictable. The sky could be overcast for days, but then over the Alps came sudden bursts of African air, the *Föhn,* blowing down on Munich, and under a deep blue sky the high mountains could be seen to the south from the streets of the city. If in the spring the sun brought some warm days, early June suddenly turned cold again. It was the time of the Alpine "sheep's cold" marked by the feast days of the "ice saints" such as Bonifatius and Pancratius. Germans saw Bavaria as having good weather, and from May to September sunshine did illumine Munich's marble lions and gurgling fountains. The rebuilt palaces gleamed in violet, churches in mustard, and Baroque facades in white and green. Above a *Platz* surrounded by outdoor restaurants fluttered the white and blue flags of the Free State of Bavaria, alluding to the white and blue sky. Crowds at outdoor cafes drank a variety of beers and white wines and ate *Kuchen* with fresh berries. Only 20 years after lying in rubble and filled with hundreds of thousands of refugees, Munich was now celebrated by cover articles in *Time* and *Der Spiegel* magazines: In the mid-1960s, it had the most publishing houses and university students, 21 museums, 19 theaters, and an inexhaustible need for workers.

The July sun chased away the chill of existence. Anxious to stay outside after months of rain and snow, I took my books into the woods and meadows of the *Englischer Garten*. (Years later I came to associate my time studying biblical exegesis with the cold of winter and my study of contemporary philosophy with summer.) The English Garden was a large meadow framed by woods. Interestingly, the meadow-garden had been suggested by an American scholar serving in the Bavarian army in 1788 and at first included agricultural schools and model farms. Ludwig I as crown prince had it transformed into a large nature park in 1803, an artless union of hilly woods, streams, paths, and meadows. While in November ribbons of water flowing to and from the Isar mirrored the gray skies and bore ducks on its rapid streams, in the spring and summer that *Wiese,* the meadow's grass, was green and deep. It recalled the Munich *Wiese,* which was the site of the mighty *Oktoberfest,* and the *Wiese* that is the festival setting in Nürnberg for the last act of *Die Meistersinger.* I also brought to the English Garden the essays of theoreticians of art such as Erwin Panofsky or the poems of Rilke—both were also philosophers. In the park around me were different kinds of worlds: nature, the city's medieval towers in the distance, and houses from the nineteenth century along the edge of the park. Blue and gray skies above the green expanse of meadow edged by brown trees were like the horizons of which German philosophy spoke, horizons that were not just settings for clouds or church towers but also for the forms of an age. On one hill there was even a Greek temple built in the nineteenth century, something from Sophocles or from the *Heiligtum* of Schiller's or Beethoven's *Ode to Joy.*

I was beginning to be at home in Germany, less lonely, almost a *Münchener.* I had made a few friends, and looked forward to visits in July from my family and from Dominicans coming to Europe to study. An influx of English-speaking students had also begun.

Baroque and medieval art had shown me different ways of thinking about Christ and the church, about myths and saints, kings and biblical events. Modern art was instructing me in a world where individual impressions and quests were paramount, where time and space were fluid. Curiously, the books I was reading about existence were written out of anxiety and pessimism, but the theologians I studied were filled with hope. At Mass in the early mornings, people aware of grace made visible in art noticed momentarily in the churches the sunlight strike a gold and white statue and were consoled or enlightened. A personal silence guarded their lives and faith while outside an old war and a cold war hovered, painful and dangerous. There was also hope for something more benign, more human.

Later, when someone asked me what I had learned at the University of Munich, I always answered spontaneously "German." The language, I meant, was the access to vast amounts of information. A few ideas, some theological, some cultural, were staying with me, seeds taking root. I was learning, however, not just information but ways of seeing how culture fashioned human life, thinking, and art. Only some years later did I realize what I had learned in that time. I had learned about worlds, gifts of time.

The summer ended and October came again, announcing through bare trees and cold days a new semester. Spurred on by Vatican II, theology was being challenged to give more human expressions to Christianity, to find new places of grace, to understand that grace-in-Christ had had a long planetary history and was loose today in the world of peoples and their religions.

●

Far away were rumors from the United States: more legislation for civil rights, the beginning of protests against a war. There were Dominicans removed by bishops for working with the poor and for not wearing clerical suits, and there were new kinds of retreats, ecumenical gatherings, and theological courses. Through a young generation of teachers and a flood of translations from Europe, priests and nuns at work in eruptive cities and among shifting populations began to carry the ideas of the Council from place to place.

---

1. Löwith, *From Hegel to Nietzsche* (New York: Holt, Rinehart, and Winston, 1964), p. 20.

2. Schelling, "Aphorismen über die Naturphilosophie," in *Samtliche Werke* (Munich: Beck, 1927), pp. 7, 238.

3. Salat, *Schelling in München* (Heidelberg: Gross, 1845), pp. 2, 56.

4. Jaspers, *Existenzphilosophie* (Berlin: de Gruyter 1964), p. 1.

5. *Ibid.*, p. 7.

6. *Ibid.*, p. 8.

7. *Karl Jaspers: Notizen zu Martin Heidegger,* Hans Saner, ed. (Munich: Piper, 1978), pp. 79, 141–43.

8. Müller, "Martin Heidegger: A Philosopher and Politics: A Conversation," in *Martin Heidegger and National Socialism* (New York: Paragon House, 1998), p. 177.

9. "Martin Heidegger: A Philosopher and Politics: A Conversation," p. 179.

10. "Martin Heidegger: A Philosopher and Politics: A Conversation," p. 189.

11. Heidegger, Letter of January 9, 1919, to Engelbert Krebs in Hugo Ott, "Heidegger's Catholic Origins," *American Catholic Philosophical Quarterly* 69 (1995), p. 147.

12. Ott, *Martin Heidegger. A Political Life* (New York: Basic Books, 1993), pp. 95f.

13. Heidegger, *Aus der Erfahrung des Denkens* (Pfullingen: Neske, 1954), p. 11.

14. Heidegger, "Forward," in *Vorträge und Aufätze* (Pfullingen: Neske, 1954), p. 7.

15. "Vorwort" to William Richardson, *Heidegger: Through Phenomenology to Thought* (The Hague: Nijhoff, 1963), p. 35.

16. Heidegger, *Gelassenheit* (Pfullingen: Neske, 1959), p. 17.

17. Heidegger, *On Time and Being* (New York: Harper and Row, 1972), pp. 16, 22.

18. Mann, *Gladius Dei, Sämtliche Erzählungen* (Frankfurt/Main: S. Fischer, 1963), p. 157.

19. Thomas Mann cited in Jürgen Kolbe, *Heller Zauber: Thomas Mann in München, 1894–1933* (Berlin: Siedler, 1987), p. 382.

20. Kandinsky, *Concerning the Spiritual in Art* (New York: Dover, 1977), pp. 31, 52.

21. Vatican II, *Gaudium et Spes,* # 40.

CHAPTER SEVEN

● ● ● ● ● ● ● ● ● ●

Theological Apprenticeship

The years of Vatican II were passing. Friends and relatives and relatives of friends came from America to visit, and in the autumns of 1964 and 1965 I ended up with them in Rome. When they left for the United States I was free to check in on the Council, to attend the press conferences on Via Conciliazione, to listen in some *collegio* to Schillebeeckx or Küng address African bishops. The sessions of Vatican II followed each other, one more filled with surprises than the last. Change had become visible.

In Rome, you could visit the tombs of the popes killed by Decius and buried in the catacombs in the third century, enter the palaces of families who produced Baroque popes, the Chigis and the Barberinis, or visit St. Peter's, which held the tombs of the popes from later times. Now the papacy was called upon to assume new forms, to accept a collegial relationship to the bishops of the world, to stop treating local churches in a paternalistic way, and to set aside claims to frequent and instant doctrinal certainty. Catholics around the world were asking: "How could the church change and stay the same?"

The trains with crowded second-class compartments taking me back to Munich from Rome passed through the sunny

Tuscan hillsides where trees and vineyards linked palazzos and farms, only to leave beyond Verona green and brown landscapes for mountain gorges and severe castles. Between the Italian and German landscapes lay Trent whose council in the sixteenth century had formed the Sunday Mass and seminary textbooks now being left behind.

After family and tourists had gone back to America, I returned to the daily work of learning about theologians and theologies, of writing a dissertation. Munich continued to rebuild and to prosper, to arrange blue and white flowers in front of ministries, and to feature *Maikäfer* (lady bugs) made out of chocolate and marzipan in the windows of pastry shops. The city entranced the new citizens of world-tourism, a migration that would make European wars obsolete. The Ecumenical Council brought forth religious journals and books from expanding publishing houses. It seemed that not only were the bishops going to school, but that the entire world had become interested in theology.

Of Time and Its Mystery

Time passed, although because I was 28 I had no feeling that anything was passing. I changed, although I never noticed I was changing. Time slipped away, and yet it was one thing I had in abundance. "Time never takes a holiday," Augustine wrote, but was my unrecorded and unnoticed life, time? Medieval scholastics had argued over time: How real was it? Was it a succession of moments in nature or a counting in the human mind? Did Albert the Great think that time was less real than his pupil Thomas Aquinas? Was time like Tillich's *kairos* drawn from the New Testament, the right moment full of possibilities, or was it like Heidegger's *Zeit,* which illumined everything but had no measure? I had passed from the time of the liturgy, symbolic and hermetic, to history's force. Politics and faith, music and migrations were directed not by angels but by time. Still, was history the quarter hours ticked off by all the clocks and watches in the windows of Munich jewelers, or was it the inner, human cries of existentialist plays and Bergman movies? No need to hurry; as the Germans said, *"Man hat Zeit,"* "You have time." Or did time have us?

When and how did cultural change arrive? Art, philosophy, theology, politics, even business, sought to see when cultures began and when they ended. A cultural shift is not something planned by biologists or forecast by atmospheric conditions. The 1960s appeared quite unexpectedly as had Romanticism in 1800. In some mysterious way, Augustan Rome or the Florence of the Medicis emerged in its distinctiveness.

The Franziskaner restaurant was like a monastery, holding room after room, and on the walls were the coats of arms of Munich families from the Middle Ages and the symbolic shields of the guilds. Next to the high, blue-draped windows were wood carvings from the seventeenth century. This place for enjoying food and drink was a time away from an ordered world. A rear *Stube,* the "student-room," was always good for liver-dumpling soup and a dark beer. Around its clock was written the German saying, *"Zeit weilt, eilt, teilt, heilt,"* "Time goes slow, goes fast, separates, heals."

Meanwhile, on some evenings, across the street at the Bavarian State Opera, the Marschalin in Richard Strauss's opera *Der Rosenkavalier* sang in distress and piety about the process of growing old: "Time is something strange....But one should not be afraid of it. Time is a creation of our Father who created us all." Time did seem to be the gift of God in the 1960s. The frowning, imprisoning structures of racism and of political and religious tedium and arrogance were being challenged. Now time was setting us free from the prisons of the 1940s and 1950s, from the ruthless and mindless scholasticisms of Rome, Moscow, and Washington.

For Christianity, time was the milieu of God's grace and revelation, a history of salvation and not an Aristotelian circle of sameness. The Trinity had created the human race in time and then had come into history in Jesus of Nazareth. Revelation and church told not of a single past biblical pageant, but of a perduring incarnation unfolding in all men and women through a long history, and so many changes came from a history of grace and need not be feared. Existence was neither permanent nor solitary but was shot through with time—personal time, biological time, emotional time, relentless time, the time that "goes fast or goes slow." Time was the condition of being alive and of fashioning culture, even of listening to God.

The cycle of feasts and festivals populated the churches and the beer halls and led people to gardens and markets. St. Kajetan's large bells tolled out the hours and half-hours every day, announcing an ordinary Sunday in Lent or, with more vibrancy, the morning liturgies of Pentecost Sunday and Pentecost Monday, feasts with their special music, their particular food, wines, and beers, and their cakes laced with brandy or *Kirschwasser.* For me in the sun or the snow, time waited outside the bookstores, libraries, museums, and churches. Months passed, even an entire year, and then two years were gone. I could not talk to the past or ask the ancient theologians how they had seen life, but the past could express itself through the visible language of light entering the architecture of a church, the choice of patronal saints, the location of the altar and the pulpit. Architecture in churches told how the Mass had been said, how sermons were preached, how laity and clergy related. And modern art exemplified human attempts to see further than the trees along the stream or the young woman's face, to see through something to the holy.

A Theological Education

The theology professors at the university were all priests. Lay men and women had recently been admitted to doctoral studies but had not yet reached faculty status. In the early 1960s, the professors wore not clerical suits and Roman collars—a garb that American ecclesiastics considered to be universal and ancient but which was, in fact, a style developed in this century among Catholic clergy in countries of English and Irish influence—but dark, heavy suits with white shirts and black or gray ties. As I mentioned, university professors were very important people in German society, well paid, but also somewhat overworked as they strove to serve a growing university population. Vatican II had drawn to Rome some of those theologians, historians, and canonists to serve as *periti,* "expert advisers," for the delegates at Vatican II during the four autumns of its deliberations. They traveled back and forth to Rome for commission meetings on drafts of texts and to address groups of bishops. A conciliar position often bestowed international fame.

Heinrich Fries, the professor in Munich for my field (fundamental theology presenting revelation and church, philosophy and culture) was a product of the Catholic Tübingen school that reached back in this century through theologians such as J. R. Geiselmann and Karl Adam to Paul Schanz, a Catholic thinker of the late nineteenth century with positive views on Galileo and Darwin. Further back lay the great figures of Johann Evangelist Kuhn, Johann Adam Möhler, and the school's founder in the first decade of the nineteenth century, Johann Sebastian Drey. Reading the writings of Schelling, Drey interpreted Catholicism through Romantic-idealist motifs: process and history, church life as an organism, intuition as mysticism. He stimulated students such as Möhler and Kuhn to express the historical unfolding of Christian beliefs and realities in a view, the church as a living communal person with its own diversity, not unrelated to that of theologians of the first centuries. The characteristics of the Catholic Tübingen school lived on in Fries: an interest in all the facets of the church, an openness to modern philosophy, an appreciation of history as the lifeblood of Christianity, and a spirit of dialogue toward Protestantism. During the twentieth century, the Catholic *Tübinger* became less occupied with idealist philosophy and more concerned with the history of Christianity and the contemporary church, particularly with ecumenism.

Fries had grown up in a small town, entered the priesthood, and pursued doctoral studies at the university as war broke out. As soon as the collapse of Nazi Germany permitted it, he had published his doctoral dissertation written under Geiselmann at Tübingen. From 1850 to 1950, a dominant German academic approach to Christianity was the philosophy of religion, and Fries's first book surveyed Catholic philosophers of religion, past and present. Over a dozen thinkers were treated, ranging from Romano Guardini and Erich Przywara to Helmut Kuhn and Karl Rahner. Fries's evaluation in 1945 of Rahner was rather strict—a young *Doctorandus* often sees too sharply the limitations of the generation slightly older. He criticized the Jesuit's *Hearers of the Word* as too existential in its view of the forms of knowing and historicity and too quick to move from a philosophy of religion to a fundamental theology. Interestingly, his study and writing in the philosophy of religion drew on John Henry Newman as well as Max Scheler.

Fries's early interest in philosophy faded, and by the 1950s he was concerned more with ecumenism and faith, with church life and authority. My short Swabian mentor came to Munich in 1958 (Hans Küng succeeded Fries at Tübingen in 1960). His several books on the church between 1958 and 1964 went far beyond anything written at that time in English and were a model conversation of the new ecclesiology, beyond Roman hierarchical forms, with philosophy ("church as event"), Lutheranism and Barthianism ("church as commission and contradiction"), and with an ecclesiology of communion between ministries, people, and charisms. "Today the church becomes credible to the extent that it speaks out of the spirit and mind of Jesus Christ....The church becomes credible today not when it embraces, anxiously, modernity and becomes relevant at any price, for then it is infected with the hectic restlessness of the age and becomes itself restless, but when it, without reservation, without addition, without limitation, and without elimination wills to be nothing other than itself in its inner being and nature, authentic and total....In the unfalsified and unbroken presentation of itself the church summons people today to decision."[1] Renewal means the end of an ecclesiological narcissism, of a static understanding of the church, of a false self-sufficiency; renewal means fidelity to the church's vocation given by Jesus Christ to mission in the world. Vatican II is not a council of reunion but of renewal, setting free believers to serve the Holy Spirit. I translated in Munich one of Fries's books for an American publisher. Through four decades, Fries remained an energetic and courageous voice for Catholic thought.

I went to courses, sat in the wooden banks of seats in lecture rooms, took down notes, and read the books of my teachers: Fries, Michael Schmaus, and Karl Rahner in systematic theology, Walter Dürig and Joseph Pascher in liturgy, Karl Mörsdorff in canon law, and Otto Kuss in New Testament.

The conciliar years were a time of special lectures and symposia in Germany. There were so many new topics to be treated and old ones to be rethought, so many theologians with ideas. These symposia were living books of essays, a tableaux of German, Swiss, and Austrian theologians. Politics, ecumenism, Christian-Jewish relations, conciliar changes, the new openness of Catholicism, theological gatherings advertised on the kiosks around the city—all attracted an audience for whom television was yet to come. *Vortrag* ("lecture") was a word I learned early, and I went frequently to a day of lectures or to an evening talk sponsored by the Catholic Academy in Bavaria. At a symposium on "Catholicism and Church: The Path of German Catholicism after 1945," Rahner addressed the topic of the "limitations of church office." At a conference on the eastern churches, Joseph Ratzinger, boyish-looking and quite progressive, reviewed the first session of Vatican II in 1963 in terms of "the essence and limitations of the church."

Theologians and historians in Germany long before the Council had pondered the relationship of Roman Catholic intellectual life to a century or two of modernity, and some had found alternatives to the suffocating papal project of neoscholasticism joined to canon law. They realized that the very history of the Catholic Church and dogma precluded a monopolistic theology and philosophy, that the issues raised by modern philosophies could not be avoided, and that subjectivity, history, and freedom did not corrupt all they touched. A conversation between modern philosophy and Catholic faith had existed in 1820 and 1860, and again in 1920 and 1960. Modern philosophy was not always an apology for atheism or a trendy analysis of terms, but was meant to describe the world behind psychology, science, and art for people alive today. German Catholicism knew that freedom and progress in intellectual life were possible. The Council was then deciding to address the modern world in a church document, *The Church in the Modern World.* In Munich, however, this was hardly a new problem. From 1920 to 1960, there had been Catholics who thought creatively about church, Christ, and modernity, and the most prominent had been Romano Guardini.

Romano Guardini, son of an Italian family living in Germany, also wrote of an open Catholicism in the twentieth century, drawing it into philosophy as well as art and literature. In the 1950s, American Catholics had few books to read beyond prayer books and lives of the saints. Along with Merton's *Seven Storey Mountain* were Karl Adam's *The Spirit of Catholicism,* and Romano Guardini's *The Lord.* The latter was a large, handsomely printed book with its jacket adorned by a painting by Rouault, a sign of a meeting with modernity. Not long after my arrival, I was surprised to learn that Guardini was living in Munich. I had read nothing of his books on modern literature and the liturgical movement, and I had no inkling of his stature as preacher and teacher. After looking at his many books, I was confused. Who was Romano Guardini? Much more than the author of *The Lord.* A fine stylist and cultural analyst, he was perceptive and critical about the modern world in the twentieth century. Much conflict in the Catholic Church would have been avoided if his perspectives on modernity had been read in the Vatican.

Romano Guardini was born in 1885, one year before Tillich and four years before Heidegger. Guardini's family was from Verona, although he spent his life in Germany. He began his studies for the priesthood when that profession was in difficult circumstances. In many European countries, anticlerical officials were in control, while in Rome, Pius X was issuing decrees against what he named modernism, discouraging all imaginative theology and dissuading priests from seeking careers in academia. After writing a doctoral dissertation on Bonaventure, Guardini received, in 1923, a position on the Catholic faculty of the University of Breslau with the initial agreement that he would serve as a visiting professor at the University of Berlin. With Adolf von Harnack's support, he became the first Catholic theologian on Berlin's Protestant faculty. The university world generally found him inadequately scientific, popular, full of insights into psychology and poetry.

Guardini viewed his teaching about faith as a dramatic journey into ideas and as a pastoral service. "Theology," he said "is reflecting upon being-a-disciple." Not only the New Testament but modern literature held a kind Christian humanism, for intellectual life and artistic vision seek what is living, what is concrete. A popular author, a moving preacher, an inspiring teacher, between the wars he brought faith and hope to young and old. He lectured to banks of students and spent summers discussing poetry and praying with youth groups at Burg Rothenfels, a medieval castle on the Main River. Masses celebrated for young Catholics led to liturgical renewal and to his own books about liturgy. He never grew tired of writing to friends and students or of giving talks in a distant city on new topics. If ecclesiastics labeled him a dilettante and academics dismissed him as a popularizer, his writings on religion or literature influenced a broad range of intellectuals and students (Hannah Arendt, at 18, decided to pursue philosophy after hearing Guardini lecture in Berlin on Augustine in 1923). He refused to be absorbed by a tired church, a pompous academy, or a fascist state. His lineage was catholic but cosmopolitan: a German from Italy, a Catholic priest in the university. His moving lectures about great figures in the West became books: Pascal and Augustine in 1935, Dante and Jesus in 1937, Plato in 1944. *The Spirit of the Liturgy,* published in 1918, has been often called the seminal work for the entire liturgical movement, and its successor, in 1923, on liturgical education drew attention to the rituals and images of the liturgy buried in mumbled Latin words, to the obscured cycles of feasts unfolding the existential gifts and purposes of the liturgy.

Thus Guardini led Catholics out of precincts of fear into some awareness of modern culture. Articles appeared on Franz Kafka and Stefan Zweig, on contemporary painting and poetry. Three years after Heidegger had begun to treat the poet Hölderlin in 1936, Guardini was writing his own study on that German poet, *Weltbild und Frömmigkeit,* "to hear what Hölderlin says: really he, only he, and the totality of what he says." Guardini lectured on Rilke at Berlin in the 1930s and published studies on the *Duino Elegies* from 1938 to 1953. Rilke was someone for the future, writing a poetry for the human being existing in the midst of modernity. He had separated himself from his Catholic background but Guardini saw his poetry as a secularized view of Christianity. Metamorphoses of "fragments of Christian belief" in secular terms, the

Duino Elegies treat life and death, as they unfold the interplay of self, world, and God.[2]

After World War II, the universities at Tübingen and then Munich gave Guardini a special professorship in "the Christian World-View." Published in 1948, *Grace and Freedom* was a theologically rich book, and 14 years after its first publication, when I bought a used copy, its ideas were still impressive. The book with its subtitle, "An Interpretation of Existence," offered an existential theology of grace played out within the categories of freedom. Seeking to move grace out of its confines of church devotions and general moral norms, it looked at redemptive grace in emotion and existence as well as in faith, in tragedy and freedom within today's society. Guardini's postwar theology of freedom was written out of Germany's situation in the late 1940s, but still bore echoes of encounters with the earlier, popular Kierkegaardian and Heideggerian stages of existentialism. No one could be more devoted to the realities of Catholicism, to monasteries and mystics than Guardini, and no one was less susceptible to a demythologization of the incarnation, although he resolutely refused to live in the past or in clerical confines, and his books expressed the deepest and most transcendent truths of Christianity in a contemporary language. "We should not say that faith has become weaker. That is often asserted, but, to me, without justification. When the modern person believes at all, that faith is more conscious, heroic— one can often say more heroic than in the past."[3]

Like Newman in Oxford or Lacordaire in Paris, for years Guardini preached at the university church of St. Ludwig, and the bookstores still had some copies of his sermons from the late 1950s published as large-format brochures. In 1959, he was preaching on the Lord's Prayer while during the week at the university he was lecturing on ethics. Preaching on the fifth petition, "Forgive us our debt as we forgive our debtors," he remained close to the Greek text but then he asked what our debt might be. A gospel parable describes how we humans would not forgive a small amount to someone in our debt, although we have been forgiven, figuratively, an enormous debt, $10,000. "What has God entrusted to us, loaned to us that we must give back to him? Let the answer come close to us: it is as simple as it is encompassing. We owe God the world!"[4] Short sermons, personal and scriptural, unpretentious but engaging, always original and direct.

In February 1965, I was walking near the university and noticed on one of the kiosks a placard that said there would be an *Akademische Feier,* an academic celebration in honor of Romano Guardini's eightieth birthday. On February 17, I made a point of going to the *Auditorium Maximum* on the first floor of the main building of the *Uni.* The crowd was dense and one could not get far into the balcony area. The first floor was reserved for dignitaries invited to this "Highly Reputable Festival Gathering." When I gave up and came down to the main floor, the assembly was already ending. I caught a glimpse of a frail figure leaving the auditorium and being congratulated. He was more fragile and shorter than I expected. This was the famous Romano Guardini, next to whom stood Karl Rahner.

The opening remarks of the academic celebration were by Hans Wolfgang Müller, dean of the faculty of philosophy. They touched upon the war years, Guardini's struggle in Berlin against the violence of the years from 1929 to 1939 and upon his removal from that university. After the war, teaching in Tübingen, he had helped to restore German university life. Coming to Munich in 1948, he had been a major interpreter of the course of modernity for Germans, young and old, Catholics and agnostics. Müller said:

> In our time of need immediately after the total collapse [of Nazi Germany], [you were] concerned to give to the young people returning to our university from chaos the right teaching for the themes of humanity and of reflection on the basic foundations of our existence....During the next

fifteen years in your courses here in Munich you gathered around yourself a large community in the biggest auditorium at our university. You, a theologian, have developed philosophically in your lectures the content of faith and interacted in the realms of the history of ideas with the religious questions of the present and the past....From the heritage of antiquity, the Church Fathers, and the great works of literature, from Plato, Augustine, Dante, Pascal, Hölderlin, Dostoevski and Rilke let appear the image of human existence, the eternal order of the world, the essence of the divine....Through your unusual personality and wisdom you overcame the problems of the unconventional academic chair for Christian world-view and the philosophy of religion within a philosophical faculty. You yourself have given to your own academic field an innovative approach. In a gifted way you have spoken to young people and drawn them into your interests.[5]

After this address, Helmut Kuhn, a professor whose lectures and writings also treated Catholicism and culture, presented Guardini with a large *Festschrift,* an honorary volume filled with contributions by professors (other professors had often ignored him as an outsider in nationality and in scientific rigor) and congratulations by bishops (few had supported him during his creative explorations of modern philosophy and literature). Among those contributing to this 750-page book were Paul Ricoeur, Gabriel Marcel, Friedrich Heiler, Fries, J. B. Lotz, and Rahner.

Inside the auditorium, the modest but energetic figure of Karl Rahner had given the main address, the *Festvortrag.* He was Guardini's successor in the interdisciplinary professorship whose field was titled "Philosophy of Religion and Christian World-View." He had taken up his professorial responsibilities a year earlier, in March 1964, with lectures on the foundations of Christian faith, a theology he later published as his mature system. Rahner ended by talking about the forces at work in

Guardini's era and about the priest's influence upon young people in the years after World War I. He mentioned the books and lectures setting forth not theories on the philosophy of religion but great artists and thinkers, the poetry and painting of Dante and Rembrandt. "In these interpretations Guardini brought his thinking through differentiation and assimilation to meet a large part of the tradition of the Western Spirit. He saw himself working at 'the end of the modern age,' in a time of transition, at the edge of a barren and hard time without any Muses. Still, the past would remain vital, unburdening itself of its contributions for our future."[6]

Guardini's response was brief and barely audible. Eighty years of age, he had been ill for some time and would live less than three years. He died in 1968 and is buried in Munich. Authorities say that Paul VI, at the time of this birthday celebration, offered Guardini a cardinal's hat and the elderly priest refused. Earlier, when he was young, ecclesiastical honors would have had some meaning, but Vatican officials and his own diocese ignored him from 1919 to 1953, arguably the important years of his theological scholarship and pastoral leadership.

Guardini was old and exhausted when I saw him, tired from having helped so many. His sermons and books were preliminary studies for Vatican II, an inspiration for theologians and pastors. Guardini gave permission to enter the *Neuzeit,* "the new time," the German term for modernity. Rahner emphasized how Guardini led the church beyond a crass antimodernism and into Pope John XXIII's *aggiornamento,* which he had anticipated. "When something grows and changes without revolution, the growth and change always appear to be natural, as if nothing else could have happened. But how much patience, caution, resignation, trust, courage and humility, loyalty to the authentic tradition, tact, ability to wait without being cowardly and strength to begin again without revolutionary passion, were required to make it possible."[7]

Karl Rahner in Munich

As I mentioned earlier, *Time* magazine announced in August 1963, just as I had learned that I could not go to Tübingen but must find a German university with a nearby Dominican priory, that Karl Rahner would move from the Jesuit faculty at Innsbruck, Austria, to be the successor to Romano Guardini in Munich. Before the Council, Rahner was not widely known internationally, although he was well known in Germany and Austria. His arrival in Munich in the spring of 1964, as he turned 60, marked the beginning of a worldwide influence and also an enormous increase in his productivity. Karl Rahner was to be the most influential Catholic theologian for the remaining decades of the twentieth century.

Rahner always stressed the ordinariness of his life. Born in Freiburg im Breisgau, he attended the Jesuit high school there and entered the Society of Jesus as an older brother had done. A person's education, like birth and culture, is partly a matter of chance, and important teachers can have a lasting influence—Rahner was fortunate there. After years of memorizing neoscholastic conclusions in the seminary, he had classes during his theological studies with Joseph Maréchal, a pioneer of the dialogue between Catholic Thomism and Kant, and seminars during his doctoral studies in philosophy at the University of Freiburg with Heidegger. "I was sent by my religious superiors to study philosophy and to pursue a doctorate. I studied mainly under Martin Heidegger, who was already known and becoming famous. He had just been the first rector of that university under the Nazi regime, and we two young priests, J. B. Lotz and I, were not anxious to throw in our lot with him for good or for ill, and so we enrolled with the professor of Catholic scholastic philosophy, Martin Honecker. Nonetheless, our encounter with Heidegger was the decisive, impressive experience."[8]

Heidegger welcomed the Jesuits into his doctoral discussions of Hegel's *Phenomenology of the Spirit,* Kant's second critique, and Schelling's Essay on Freedom. The two Jesuits had chosen studies in philosophy instead of theology not only out of interest but because there was uncertainty about the degree of Nazi discrimination toward Catholic theology students. Heidegger was the only teacher whom Rahner saw as particularly gifted. "It is not a specific teaching I have taken from him but rather a style of thinking and of investigating which has proved quite valuable....My theology does not really show the systematic and thematic influence of Heidegger. What he communicated was the desire to think, the ability to think." The introduction to a renewal of thinking, however, did not mean that ontological existentialism provided the material for Christian theology. "Whether the truly theological subject matter and enterprise [in my work] is very much influenced by Heidegger and dependent upon him I really have to doubt."[9]

Rahner and Lotz became friends with another student, Max Müller, and in their rooms they worked on Plato and discussed their teachers. Decades later, Müller described Rahner as someone caught between the neo-Thomist Honecker and the prestigious Heidegger. Honecker, not a creative intellectual, was intolerant of nonscholastic viewpoints, oversaw Rahner's dissertation, but then did not accept it upon completion. Müller recalled:

> Rahner wanted to be granted the doctorate with a study on Thomas Aquinas, *Spirit in the World,* but his work was not accepted by Martin Honecker....Honecker had rejected the work as the main director, but Heidegger too, as a reader, did not support it. How did that happen?...Why did the remarkable work of the highly gifted Karl Rahner fail? Siewerth, Lotz, and I had attempted to "locate" speculatively, through our then rather original interpretations of Thomas, this thinker in the great speculative, European tradition of metaphysics in which Aquinas belonged; Rahner, however, tried something in

> another direction: an existential-anthropological inter-
> pretation of human knowledge in Aquinas. For Honecker
> this was too "Heideggerian." Since Heidegger was right
> there in Freiburg, in Honecker's view he should have rep-
> resented the dissertation.[10]

Heidegger would not direct the dissertation. He was at that time in the midst of his *Kehre,* his turn, a shift in focus from human existence to Being, a return back to the themes of truth disclosed in history and intution, themes of his writings before the charter for "existentialism," *Being and Time.* In the mid-1930s the modestly transcendental and existential directions of Rahner's thesis were for Heidegger already something of the past. Why, moreover, should he be linked to someone whose connections with neoscholasticism and the Catholic Church would remind him of his own origins, of the years of his finan-cial support from the church? Because Honecker—years later I heard Rahner refer to him as *"der dumme Honecker"*—did not accept the dissertation, Rahner left Freiburg without a doctor-ate. His superiors assigned him to teach not philosophy but theology, and he quickly wrote a theological doctorate for the University of Innsbruck on an aspect of the sufferings of Christ in patristic theology. If Karl Rahner had failed the standards of German academics and had yet succeeded in life, then, I thought, there was hope for me whether this European adven-ture had a happy outcome or not.

Rahner was a gifted and knowledgeable reader of Aquinas, although he exercised a relentless critique on neoscholasti-cism, the *Schultheologie* dominating all seminaries and many universities throughout the Catholic world. "School theology" meant to Rahner two things: (1) the theology taught in semi-nary classrooms from 1880 to 1960 and found in seminary textbooks, manuals with blocks of information; (2) forms of neoscholasticism in the nineteenth and twentieth centuries. In the second a boring, abstract system, more philosophical than

Christian, addressed no living issues, no living people, and also disdained human cultures. He did not consider the great figures of the Middle Ages to be well presented in that theology. New theologies were replacing the "ecclesial autarchy"[11] ruling between 1860 and 1960. "The new theology must not view neoscholasticism as a defeated predecessor it can simply leave behind. This aspect of past history remains a reality whose values are to be acquired anew....On the other hand, despite spasmodic efforts, there can be no return to neoscholasticism."[12] Rahner went ahead, not repeating Aquinas but employing some central motifs of Aquinas's theology to express Christianity in modern thought-forms. Of the attitude of his own generation he wrote: "We read the works of Thomas: we allowed him to alert us to certain problems, but ultimately we approached him with our own questions and problems. And so we didn't really practice a Thomistic scholasticism but tried to maintain toward him a stance comparable to that toward Augustine, Origen, and other great thinkers."[13] There was not just one way of looking at reality or at Jesus Christ.

Nevertheless, in 1962, as the Council began, not all thought like that. Prior to the first session of Vatican II, a well-known Roman, curial theologian Dino Staffa wrote an essay on the unity of the Catholic faith and church he found in three sources: neo-Thomism, the legal structures concretized in the *Code of Canon Law,* and the Latin language.[14] That remarkable isolationism explains why during the first half of the twentieth century in Rome and in theologically limited English-speaking countries there were few Catholics looking for new ways to present Christianity. Rahner had no interest in repeating philosophies from the nineteenth century or liberal Protestant theologies, that magisterium of individual German professors reducing the content of Christianity, discerning an ever longer grocery list of what could not be believed because historical revelation was opposed to science and implied a supernatural divine presence in people. Still, modernity was not evil but an epoch offering opportunities to Christianity, and a Catholic could begin with the subject and take seriously the history of thought and culture. "If Christianity ultimately (I say 'ultimately,' not 'alone') announces that the absolute, infinite, holy, and living God is the total fulfillment of human existence, then with that comes a joy and a fulfillment of a fundamental kind exceeding everything else. Whether, and how far, an individual man or woman in the concrete situations of life, limited by one's lifespan, by one's work, depending also upon one's individual, intellectual and other abilities, is able to really appreciate such an awesome message is quite another question. Nevertheless, Christianity preaches an absolute joy."[15]

Despite my meager understanding of their German philosophical backgrounds, I could see that Rahner and Paul Tillich had some similarities. Though not of the same age, both had neo-Kantian and existentialist mentors, both sought a theology that left room for the gospel amid modernity, and both theologians stimulated positive appreciations of the world religions. They had, however, very different views of the reality and history of God's grace. Despite Tillich's sweeping permission for histories to exist on their own, history in the church and the gospel rarely escaped being mental constructs, and dogmas and sacraments were symbols. Rahner, however, affirmed oil and Eucharist and bishops not as symbols but as culturally conditioned forms of divine presence. They continued the incarnation but had their own history, understandings of Jesus Christ in churches East and West, the sacrament of penance in many forms, and the Petrine ministry in the fifth or fifteenth centuries.

An inquiry had come from the philosophical faculty in Munich in February 1963—would the Jesuit entertain the idea of being Romano Guardini's successor? "I certainly felt," Rahner wrote later, "that this was something very appealing and quite an honor, because the appointment came ultimately from Romano Guardini himself. I discussed it with him beforehand and I gladly accepted it, even though later much happened that was not originally planned."[16] Some years earlier, the Jesuit superior general in Rome had forbidden him to accept a call to the University of Münster, but now permission was given for Munich where he hoped to find in a German university protection from Vatican interference, and assistance in producing several multivolume works he had undertaken to edit. Karl Rahner came to Munich from Innsbruck to assume the chair of Philosophy of Religion and Christian World-View in May 1964, as the summer semester was beginning.

Rahner arrived in Munich at the time of his 60th birthday, and the daily paper, the *Süddeutsche Zeitung,* published on March 4, 1964, the day before his birthday, a long article in which Heinrich Fries wrote that Rahner's widening influence was due to the fact that he took people as they were and affirmed their lives. The 840 entries—articles, books, and translations—in Rahner's bibliography at that time showed not only his productivity but the receptivity of his audience. A two-volume collection of essays, *Gott in Welt,* celebrated the birthday, and the several dozen articles in 1,300 pages were introduced by 61 pages of congratulations by theologians, bishops, and philosophers. The Jesuits Lotz and Emerich Coreth wrote on modern ontology; Bernhard Welte and Otto Semmelroth treated major issues of fundamental theology such as freedom and personalism. There was a posthumous contribution by Gustave Weigel that drew together Tillich's method of correlation and the address of John XXIII inaugurating Vatican II to emphasize that faith should be expressed in a language and mode that could be understood by people. Rudolf Schnackenburg gave an exegetically nuanced picture of how Jesus founded the church, while Fries wrote an overview of the problem of myth and revelation, and Congar examined the conciliarity of the church. Bernard Häring considered the relationship of morality to church and Herbert Vorgrimler that of theology to art; Joseph Ratzinger treated the world religions, and Erich Przywara wrote on Catholicism and ecumenism.

Again and again, one read of a quest for a theology that would speak to people. Welte, a professor at Freiburg, concluded: "Theology must enter upon the long path of a historical understanding of the witnesses of revelation and the theological synthesis of its documents. But even then something decisive still remains for it to do, namely, to draw the faith out of its sources and to reach individual existence."[17]

Soon after my arrival in Munich, I purchased Rahner's two early works. *Spirit in the World,* the rejected dissertation that analyzed three pages from Aquinas's *Summa theologiae* on knowing in light of Kantian philosophy, didn't interest me. I was tired of neoscholastic concepts and phantasms. The second book, *Hearers of the Word,* inquired into the conditions for a revelation from God to us; it asked, how could God speak to men and women, that is, which aspects of men and women permit and receive revelation from God? A human self, an existence, a community, a language, a time—these compose the grammar through which the word of God speaks, plants words in human consciousness silently in a self-communication that is both revelation and love. Consequently, revelation will be neither a celestial language nor a religious myth but a special, silent, constant presence: "The human being is that being who in free love from God stands before the God of a possible revelation. The human being is paying attention to that address or silence of God as it opens itself in free love to this revelatory message of a speaking or silent God."[18] Revelation comes to people who are free to respond to God. It comes to them in their history, emerges inwardly and then publicly in a long history of religions, finding a climax in Jesus of Nazareth. Christianity should and can take into consideration the individual, the freedom of people in society, and history. "The new is always uncomfortable and frightening. We want through 'new knowledge' only to confirm ourselves. Real truths, when they penetrate in a new way into us, frighten us away, affect us, threaten us, change us, force us into realms of the spirit in which we cannot confuse normalcy with new insight, in which we don't feel at home."[19] Plato, Aristotle, and Aquinas will remain thinkers from which Christians can learn, but philosophy and theology cannot only imitate the past. Idealism, phenomenology, existentialism can be un-Christian when they turn the autonomous subject into an idol, but does not the preaching of Jesus about the dignity of all, does not the understanding by Paul of the Spirit active in each life focus on the free subject? Christianity cannot remain in a library or in a sacristy of statues and chalices but must look at each stage in history.

Rahner arrived to join the university in April 1964. One afternoon in May, I crossed the Schellingstrasse, went into the *Lichthof* of the university's main building, and found a seat in the crowded *Auditorium Maximum* to hear his opening lecture. Rahner's debut was modest: A short figure in black suit and tie, he began to speak on his intention to unfold the most basic ideas of Catholic Christianity. This general course was his early draft of a new modern Catholic theological system, one of the very few in this century. Rahner appeared during his lecture as both meditative and energetic; his determined and resonant voice expressed a respect for the subject of his course that he inevitably stated to be "that infinite, eminently active, ineffable Mystery which in both silence and power is always but secretly contacting each and every one of us in a nonreflexive way." He was, I would learn, unassuming and approachable but there was also passion: Rahner was not just addressing philosophers or dutiful students but the church and the world.

It was clear early on that Rahner would not be Guardini's successor in the sense of attracting a university-wide audience of hundreds of students and faculty, nor did he offer aesthetically engaging commentaries on trenchant points in contemporary religion or poetry. Rahner was a precise theologian who wanted to unfold the dynamic motifs of Catholic life, a theologian concerned with explaining to people from all walks of life the constant reality and a contemporary interpretation of Jesus' message. After a few weeks, I noticed that my student-neighbors were losing interest; attendance dropped; the lectures were too advanced for nontheologians.

Rahner, however, did not disappoint me. His lectures, like his articles, prepared one to be a contemporary explorer into faith. In 1964 and 1965, he presented what would be published later in English as *Foundations of Christian Faith,* a new expression of the depth and expanse of Christianity. Somehow, I kept a few pages of my notes from that opening lecture in Munich in the spring of 1964. "The student," I wrote down during his opening lecture, "has a responsibility to understand courageously the intellectual and cultural powers of the time." Theology addresses humanity as it encounters "the ground of human existence that we call the ineffable God," mystery pure and simple. The course was not to be the academic study of religion, not a theological course for seminarians and schoolteachers, but a look at Christianity from the point of view of the person who in freedom realizes—it might be vaguely or explicitly religious—a movement toward God. These opening lectures marked the summer, and a group of us discussed translating them into English for publication, but nothing came of it—Rahner only published the course a decade later. The course and book bore the subtitle, "An Introduction to the Idea of Christianity," and the "idea" of Christianity recalled the great philosophers of the nineteenth century. "Thus the book endeavors—to the extent that the historicity of salvation history and of God's freedom permits—to reduce the whole of Christianity to an idea, to reflect on the ultimate oneness and authentic inter-relatedness of all that Christianity proclaims."[20] To hear Rahner was to hear someone who believed deeply, someone who could think and who liked to think. No matter how preoccupied or unassuming Rahner was, you felt you were in the presence of a gifted thinker whose ideas pointed to something deeper, not to a theory, not to a self, but to a reality: the active presence of God. That immanent mystery permeated his daily life as well as his ideas, and it was clear that he saw himself as a worker, an engaging teacher, and not as an ambitious cleric or academic.

While we in the *Audi Max* waited twice a week for his lecture to begin, Rahner might have been snatching a few extra minutes to direct the many projects he had assumed. Whether serving publishers or cardinals, his life existed in long days of writing, and in directing projects executed by teams. There was a new edition of the German Catholic encyclopedia, *Lexikon für Theologie und Kirche* and a new edition of Denzinger's collection of documents by popes and councils from more than 2,000 years. Living in a Jesuit house near the English Garden, beginning early in the morning after prayer, Rahner was assisted by a small staff helping him to write essays, conciliar talks, and articles for encyclopedias. One of his assistants recalled:

> In the mornings when Rahner came to the Institute, he had already put his handwritten letters in the mailbox. Then he went, not infrequently with a sigh or grumble, to the work before him: writing, dictating, reading the newly arrived mail of the day, and then a pause for coffee. After a break at midday the same work continued, although to it was added appointments with visitors. Even the time between the appointments was used for work. And yet, how relaxed and free he could be when he was conscious that the day's work was done. He enjoyed ice cream on a hot summer afternoon, and an evening in winter at the Circus. Still the basic world of those years was work, work not understood as research, and certainly not as a basic reexamination and explanation of his own positions, nor as lectures (although Rahner liked to call himself a "school master")—that was all too systematic, theoretical, and easy—but rather as "information." Information as answers to basic questions being asked today in educational institutions, information as articles for collections, and information as answers to the questions asked by people in different circles.[21]

As the Council drew to a close, Rahner and his helpers were assembling two thick paperbacks: a theological dictionary and a commentary on every document of Vatican II. Equally time-consuming were multivolume theological works whose articles were written by leading theologians, but whose editorship and composition of large sections fell to him. The first volume of a large *Handbuch für Pastoraltheologie* appeared in 1964 while a few years later came a more extensive theological encyclopedia, *Sacramentum Mundi,* and a postconciliar textbook, *Mysterium Salutis.*

Rahner's theology has three great themes: the existential and transcendental-psychological analysis of the human person; the self-communication of God as grace and revelation; history and people in their history. "God's real supernatural and personal revelation is always being given. Hence the history of the human person and the history of revelation are coextensive. What we usually call revelation history (from Abraham and Moses to Jesus Christ) is not, strictly speaking, *the* history of revelation but a special and privileged part of that global salvation history constituted by God's self-communication as part of human existence and encountered throughout humanity's history at different levels."[22] Despite the Teutonic language, Rahner's interest was in making Christian truth, church life, and liturgy intelligible and attractive to people; he did this by finding within memorized creeds and burning candles the word and presence of God. Rahner was a master at showing how different cultural forms offered one religious reality: For instance, the same sacrament assumed different rites for different peoples. This was important because Catholicism around the world was passing beyond the fixed monopoly of Latin phrases and late Baroque forms. If fearful critics saw him as too modern, Rahner viewed himself as quite traditional. Sometimes he observed that he was not a theologian, if theology meant footnoted research; he just wanted to make vital and clear "the real, immediate preaching of the Good News of the Gospel."[23]

As I mentioned, I learned early on that Rahner would probably be denied permission to direct students working toward doctorates in theology, a permission he thought had already been given him. Through 1964 that uncertainty dragged on, and I switched to Fries and began to write my dissertation on Tillich, although I never missed a course Rahner taught. He recalled: "I received a call to Münster, and with the approval of the Minister of Education at the time and of Cardinal Döpfner, I said, 'I'll stay in Munich if I'm allowed to have doctoral students.' That was because I wanted an assistant and co-workers who would receive doctorates in theology and then could advance academically in that field....For all practical purposes the theology faculty refused me this rather harmless and in other respects obvious and common enough request....Guardini was very disappointed in me and vexed about the matter, but there was really nothing else I could do"[24] The Jesuit theologian was honored during his Munich years by honorary doctorates from universities as different as Strassburg and Helsinki. He accepted a theological professorship at Münster in the spring of 1967. This was, according to Fries, a solution that did not please him or all of the professors. "Munich always retained for Rahner," Fries summed up, "a particular attraction. He was in his faculty highly respected, met many friends and gained new ones; he had in Karl Lehmann an outstanding *Assistent* and enjoyed the particular trust of Julius Cardinal Döpfner."[25] Rahner's last semester in Munich was the one in which I took my comprehensive exams and graduated, and to me his departure passed unnoticed. In Münster, he had a number of American students who were to influence American theology greatly. Then, after his retirement in 1971, he came back to Munich for some years.

I heard Rahner preach once, at the university church, the Ludwigskirche (where Guardini had preached so often). He had preached for almost ten years every Sunday in the university church in Innsbruck, and I bought the published collection of those sermons in 1965. The small figure was a little lost in the large pulpit in front of Peter Cornelius's vast *"Last Judgment"* whose swirling figures and colors wanted to imitate Michelangelo. A respectful and monotone but energetic voice depicted, not asserted, interplays between the human and the divine. Did not Christian faith mean laying bare the encounter of grace with the transcendental and existential facets of each human life whether in the age of Mary Magdalen and Paul or today? That night—I believe it was during Advent 1965—I sensed he was rather tired.

Conciliar Theologian

During his lectures Rahner seemed slightly preoccupied, no doubt by his many writing projects but also by his days of constant work for Vatican II. Often, on the very day of his lecture, he had flown in from Rome. I would see Karl Lehmann off to the side talking to him about some problem, perhaps about conciliar issues or publishing schedules.

The Jesuit's contacts with Rome before the Council had been few and negative, repeated Vatican insistence upon prior censorship of writings. He had gone to Rome for the first time only in 1955 when, more than 50, he had been asked to give the Ignatian spiritual exercises at the German seminary. Shortly before, his study on the assumption of Mary, proclaimed a dogma in 1950, had been forbidden publication. At the end of 1954, Pius XII had criticized his theology on "the multiplicity of Masses and the one sacrifice," a theology that ten years later, Rahner observed to Paul VI, had become widely accepted in concelebration. Pope John XXIII appointed him over the objections of influential Jesuits at the Gregorian University to a preconciliar commission on the sacraments in 1961, although he was not invited to Rome for any of the early sessions of his commission. As the opening of the Council neared, bishops were permitted to select a theological adviser, and Cardinal König of Vienna chose Rahner. "Rahner," the cardinal recalled, "was startled at first and asked to think it over; he said that he had never been in Rome, that his name was no recommendation for me, and that he feared difficulties in the place where his censures had originated. His first theological works marked by existential philosophy and new aspects of anthropology had found in many circles astonishment and contradiction. After some hesitation he came to accept my invitation."[26] In Herbert Vorgrimler's view, Jesuits in Rome were of little help to their theologian (just as some Roman Dominicans had ignored their gifted French colleagues). "The Jesuits in the neighborhood of the Holy Office were either his enemies such as the dogmatician Sebastian Tromp and the moral theologian Franz Hürth, or they were cautious tacticians like Augustin Bea. The General of the Society, J. B. Janssens (who died in 1965), was an amiable and benevolent enough man, but quite helpless in the face of the Holy Office."[27] Janssens once observed to Henri de Lubac, who himself was under a cloud for supporting Teilhard de Chardin, that curial officials often did not obey the pope. Regardless, Rahner was kept away from the preparatory work for the Council, a measure that brought protests from German theologians and bishops and remarks of displeasure from John XXIII.

What was the background to these Roman tensions? Curial officials had investigated Rahner over the years because he wrote in a contemporary style and a nonscholastic format. In June 1962, the General of the Jesuits informed Rahner that everything he sought to publish was to be subjected to scrutiny by a special censure, although Rahner had indicated that he would give up writing rather than submit to such a process. A letter containing 250 signatures (including that of Konrad Adenauer) was sent to the pope who eventually intervened. "In May 1963 the Jesuit General told Rahner that in the future, he would choose Rahner's censors, as before. With this the Holy

Office retreated, and from then on until his death Rahner was spared further canonical penalties. In fact he came to have a genuinely friendly relation with his former enemies and contributed essays to the *Festschriften* for Ottaviani and Parente."[28] When Rahner was named by the pope to be an adviser of the Council, the threat of censorship was removed, and so Rahner arrived at Vatican II as a conciliar expert in a curious situation: For him, no time had intervened between heretical suspicion and conciliar accreditation.

Rahner was drawn into an enormous amount of work, and during the first two sessions his numerous addresses in Rome strengthened the bishops to seek out new directions. "The schemata of the preconciliar type, put together by the Roman theologians before the Council and for the Council, were so full of neoscholasticism that in many ways one can really thank God they were dropped....I would not say that I performed anything special that one could pin down. I did work very hard, and it was terribly tiring work. It is hard to imagine how a particular decree, in some cases after hundreds of suggestions for corrections from bishops and others, finally found a formulation which was then accepted by the Council."[29] His letters back to Innsbruck and Munich spoke of daily problems, of slow progress through meetings and drafts; he was never seized by conciliar euphoria and later evaluated the success of the Council as modest. "I got back from Rome yesterday, tired. But one can always see to it that the worst does not happen and that small points of contact for a later theology are put in the schemata. That's not much, and yet it's a great deal."[30] Rahner saw that small steps forward took hours of work. Like some of the German bishops and other theologians, Rahner sometimes found the drafts too optimistic or too vague, too French, lacking precision in treatments of dialogue and atheism. Theology must not be afraid of looking at people as they are and of developing its ideas and structures from pastoral and ordinary issues.

In the meeting rooms within the Vatican, Rahner's stream of ideas was assisted by his competent, even elegant Latin. Tireless in revising drafts, he worked hard on documents treating the theology of the church. Somewhere I acquired mimeographed pages of Rahner's observations on the schema *De Ecclesia in mundo huius temporis (The Church in the Modern World)* in the draft of May 26, 1965. It was written in the first weeks of the spring semester in Munich, the spring before the last session of the Council. Comments were divided into general and specific (He also observed that the Latin style needed extensive improvement!). "This schema constructed, despite many difficulties, by so many different people working so intensely in different areas is still deficient in many ways." A first observation noted that it is not clear how the contemporary person is to think about Christian revelation guiding the church in the wider world. If statements, often vague, leave behind prior neoscholastic terminology, an engaging manner of expression is still missing from the text. One asks, in what way is this theology contemporary? Rahner suggested adding to the document a Christian anthropology that would include sin and also have an eschatological dimension. Yves Congar recalled Rahner at the Council: "Rahner spoke a great deal but always had something to say (perhaps that was an indiscretion). When Rahner spoke it was with heart and soul."[31]

The end of the Council in December 1965 was marked in Munich by a special lecture delivered by Rahner in the Herkulessaal of the royal residence, an auditorium for symphony concerts. He spoke of the basic goal and meaning of the Council, that more faith, hope, and love might flourish among the human race. The Council and church must seek out what is personal and intimate; otherwise their deliberations are a sad and deceptive theater. One should not think that conciliar measures must have all their results in ten years, since it took the Council of Trent a hundred years until it had sustained its measures. Vatican II was a great Council, a Council introducing a new period in the church, the first council of the church stepping forth as a true world-church. Was renewal bestowed by the Council? No, but the event was a decisive beginning: The church cannot go backward to the age before it.

Grace, God's share of the divine life, was at the center of Rahner's theology. An existential and transcendental theology of grace meant going beyond the scholastic and Baroque electric company of passing graces to recognize an intimate, personal presence of the Triune God in individuals. Jesus preached the kingdom of God, and that reality St. Paul and theologians came to call grace. Grace could no longer be depicted as a commodity to be acquired, as an extrinsic force summoned up by laws; grace was something dynamic and inseparable from human life. The believer is not simply an object present at church services and required to have external and internal religious badges. Rather, each man and woman is a subject, complex in freedom and personality, for whom faith and liturgy, prayer and religious experience make present Someone unseen seeking to become known to them. Not only are death, language, and temporality facets of our personality, but there is also a "supernatural existential," God's constant offer of love. Wouldn't, I wondered, such a personal understanding of life and grace, liturgy and creed help Roman Catholicism to become less moribund, less automatic, less cold?

And the church? Did anyone today need the church, a church of faded performances and rigid structures? Wasn't the church static and boring even for the devout? Rahner showed in essay after essay, talk after talk, how the church could not only survive but also flourish and serve.

Individual persons and God meet in a community, in a local church that is itself a collective living person. Rahner saw in the 1950s that the church was overly monoform and institutionalized. Bookstores still held his book, written in 1957, called *The Dynamic Element in the Church.* Far from there being just an occasional mystical charismatic like Vincent de

Paul or Damian of Molokai, the life of the church held many charismatics (then to use the word *charismatic* was controversial). A dynamic church included more than bishops: Why were hierarchical structures involved in a conspiracy to keep all that was dynamic repressed? The charismatic is not the extraordinary, not the miraculous but the Spirit subtly at work in myriads of people, in their lives and love for each other. That book invited the church to pass beyond the barricades set between institutions and God's grace, to let the Spirit unfold in various forms serving the community. Catholics who were not priests or nuns had a dignity that went beyond pure passivity. Although the alternative was not democratization, there should be a new reunion of Spirit and church. A bishop, expected to be more than an aloof and annoying bank president, should have the qualities of a leader, a leader in public preaching and in serving what the Spirit wanted for the church. The pope is not the only active subject in the church but to some extent discerns and receives the powers that the Spirit of God pours into various people in the church. The Spirit is preparing new charisms of ministry for the laity, for a community in which there is no lack of people reading and willing to respond. "That prophets [from the distant past] are praised and canonized is fine—then they are dead and their charism can be institutionally accepted. More important is the discernment of charisms of the Spirit when they emerge; the furthering of charisms and the avoidance of letting them suffocate from misunderstanding and neglect, even from hatred and mean-spiritedness. That is not so easy, for while the institution is always the same..., the charismatic is essentially new and surprising."[32] It is dangerous for the church to fight against the gifts of the Spirit.

Rahner was unassuming, approachable, and direct. He did not fit the type of the *Herr Professor.* He had no interest in prestige, in power, and certainly not in money; in interviews he described himself as without anything distinctive, ordinary, living amid people to whom he was trying to make the gospel credible. Around 1965, the English-speaking doctoral students in Munich founded an association. We would invite a professor to an officers' club at an army base where he would give a brief talk followed by questions; in this way the faculty could come to see that the English-speaking students were serious. One time Rahner came. Toward the end of the evening, his *Assistent,* Karl Lehmann, turned to me and asked if he had understood correctly that there was to be a small honorarium. I replied that there was, 100 marks (then about $23). He asked if it were possible to have it that night. "You see, we are driving to Innsbruck tomorrow and we're leaving early and we don't have enough money for gas." When I showed my surprise, he replied that they never had any money because all of Rahner's salary, fees, and royalties went directly to the Society of Jesus, and the professor never remembered to ask for money. I had the impression that the overworked and little paid Lehmann was often providing money for gas and ice cream.

For the winter semester, 1965–1966, Rahner was scheduled to teach a seminar, but when we arrived for its opening session, well over 150 people were seated in the large slanted classroom. He solved the problem by developing brief but insightful monologues on various subjects. Continuing his tradition at Innsbruck of holding colloquia to discuss all kinds of topics, the seminar became a theological investigation of themes suggested by the students. That opening meeting turned out to be particularly interesting and remains in my memory 25 years later. The seminar topic was supposed to be "The Theology of Nonbelief." That afternoon for two hours Rahner simply suggested topics we might discuss. One seminal and significant subject followed another, each left suspended in the midst of various historical realizations and meanings. The slow German voice began wondering, pondering about what sacrament, creed, or penance for sins might mean. "It would be quite interesting, if only in a provisional way, to ask about the reality of this sacrament for today's Christians, for those who accept this sacrament in a believing way and practice, but who understand little concerning its origins with the early church or its various culturally conditioned and Spirit-led transformations in rite and text through history, not to mention its connection to and realization of the dynamic of Jesus in his earthly life and teaching, a sacrament, which, if not explicitly, nonetheless implicitly, and in a deeper way, intentionally was his gift. But first,..." Theology was historical discovery and cultural insight, a mystagogy into religion amid people, a contemplative guidance into an unseen Mystery present in the halls of time.

That afternoon time sped. "It would be quite interesting, if only in a provisional way, to ask about the purpose of...." The potentiality of a Latin word, a Greek proposition, a Baroque rite, a philosophical category unfolded, resulting from the style of thinking he had learned from Heidegger, who spoke of thinking as piety. The goal, however, was not the condescending extraction of the mythical or the secular rejection of the supernatural, but the uncovering of the incarnational, of divine reality emerging through cultural and historical circumstances, not as a dilution but as a gift. Questions should be posed in order to further discussion, not to end it. "The infinite horizon of human questioning is experienced as an horizon which recedes further and further the more answers a person can discover."[33]

Similarly, in his numerous essays, he would unfold after an opening historical dialectic a new way of looking at a theological issue—"Even dogmatically permanent and divinely ordained structures in the Church have always had a historically conditioned concrete form."[34] In the 1950s, his articles had begun to be collected into volumes called *Schriften zur Theologie:* the first volume, *Theological Investigations,* had appeared in an English translation in 1963. It was a book of essays on the evolution of dogma, Christ's knowledge, evolution, and nature and grace, and was the only realization I had had of Karl Rahner and his theology before arriving in Munich.

A book of Rahner's essays accompanied me as I walked in the damp and gray days of winter in the gardens of the Nymphenburg palace waiting for spring. Later, it would be clear that in the 1960s Rahner was passing quietly into the third stage of his theology. First, there had been the analysis of the believer in light of modern philosophies; then came the theology of God's self-communication present existentially to each man and woman in various modes beyond the electric company of laws and forces to each man and woman. History now held an important role: the history of salvation beginning for tens of millions of people long before Abraham, of human religions, the history that held a climax in Christ, of the church's forms and ideas. Rahner's theology was moving beyond ecclesiastical difficulties to Christian dialogue with European atheism and Marxism, and then to an even wider "ecumenical" horizon of the world religions, the great issue of the coming centuries. "Contemporary theology must be theology of a world-church....The plausibility of Christianity for other cultures can no longer be grounded in the superiority of Europe and the West. We must come to a Christianity that has genuinely achieved an inner and essential synthesis with other cultures. There are signs that this is beginning to happen."[35]

Rahner helped me see that the challenges facing Catholicism were much greater than simply absorbing some insights of the Protestant reformers or understanding the trendy terminologies of Tillich or Bultmann. Catholicism had its own history, very broad and very old, and those riches repressed should emerge. The challenge was no longer Protestantism but modernity, and its opportunity lay not in Aristotle's metaphysics and neo-Gothic buildings but in science, person, and worldwide humanity struggling to become aware and free. Above all, he showed how the salvation of a generous God found a positive, visible climax in Jesus, but was not withheld from the hundreds of millions who existed before Plato and Isaiah or who prayed at a Muslim or Hindu shrine.

In Munich, I did not think about whether Rahner was influencing me (in 1965, in Munich, there were doctoral students who had no interest in Rahner). A great thinker does not have an endless string of new ideas but only a few insights, insights, however, appearing in a kind of code. If the thinker is great, if the ideas are rich and liberating, the teacher's words illumine life. Rahner's lectures and publications held no radical statements about Jesus or the papacy; they were inevitably about something beneath the many things and ideas of Christianity, something implicit, elusive, and luminous, something about the real presence of God in history.

Bildungsroman

To discover, to learn, to make choices, to love and be loved, to sense the future arrive in the streets or in the woods—all this shapes a life. Each person's trajectory leads out from family, nationality, religion into the open mystery of one's life. Someone has loved me into existence; no one like me has lived before; and no one in the future will be the individual I am.

German philosophy and German art pursued stories of the self. Schelling's philosophy narrated how through conflict and freedom even the divine Trinity of powers was becoming itself: God was becoming God. Heidegger's existence and Freud's ego sought to explain the pattern of an individual. The Germans had a word to designate the story of becoming oneself, *Bildungsroman. Roman* is a romance, a novel; *Bildung* has a rich linguistic family in which *Bild* means picture and *bilden* means to educate in a cultural way. *Bildungsroman,* a novel about the people and events influencing the personal formation and education of an individual on the road to identity, was born in the late eighteenth century along with modernity. Goethe's *Wilhelm*

Meister, Dante's *The Divine Comedy,* George Eliot's *Middlemarch,* Mark Twain's *Tom Sawyer* are novels of a man or a woman becoming a person amid life's conflicts. The novel of self-discovery usually involves a journey as someone young leaves family and community and walks out into the world of promise and alienation to find mentors who are both troubling and wise.

During my first summer in Germany, I read some of Thomas Mann in German; in the autumn, I bought the two-volume paperback edition of *The Magic Mountain,* passing over a remarkable number of unknown words as I read it. Not a few critics found Mann's *The Magic Mountain* to be the great *Bildungsroman* of the twentieth century. In Mann's story, experiences, people, conflicts, even illness form an ordinary, unimposing, "simple young man," Hans Castorp. *The Magic Mountain* takes place in a Swiss tuberculosis sanitorium located high in the mountains where the patients for most of the year look out on endless snow. The hero has come to visit his cousin, a military officer with tuberculosis, for two weeks, and he stays for years, since he accepts the diagnosis of the doctors and psychotherapists that he, too, is ill. The isolation of the sanatorium is a school for discussions about liberal and reactionary politics, sexuality and science, art and humanism. The hero of this novel of time was not just Hans, "worrisome child of life," the problematical "man of God,"[36] but the modern person who has questions about his or her place in the universe, about the mystery of existence.

A novel of the self is not always one of achievement or violence or mounting sensuality but can be the story of reflection and awareness. "Some," Mann wrote, "have called *The Magic Mountain* a novel about education. Since at its center is the human problem, the puzzle of being a person, I am not too hesitant to call it a religious book....No wonder and accident for from the beginning religion and myth in their historical form—a world of the most touching intimacy and isolation and one in which from the beginning all is present—have totally overpowered my interest in the human and the humane."[37] In the enclosed atmosphere of the medical resort, Hans's experiences are heightened, as the young engineer comes to know not more about science but more about life. Mann's novel—it is not much of a story—reaches a humanist climax: Hans's vision in the sudden Alpine blizzard when he is urged to choose life over death. "Man should for the sake of goodness and love give death no place for ruling his thoughts."[38]

The novel is very much about time, about temporality understood as chronological time at the edge of World War I, or as interior, human time running slow or fast. "The book is itself about that which it narrates. For inasmuch as it describes the hermetic education of a young hero into the timeless, it strives through its artistic means to dissolve, transcend and realize time through the attempt of a musical-ideal total world which it encompasses, in each moment it wants to give a complete presence and yet to present a magical *'nunc stans.'*"[39] The characters' conversation and attitudes express a little of new theories on time from the first decades of the twentieth century: the élan vital of Henri Bergson, the temporal relativity of Albert Einstein, the historicity of Heidegger, the simultaneous tonality of Arnold Schoenberg. Although its theme is time, nonetheless, in this novel little happens: Dramatic conflicts are few and conversations are many and long. There are theories on everything from medicine to war; its world is an inner world where a self is observing, puzzling, changing. Time barely moves.

Not surprisingly, in Europe I liked to read about others seeking their self out of uncertainties and conflicts, for in reading about individuals I was studying that modern psychology and philosophy excluded from my education. Literature could be psychology. Thrown toward the future, caught between the past of Rome and the future of America, my limited and repressed personality sought to understand. If, in my first years in Europe, my solitary ego had shrunk before the eyes and language of mentors in philosophy and theology, nonetheless, my life and education were expanding. Hadn't Catholic years in the Midwest bestowed on me an optimism about change and the future? The lives of the saints, stories read in grade school that appeared later on the feast days of the liturgical year, were stories of heroism when individuals garbed in togas or medieval robes found adventures ending in martyrdom, foreign journeys, or caring for lepers. So many religious movements, so many monasteries and bands of preachers, so many schools of mystics, all of which began with some man, some woman who, in a new way, transcended self-absorption and found a conversation between self and God. The mystic Meister Eckhart had concluded: "Life gives the most noble lessons."

As the monoform days of snow surrounded Hans in the Alps, so the cold and overcast Munich months intensified my experiences. I also was without distinction, ordinary, a somewhat orphaned and bewildered antihero, someone emerging from a period of temporal suspension and now in a further exile, a young man finding an education in daily life as well as in seminars, in architecture and politics as well as in old texts.

An exile in Europe, however, could be dangerous, mortally dangerous. Some foreign students found the independence and the lack of academic requirements to be a slide into passivity. So much freedom for reading and research never resulted in anything written, and merely living in a foreign country (using the library or the post office) occupied time. Years would pass and nothing was accomplished. Some would not have even learned the language: Eventually, inactivity brought depression and paralysis. Moreover, as the 1960s progressed, isolation in Europe provided an escape away from the changes in the church and society back in America. Newness in the church and the desire to return from my European education kept me awake and active.

Die Meistersinger and *Der Rosenkavalier* were Munich's favorite operas. The first, by Wagner, premiered in Munich in

1868. The second, from fifty years later, was by Richard Strauss, a Munich boy whose father played the French horn in the state opera and whose mother was the daughter of the family that owned the large Pschorr brewery. Both operas were stories of young people growing up and others growing old, about time and subjectivity. Nürnberg in the sixteenth century and Vienna in the eighteenth were the settings for these plays about youth, for stories of an aspiring young man amid immature apprentices and academic masters, or of young people in the Viennese society of arranged marriages.

In my first summer I heard *Die Meistersinger* in the newly rebuilt Bavarian State Opera. It was very long, but the action was funny and held Bavarian words such as *Mädl* and *Sprüchlein.* The *Lehrbuben,* the apprentices, were always fooling around by mocking people just as at St. Kajetan the *Messbuben,* the altar boys, occasionally arrived in the sacristy for High Mass with only seconds to spare or stood around afterward in their red cassocks and laughed at my accent and grammar. In Wagner's opera a young knight, pretty much alone in the world, arrives in the big city of Nürnberg to enter the guild of master singers. At the beginning of the first act, he meets a young woman, Eva, and learns that his desire to be a master singer is also the only way, to win her for marriage. He doesn't lack confidence. He has learned to sing "in his own way," instructed in music on his rural estate in the winter nights by ancient books, and in springtime by birds. It was an opera of rustic energy pitted against academics and of an unknown young man with lonely aspirations meeting brusque rebuffs from various institutions. "If I have to fight for her by singing, I can only win!" In Walther and his young mentor, David, and the wise Hans Sachs, I saw something of my own situation. David does not think Walter has much of a chance—"the rank of master singer you don't earn in a day"—and gives him technical instructions on how to prepare for the examination: "You must be both singer and poet before you turn into a master."

Walter's examination song is filled with talent and emotion but breaks too many rules, although the wise Hans Sachs, cobbler and poet, realist and idealist, defends him: "If he shows an empathy with true art and employs it well, who cares about who his teacher is. The young knight's song and melody I found new but not confused; if he left our paths still he walked firmly and without error."[40] Amid the uproar of the apprentices and the posturing of the masters, he fails the first test and is *versungen und vertan,* "miss-sung and miss-done." Sachs meditates on the sad human condition, wondering if the traditional explanations of spooks or lilacs making people a little crazy are not as good as any other excuses for human folly. He rouses himself and sets in motion an intrigue that leads to a happy resolution for Walter, Eva, and art.

Life was a risk. There were always plenty of pompous authorities around to disrupt things. The replacement of art and love with rules was one of the oldest stories in the human race. I hoped that the difficulties of the opera would not reappear in my life, but rather that, in David's words, my doctoral dissertation and exams would be crowned with success.

As Shakespeare Said: ## "Ende Gut, Alles Gut"

What had I learned as the years passed? In 1964, 1965, 1966? I understood little and a little. Some of what then seemed important would over time be absorbed and taken for granted: general ideas about the theology of the church, the theology of the different reformers, principles of ecumenism with Protestants. I knew a little of Schelling, nothing of Hegel; I saw how Catholic theologians and exegetes used the Bible and Heidegger; I studied Rahner's conclusions more than noticing his vision. Idealism or existentialism, medieval or Greek metaphysics, French and German theologies of the seventeenth or nineteenth centuries—all were different ways of seeing, of reaching out to the real. Other ideas to which I had hardly adverted would gain importance, for instance, culture and grace, Christianity and the world religions, the theology of the local church, the history of sacramental rites.

How utterly different my life would have been if I had studied in the United States. I would have missed being a witness to the event and experience of the Council, remained a Puritan without the sacrament of cultures. I would have been drawn too far into American Enlightenment religion and liberal Protestantism, which then seemed so important, but which were headed toward decline, destined to continue more as books and theories than as churches. However, in those years in Europe I rarely averted to what was happening in America.

The late autumn sun showed some mornings that south of Munich an early snow had fallen on the Alps; six months later, in May, the waiters were setting up their tables in the Marienplatz. From the moment I arrived in Munich there could be only one happy ending, to gain my doctorate. This would be accomplished first by attending seminars so that professors had at least seen you before they examined you, second by writing a dissertation, and third by passing comprehensive exams. In Germany, those exams were taken after the completed dissertation was approved. They were held in eight areas of theology, ranging from Hebrew scriptures to canon law, and in each area there was a long written exam—the professors would have to be patient with both my German grammar and handwriting—and then an oral exam. Professors assigned a student large areas for the examination: For instance, in the New Testament I was given the Greek grammar and exegesis of six chapters of the Gospel according to John and of ten chapters of Acts of the Apostles. During the oral exams, however, the professors proved to be sympathetic and interested.

After the exams, in June 1967, obstacles still remained to my receiving the degree, rituals surrounding the ceremony bestowing the doctorate: These medieval customs and academic protocol were the last obstacles in my apprenticeship. As in universities centuries earlier, I was to select thirty theses for public disputation, theses formulated in Latin, published in a four-page brochure, and then briefly defended at the ceremony granting the degree. Fortunately, a German Dominican scholar—one of his fields was the presence of Western theology in Greece and Armenia during the Middle Ages—passed through and improved the vocabulary and grammar of my Latin. I was given the name of a printer who did that kind of work for the university, and in a few days I had the copies of my theses with their modern topics stated in the language of Cicero. The ceremony of my "promotion" was announced to the members of the faculty of theology as I gave each professor personally a copy of the theses. That direct bestowal was not so easy, for the faculty was busy, moving rapidly from office to lecture hall. I searched them out as they entered or left their lectures but made the mistake of leaving the copy for one retired professor at his residence; he called me up to tell me it must be given to him in person—one last anxious situation.

The day of the doctoral ceremony approached. I recall mentioning to the Dominican rector of St. Kajetan who attended the ceremony with me that only now, three days before its conclusion, did I think that I might finish this enterprise. That morning, the theological faculty with its dean assembled for the ceremony, an academic ritual resembling an ordination. There was a beautifully printed document of the ceremony with texts in black and the directional rubrics in red. We students—I joined two others for the final ceremonies—were examined for a few minutes on one or two of our theses and received a robe, a hat, and a ring (not to keep). Then each of us had to read the opening of his inaugural lecture in Latin, but we were interrupted, as we knew we would be, after two or three sentences. The ceremony ended with congratulations.

That afternoon I was in the Herder bookstore, and the friendly woman clerk whom I had known over the years addressed me not as *Herr Pater*, but as *Herr Doktor*. An important and known change had taken place in me, if not a substantial change, certainly an existential one. Fries invited me to dinner, and the next day I flew to Paris, and then to America. I could hardly wait to return to the United States and its church unsettled and set free by the Council.

---

1. Fries, *Kirche als Ereignis* (Dusseldorf: Patmos, 1958). pp. 25, 27; see "Die ökumenische Bedeutung des II: Vatikanums," in *Glaube im Prozess* (Freiburg: Herder, 1984), p. 335.

2. Guardini, *Rilke's Duino Elegies: An Interpretation* (Chicago: Regnery, 1961), p. 250.

3. Guardini, *Freedom, Grace and Destiny* (New York: Pantheon, 1961), p. 10.

4. Guardini, *Die Vorsehung* (Würzburg: Fränkische Gesellschaft, 1959), p. 3.

5. Hans W. Müller, "Grüsswort," in K. Foster, ed., *Akademische Feier zum 80. Geburtstag von Romano Guardini* (Würzburg: Echter, 1965), p. 10f.

6. Rahner, "Festvortrag," in K. Foster, ed., *Akademische Feier zum 80: Geburtstag von Romano Guardini*, p. 23.

7. Rahner, "Thinker and Christian: Obituary for Romano Guardini," in *Opportunities for Faith* (New York: Seabury, 1975), p. 130.

8. *Karl Rahner in Dialogue: Conversations and Interviews, 1965–1982* (New York: Crossroad, 1986), p. 337.

9. *Ibid.*, p. 13.

10. Max Müller, "Zu Karl Rahner's 'Geist in Welt,'" in *Karl Rahner, Bilder eines Lebens* (Freiburg: Herder, 1985), pp. 28f.

11. Rahner, "The Present Situation of Catholic Theology," in *Theological Investigations* 21 (New York: Crossroad, 1988), p. 71.

12. *Ibid.,* p. 73.

13. Rahner, "The Importance of Thomas Aquinas," in *Faith in a Wintry Season* (New York: Crossroad, 1989), p. 45.

14. Dino Staffa, "L'Unità della fede e l'unificazione dei popoli nel magistero del Sommo Pontefice Giovanni XXIII," in *Divinitas* 6 (1962), p. 21f.

15. Rahner, *Faith in a Wintry Season,* p. 10.

16. *I Remember* (New York: Crossroad, 1985), p. 73.

17. Bernhard Welte, "Ein Vorschlag zur Methode der Theologie heute," in *Gott in Welt* 1 (Freiburg: Herder, 1964), p. 285.

18. Rahner, *Hörer des Wortes* (Freiburg: Herder, 1963), pp. 9, 133.

19. Rahner, "I Believe in the Church," in *Theological Investigations* 7 (New York: Herder and Herder, 1971), p. 103.

20. Rahner, *Foundations of Christian Faith* (New York: Crossroad, 1978), pp. 1, 4.

21. J. Splett, "Auf dem Lehrstuhl Romano Guardinis," in *Karl Rahner, Bilder eines Lebens,* p. 72.

22. Rahner, "Reflections on *Foundations of Christian Faith,*" in *Theological Digest* 28 (1980), pp. 209, 211.

23. *Karl Rahner in Dialogue,* p. 210.

24. Rahner, *I Remember,* p. 75.

25. H. Fries, "Professor in München (1964–1967)," in *Karl Rahner, Bilder eines Lebens,* p. 70.

26. Franz Kardinal König, "Der Konzilstheologe," in *Karl Rahner, Bilder eines Lebens,* p. 62.

27. Vorgrimler, "Karl Rahner: The Theologian's Contribution," in A. Stacpoole, *Vatican II Revisited by Those Who Were There* (Minneapolis: Winston Press, 1986), p. 38.

28. *Ibid.,* p. 44.

29. *Karl Rahner in Dialogue,* p. 262.

30. Vorgrimler, *Karl Rahner: An Introduction to His Life and Thought* (New York: Crossroad, 1986), p. 182.

31. Yves Congar, "Erinnerungen an Karl Rahner auf dem Zweiten Vatikanum," in *Karl Rahner, Bilder eines Lebens,* p. 67.

32. Rahner, *The Dynamic Element in the Church* (New York: Herder and Herder, 1964), pp. 82f.

33. Rahner, *Foundations of Christian Faith,* p. 32.

34. *Karl Rahner in Dialogue,* p. 236.

35. Rahner, *Faith in a Wintry Season,* p. 165.

36. Thomas Mann, *Der Zauberberg* II (Berlin: Deutsche Buch-Gemeinschaft, 1957), p. 183.

37. Thomas Mann, *Über mich selbst* (Frankfurt: Fischer, 1983), p. 380.

38. Mann, *Der Zauberberg* II, p. 209.

39. Thomas Mann, "Einführung in den 'Zauberberg,'" in *Gesammelte Werke* XI (Oldenburg: S. Fischer, 1960), pp. 611f.

40. Richard Wagner, *Die Meistersinger von Nürnberg* (Munich: Goldmann, 1983), p. 83.

CHAPTER EIGHT

• • • • • • • • • •

Returning to a New World

The Council had ended. Americans were coming in numbers to Europe to study at French, Dutch, and German universities where theologians, more or less famous, taught theologies of the Bible and of Vatican II, theologies about the local church or about a deeper and wider sacramentality of God at work in society and the world. A force of change brought confidence and expectancy in a period that was to be known as "the postconciliar era."

And I returned to the United States. On a happy day in August 1966, one of the blue buses finally took me from the *Hauptbahnhof* to München-Riem airport, and to a TWA flight for Chicago. Less than four years had passed (they seemed to me a decade or more), years that had jostled centuries, shaken institutions, questioned religion, years ending much and beginning more.

A conviction was moving through the world that something better was possible than the dictatorships of racial, economic, and ecclesiastical rigidity. The Council's texts spoke of encouraging society's quest for peace and justice. In America, in the 1960s, the Catholic Church and the gospel of Jesus met changing societies in which people were struggling to see things differently—blacks need not be isolated from society; war was not normal; a monastery or a school was not a prison; a parish was not a fiefdom. If some thought the Council would be followed by a brief regulated time of application, the freedom after the pressure of 400 to 700 years of sameness did not permit that. Blasting caps had been detonated, seeds sown. The future, the decades to which I was returning, was to be filled with renewal and upheaval, with changes and collapses in what I had known as permanent institutions, with liturgies and educational programs undreamed of in 1960, and, above all, with ceaseless work.

I had seen how past times brought ideas to life, and now I would watch how transcendent forces would alter society and disrupt institutions. I was young and did not ask where church and society were headed because I did not want to hold them or me back from the future. As soon as I left Munich, that city was forgotten, and I could only think of what was happening in the United States. In August 1966, I was impatient to leave behind days in foreign countries marked by rain, trains, dark beer, and hard rolls. Nonetheless, what I had studied and experienced was not just stored away but was also silently at work. Years later, I realized how not only books and ideas but also church buildings and experiences had become the lenses through which I would meet life. The decades after my return were no longer an education but a realization of what I had seen and learned. (The reader must be warned again that the narrator of these pages will not soon achieve important status or enter circles of power. Figures making world history in oval offices, composing atonal string quartets, directing movies, or drawing up Vatican rescripts will not appear. My destiny was not New York, but Iowa.)

Arrival

The plane from Munich brought me back to America on an August day. Beyond my Bavarian idyll and my European school of culture, I rode past the suburban houses with their green lawns down into the center of Chicago to the priory and parish of St. Pius for a week before going out to Iowa to teach. The night was stifling: Chicago, in late August, was enclosed by a heat and humidity I had forgotten in Europe. My brothers and friends from seminary days, now priests, described to me their new world, telling me how the Order and the church were changing. A church now existed that talked to Protestants, spoke of social injustices, bought books on theology, and went to school to study political science or biblical languages. The church was already different from the neo-Gothic priory set in the countryside or the Baroque shrine in the changing city. Some English in the liturgy had led to experimental, informal liturgies of songs and guitars for Masses in classrooms, homes, or parks because Catholics felt the need to celebrate the Eucharist outside of the dark church. Bible study groups had sprung up, rediscovering themes of the New Testament, such as baptism, that overflowed into community and ministry. A growing number of priests and nuns were working in slums whose racism and poverty had suddenly broken into public sight. Young Catholics wanted to work with the poor. Breaking out of enclaves of seminaries and novitiates, they were spending summers amid the drama and romance of the destitute. Excitedly, the Dominicans told me about more and more opportunities to meet all kinds of people and develop new ministries.

Along with social action, ecumenism, theology, and liturgy, psychology had arrived. Psychology is America's modern philosophy, its own form of transcendental idealism. Now it was legitimate for Catholics to talk about the struggles of life, to reflect on personal emotions and frustrations. Instead of being forced on some cold weekend to listen during a retreat to a priest's sermons that were lectures written up decades earlier, high schools students and young adults rushed to make weekends of encounters with self, friends, and God—heady stuff in a church for which *experience* had been a bad word.

In 1966, the Mexicans and Mexican-Americans in Chicago were fashioning around St. Pius church a "little Tiajuana." Ten years earlier, in white habit and black cappa, carrying a red rose, I had processed on Rosary Sunday through that area composed of Slavic ethnic groups. Six years afterward in 1962, as a young priest working there during the holidays, I had talked with recent immigrants whose apartments had burned on Christmas night. This local parish, within whose boundaries a half dozen other churches were set aside for middle-European groups, had become largely Hispanic as more and more of the Polish had pursued their dream and moved to the suburbs. On the night of my return, aromas of spicy food moved through the damp heat, and the poor Pilsen neighborhood was decorated with colored lights because this week was the parish festival, the *kermes*. The sounds of the people outside my window announced a crowded, diverse, needy church. The parish and the neighborhood cluster of parishes were a communal self with its social life, problems, and aspirations, part of America's sudden engagement with poverty and racism, a new kind of church, classrooms, and centers in the inner city. That August, just six months after the Council, American Catholicism was simultaneously plunging enthusiastically into two worlds: the multifaceted church renewal of Vatican II, and the serious problems, now surfacing, of the society in which it lived.

Freedom for the New

The world, East and West, was changing. Former colonies were entering the United Nations. The old America of Henry James and Calvin Coolidge soon would hardly exist in Atlanta, Denver, Phoenix, Seattle, or Los Angeles. Even the Roman Catholic Church could change. The texts of Vatican II set loose deep forces: the church as a communion of communities, theories of collective justice over individual aggrandizement, a richer history of salvation within human history, grace in men and women, new liturgies, an organic communion of churches. The ideas of French biblical scholars and German university theologians filled the new journals and books that had sales far beyond the previous offerings of American publishers. It was time to verify faith in experience and relevance, and the American mind spontaneously united theory and praxis. Nuns no longer wore clothes from the seventeenth century, and young priests preached from the pulpits about racial discrimination. Christian doctrine was no longer replaced by metaphysics, but found exploration in new texts for high school and colleges; above all, adult religious education appeared, inquiring into the reality of original sin and the presentation by the Gospel of Luke of the kingdom of God. The parish expanded its ministries beyond the Sunday Mass and the parochial school. The years after the Council introduced what was partly just common sense: expecting liturgy and sermons to have some impact, assigning people to ministries for which they were suited, and curtailing a clericalism with its implied contempt for others, even for its own members.

The liturgy changed under directives from Rome and national offices. The silent Mass that had not seen a Latin word altered for centuries offered a variety of readings. There were Masses for the elderly and sick, for children, for camping trips, for neighborhoods in a parishioner's home. Bridal couples understood and selected the biblical readings for their marriage liturgy; seminarians wrote eucharistic prayers; guitar players composed hymns and chants in the style of the new folk music. The American Catholic Church had very little music of its own. Gregorian chant and Palestrina were difficult and rarely performed, while the few vernacular hymns from Ireland and France were simple but sometimes unintelligible—during my grade school years, I wondered about the aeronautical meaning of the line we sang occasionally, "Nor fly thy sweet control." Mass outside of a church was something unimaginable, but now the celebration of the Eucharist blessed the ordinary life of a neighborhood gathered at someone's home or entered the streets as a proclamation of social justice. The repetitious devotions on a weekday night in parishes had offered an opportunity to pray and sing in English, but they faded away as the Mass itself was celebrated in English and in the evenings. Why attend novenas to St. Anne or Benediction when you could participate in the eucharistic liturgy through word and hymn—not just at dawn and not by listening to Latin but in the evenings in English. The Eucharist rendered its post-Baroque substitute superfluous, the repetitious prayers and mediocre hymns to a saint. There were Eucharists of all kinds receptive to human needs and aspirations of people. During the anti-Vietnam meetings and rallies in the spring of 1970, I attended Mass with dozens or thousands of people, liturgies where gold cups had been replaced by glass ones, brocade vestments by rough woolen stoles. In 1977, in the mountains of Japan, we sat on mats, with shoes off and caps on, as the readings led through long periods of silent meditation to a communion of consecrated bread and wine. And yet, the structure of the Eucharist was the same. The conciliar aftermath led Catholics in a few years out of a ghetto in a Protestant land into being the visible, seminal religious force in America.

American parishes, Latin American-based communities, and movements in Africa flowing out of liturgies of healing were graced points in the collective personality of a church struggling to find new forms beyond Europe, and soon Europe would draw some ordinary but vital pastoral formats from the Americas. The worldwide church and American society were eager disciples of renewal. Everywhere there were profound questions and interesting suggestions coming not from clergy but from a high-school French teacher or a tractor salesman about why the church should change and how it could change.

As the forms were altered, people understandably asked, which forms were divine and which were human? How could the indestructible and infallible church change? Were venerable and ancient customs, in fact, quite recent? An optimism about God's love and grace set aside the view that every infant who died apart from a ritual of washing or every unconscious senile person was excluded from heaven. One striking innovation was the liturgical mourning and celebration of the death of a Catholic Christian. The renewal of baptism and funerals brought to the liturgy of burial white vestments and Pauline readings of resurrection, implying that the destiny of the Christian was not primarily purgatorial fires but eschatological life.

Changes were clearing away what John XXIII and Paul VI had called the decrepit and moribund aspects of the church. What seemed new, however, was more often than not ancient and biblical, although it took some education and faith to understand the new. Change brought more change—all of which the *National Catholic Reporter,* a recently founded, valuable chronicle of the upheavals and progress of the American church, described. Some Catholics were surprised, some even shocked, by change. Why, however, would change be unusual, considering that little had changed in the church for centuries. In 1968, my aunt on an Iowa farm asked me how long "the changes" would continue. I answered unrealistically, but to her dismay, "for a few more years."

This postconciliar period, the fallout of a Council that lasted only four years, would for my generation never end. We were to live in the Catholic Church twice, before and after Vatican II, to live in a church and a society on both sides of the electric line of 1962. Experiencing two eras as different from one another as the age of Richelieu and that of Sartre, we did our theological education twice. After years in a neoscholastic seminary, at age 26 or so many went off to European or American faculties to undertake a second theological education. Schooled in a Baroque or modern style of neoscholasticism, we knew a lot about Duns Scotus and Albert the Great or Cajetan and Suarez, and then we came to have some acquaintance with Kierkegaard and Tillich, with Jungian psychology and urban sociology. Catholic theology at the beginning of ecumenism needed to be familiar with some Protestant theologians, past and present. In terms of generations, there was the age of "the greats," of Congar and Rahner, of Liégé and Jungmann. Then came the next age group that in Europe, with theologians such as Fries, continued the new directions in church and theology as did some in the United States. Then there was my generation, dedicated to the application and expansion of the Council: We might be called the "learners" and the "workers."

I was right, if boyishly exuberant, that September afternoon in 1963 at the New York airport when I exclaimed to the Maryknoll nuns that Vatican II was as important as the assembly of Nicaea in the fourth century. The later Council, however, was not a text but an event, not a dogma but a pastoral instruction.

Change is unnerving, and religious change is particularly disturbing. Changes in the church brought tensions between the advocates of the old and the new. *Polarization, pluralism,* and *renewal* were heatedly discussed. Alienation and fear among a few, however, could not stop bursts of change after centuries of sameness. The opposite of the future is not the past but the frozen present, the *nunc stans,* a milieu of neurosis rather than of grace. In Goethe's *Faust,* the devil introduces himself as "that spirit who always says, 'No.'"

The 1960s were new. They were modern. And yet their modernity recalled the past century's Romanticism of the individual amid nature and history, theories of the divine and human self-in-progress that I found in Munich libraries. The searches for community, the openness to personal journey, a mystical quest for some kind of revelation in ordinary life, an antipathy toward technology and a sympathy for people—these themes of the 1960s signaled the arrival of a new Romanticism, a return utterly unexpected, a mood expressed in the words and beat of the new music, music composed by those turning against oppressive establishments, music with an immediacy and sensitivity to individual life far beyond the songs of Broadway musicals. There was more to humanity than value-free science and more to Christianity than anguished existentialist versions of the aphorisms of Jesus.

Inspiring pages were found in paperbacks passed around, written not by Camus but by Pierre Teilhard de Chardin. This French Jesuit's passion was for the long history of earth revealed in paleontological exploration, and, in his view, the long evolutionary history of the earth did not imply a long development of God's grace at work in people. The Vatican, in the 1950s, refused the Jesuit permission to publish his works, but after his death they sold hundreds of thousands of copies a year. People were yearning to live in one world and to find there a personal and communal identity without violence. Teilhard spoke of a human history of slow, social progress moving through hundreds of thousands of years. As a scientist, he saw evolution unfolding in galaxies, stars, plants, and animals. Could not that same development be found on another level, in divine grace touching the human spirit in the history of religions and finding its climax in Jesus? The Bible was an evolution toward Jesus born at Bethlehem and toward the Christ coming at the end of time. What Teilhard called the *noosphere,* a realm of human freedom and consciousness, was exploding—not in esoteric spasms of inevitable violence born from sin and decline, not in a miraculous myth but in challenges to maturity. What blood and sex were to animals and sap was to plants, love was to the human race. Within cosmic and biological evolution and within the drive of culture there was a deeper unseen love given by God to form community, the *agape* preached by Jesus, a *Christosphere.* God's complete reign, the second coming of Christ, might be as far ahead as the time of the mastodons were in the past. This generous view suited the Council's openness to humanity and history, to its passage beyond the unhappy spirituality of legalistic routines and a pious, anxious disdain for the human. "We must try everything for Christ," Teilhard wrote, "we must hope everything for Christ....To divinize does not mean to destroy, but to sur-create. We shall never know all that the Incarnation still expects of the world's potentialities. We shall never put enough hope in the growing unity of humanity."[1]

The Council, whether it intended or not, brought freedom: There was not just one theology, not just one eucharistic prayer in Latin, not just one ministry of priesthood, not just one way of being a parish. The unquestioned past, a monolith in which every form and rule had its fixed place, shook and dissolved not into secularity but into sacramental variety. The Latin Mass in 1960 did not have the same texts and forms as those used in Rome in A.D. 260. The ideas of Jesus were not quite the same as the conclusions of seminary manuals. If human authority united everything in the post-Baroque church—forgetting a rubric at Vespers or neglecting to receive a minor dispensation from an obscure Vatican office was little different from the exploitation of factory workers or rape—the 1960s brought to Catholics not evolution but liberation from the bland, a freedom from the recent past for something richer, for a return to the mission of Jesus and the Apostles, for a church resembling the communities of the first four centuries of Christianity.

The American Catholic Church was young; a large percentage of laity, nuns, and priests were young. They were unanimously in favor of the new directions of the church involving the centrality of scripture, liturgy in the vernacular, an emphasis on community and activity in the local church, and freedom for theology to learn from other faiths. If Catholics fell into a postconciliar nomenclature and grouping of conservatives and liberals, those terms were concerned not with new dogmas but with the degree of change and originality to be urged for the concrete expressions of parish life. The shock waves of the

Council's texts bewildered teachers of scholastic logic and church law, as well as autocratic pastors and bishops. Two years after Vatican II had ended, I recall overhearing a professor of canon law being asked in a friendly way, "What do you teach?" He responded as he turned away, "I wish I knew." Some reacted to the new freedom by leaving the ministry, even by leaving the church. Some of what had been held up as divine appeared to be quite transitory, all too human. It made no ultimate difference which "Preface" was used at a Mass or what one ate on Friday. It was, however, important to help a poor person. One was free to be a Catholic or not, free to remain a priest or a nun or not. Naturally, church attendance fell from the unrealistically high numbers of people packing a church for 30 minutes to fulfill a duty, but it remained, in the light of history and in comparison to other countries, quite high.

The human, the pastoral, the social would be tested according to the Council *per modum experimenti,* by experimentation. Freedom sought the life of the gospel beneath the laws of the church, sought out each life as an individual life and not as a failed attempt to replicate the biblical Ruth or the French Vincent de Paul. Little by little, the American church became one of adults who had freely chosen to belong to it actively. Roman Catholic optimism expected this time to be a smooth progression, but years of activity and debate unfolded as the Council's themes revealed more and more issues. Over the following decades, Catholics would remain in favor of the directions taken by the Council. If they stayed traditional in dogmatic viewpoints and strong in their support of church institutions, they were liberal on some social and moral issues, and they expected the ministries in parishes to be realistic and effective.

What force was behind it all? Time? Tradition? The Holy Spirit?

The ecumenical contacts among the seminaries in Iowa I described earlier heightened when Vatican II admitted that

Protestant churches were churches. Clearly, the renewal of Catholicism included a number of things the Reformers had emphasized in the sixteenth century: vernacular liturgy, expansion of ministry, the sovereignty of God, the reduction of Mary as a quasi-goddess, ecclesial groups complementing the papacy. Harmonious existence among the churches moved rapidly from novelty to norm, and one could hardly imagine the previous era of Christianity when a furtive glance inside a Methodist church might be a sin and when a Catholic priest might be a devil. The three seminaries in northeastern Iowa were pioneers in ecumenism, developing one unheard of project after another: jointly administered libraries, coordinated class schedules, cross-registration of seminarians, and joint summer sessions. Courses in the Old Testament and history were often taught by a team, as were advanced seminars comparing major Protestant and Catholic theologians. Catholics benefited from Protestant scholarship in history and the scriptures, while Protestants profited by Catholic interest in worship and ethics. The seminaries offered the traditions of the past—Catholic, Lutheran, Calvinist—and presented contemporary theologies of importance. There were experts among the Dominicans on Thomas Aquinas and Yves Congar; among the Wartburg faculty on Martin Luther and Paul Tillich; and among the Presbyterians on John Calvin and Karl Barth. In June 1965, the Association of Theological Faculties in Iowa was founded—the seminaries' cooperative union involved at that time the University of Iowa's School of Religion. Soon this enterprise would be overshadowed by clusters of seminaries in Boston, Berkeley, and Chicago, but Iowa fashioned the first group of Protestant and Catholic seminaries not only in the United States but, perhaps, in the world. In the 1960s, a number of famous Protestant churchmen pushed forward the new ecumenical age: Max Lackmann, pioneer of German ecumenical and liturgical communities, and the Presbyterian Eugene Carson Blake, head of the World Council of Churches, while the

Dominicans hosted lectures by Karl Rahner and Edward Schillebeeckx. These lectures were followed by symposia on the charismatic movement, Christianity and Marxism, and social justice related to justification by faith.

The teachers in the seminaries in the 1960s saw ecumenism as a mission, a ministry to spread the word of church unity. Professors went out to the towns of the Upper Mississippi Valley to offer in a high school gymnasium a new view of being Christian in America. The seminaries in Dubuque, exemplifying positive relations among Christians, thereby changed the climate of Iowa and the bordering states. One October, in 1968, I went to a small city in South Dakota. To a large assembly filled with people from the area's churches, I explained carefully why it was permissible for Catholics and Protestants to associate with each other, to sing and pray together, and how as Christians we shared much of our faith. As the concluding hymn with words by John Wesley faded away, there was spontaneous applause. I noticed how many people in the audience of Catholics, Methodists, Lutherans, and Presbyterians had tears in their eyes. Echoing their own deep but unexpressed intimations, they had just heard at church that it was all right not to hate.

The Year 1968

I had returned to Iowa to teach, to write, to live in a monastery far away from great cities and events, and yet change was all around.

The year 1968 was certainly an American *kairos,* a year of cultural and social change impelled by optimism and bordering on utopianism. Returning from Europe, I had noticed that disparate areas in the United States (the military, the university, the church) were challenged by the same ideas. The same kind of music protested war, celebrated liturgy, and spoke of ordinary life, a direct, rhythmic music unlike that of cocktail lounges where smoke got in your eyes. The postconciliar era met the age of Aquarius in the songs of Peter, Paul, and Mary and in movies such as *The Graduate* where, at the end, Dustin Hoffman locks people assembled in the church for a misarranged wedding with a crucifix set in the door handle. People in religious orders and universities, in the military and the government questioned the control of their respective aristocracies, which always opposed improvement and presumed a sovereignty, excluding just procedures or courts of appeal. The protests of the 1960s were aimed at bland and frozen institutions. New ideas were not accepted in the war-planning Pentagon nor in state legislatures procrastinating over civil rights, while the ivy-lined buildings of the university tranquilly portrayed in films had slipped into war research and useless projects, supported by state and federal taxes and the students' fees. The university prized itself on being value-free as it prepared weapons or ignored segregation and urban poverty; its cold secularity indirectly drove students to bizarre religions, to cults or drugs, to protest. Behind the protests, the polarization of generations ("Trust no one over 30!"), and the anger of the institutional directors dismayed by change were cultural plates plowing into one another, removing and creating thought forms, styles, and goals. By 1968, movements of change found intense forms in protests against a foreign war, public marches against domestic racism, and even rebellions in seminaries.

The young asked: "Who gave a few the power to command others, to reject or libel them, even to send them off to be killed?" Who were these people, so condescending, to have such power? It was clear that religious leaders, presidents, coaches, colonels, or mayors did not necessarily know best nor did they have any great interest in those they were supposed to assist. Corporations, political machines, seminary administrations, and White

House advisers had a tremendous investment in the status quo of the 1950s; the America of Doris Day and Eisenhower should last forever. How betrayed they must have felt because their subjects dared out of energy and hope to call for change. American and Western institutions were challenged not just by a new generation with a short list of improvements but by questions. The word "radical" entered the popular vocabulary; it meant honestly looking at the present and into the future. The 1960s were not revolt but speaking out, questioning, and protesting.

While some groups of the protest generation acted in violent ways and sought freedom and transcendence in sensuality, the mode of people from the churches was nonviolent. The marches, songs, placards, demonstrations, and resistance aimed at justice and peace. What journalists called "a new consciousness," Catholic activists understood as the Beatitudes of the reign of God visibly at work in society.

Of course, I recall this from the perspective of youth—I was a little over 30—and my recollections of those months come from my experience of the church in the Midwest.

The end of my second semester of teaching in the Dominican seminary and theology school fell in December 1967. The Dominican professors had the tradition of holding a Christmas party away from the priory, and that year it took place in a winter lodge on the Mississippi rented for the evening. As we were sitting down to dinner I noticed a certain commotion, people leaving and returning. Then, as we were enjoying the holiday meal with its wine, the subprior announced that he had just returned from taking the prior to the train station. The prior was leaving the Dominicans and the priesthood (and, one got the impression, the church and the faith). His was a rigid personality, a teacher who, over some years in strict and humorless classes, did little but repeat abstract neo-Thomism. The previous summer, however, he had gone to the Protestant Union Theological Seminary in New York for a few months of courses by Protestant and Catholic professors in exegesis and theology and had returned to lecture enthusiastically on modern biblical criticism and ecumenical issues. He had become more personable but also more sardonic, giving signs that he found much in religion amusing and a little fraudulent; he had assumed a certain liberalism but his liberal mentality was itself rigid.

The departure of a religious superior was at that time something unprecedented, a scandal. We heard that dioceses and other Dominican provinces looked down on us, unaware as they were that departures of superiors, bishops, and university presidents would soon touch them too. A month later, as 1968 began, two other Dominicans in our house left the Order. I had watched a postconciliar disease take hold of them: the arrival of new ideas and liturgical procedures, traditional but to us new, left them paralyzed. They became incapable first of teaching, then of preaching, and eventually even of celebrating Mass. Apparently, small alterations in the machinery of 1950s Catholicism made some priests so uncertain about everything that they could not function at all. They left sad and bewildered by a church and an Order, still quite traditional and monastic, whose unclear future of renewal and work frightened them.

Those departures were soon eclipsed by a greater disturbance. The Dominican school had three sets of students: Dominican students, diocesan seminarians, and a small group of nuns and lay people. The Dominicans had come to Iowa in the late 1940s to staff a seminary located across the road from the Dominican priory and school, where future priests were educated for the four dioceses of Iowa and for other dioceses reaching from Illinois to Montana. The Dominican faculty had changed in the three years after Vatican II as young professors returned from better educations in scripture, history, and moral theology. The diocesan priests on the other side of the road who directed the seminarians' formation (the daily rules, the liturgy, consultation about the personal, spiritual life) stayed the same as they had been in 1958. Either ignorant of the sea changes around them or hostile to the directions of the Council, the rector and his staff continued an inflexible regime of petty rules and punishments, a mixture of infantilism and clericalism repressing individuality and energy. (When the rector drove with his mother she always sat discretely in the back seat.) I was once drawn into this penal world when I was summoned to the rector's office to explain why I had given a seminarian, who, unknown to me had been restricted to campus, a ride back from a student party on a cold winter night. I explained that we received no information on seminarians being disciplined and that, regardless, considering the bitter cold, I would have given him a ride anyway. The rector objected to this affront, and I countered with a respectful reference to the behavior Jesus advised in the New Testament. To my allusion to the inspired word of God he replied with exasperation: "You see what comes from associating with Protestants."

After several semesters of frustrating situations, the seminarians had reached their boiling point and were drawn into serious conflict with the priest-directors. Some petty disciplinary move by the rector escalated the situation. Upon their return from Christmas vacation in January 1968, the seminarians went on strike and refused to attend classes within the seminary (elsewhere, in Boston and Washington, there were also strikes and conflicts in seminaries). The dioceses of Iowa were faced with the loss of a generation of priests, and in an unprecedented concession the bishops came to listen to the student complaints. At the end of the interviews, the seminary staff was replaced.

The Dominicans were careful to keep out of the strike, but there had to be someone for church authority to blame, namely, our young faculty. After all, it would be less awkward to blame the religious order than their own future clergy.

The 1960s was a time of hope. When the realities of racial persecution and war appeared on television, protest exploded. Couldn't the structures be removed that had been accepted as normal but had, instead, injured lives? Hope protested the slogan "business as usual" and replaced it with Martin Luther

King's "I have a dream." In April 1968, Duke University organized a symposium on the theology of hope and a number of Dominicans from the Midwest attended the assembly. The central speaker was to be a Protestant theologian, Jürgen Moltmann, who had recently published *The Theology of Hope.* It was a critique of liberal Protestant theologies from 1925 to 1965, of theories reducing the historical and the miraculous in the Bible to myths. After World War II, progressive Protestant Christianity became existentialist, substituting for the historical deeds of the divine Savior inspirational biblical texts sustaining a doubt-filled existence living apart from time or community. The New Testament, however, as theologians such as Moltmann and Teilhard de Chardin observed, was more. Jesus' kingdom pushes into the future, and the Bible's central affirmation—God is at work not just in heaven but on earth—leads through a theology of hope to social criticism and social betterment.

Duke pursued its sciences in buildings built in a neomedieval style set amid a spring of purple and scarlet azaleas. Hundreds of teachers and ministers attended the symposium. The crowd forecast the coming of an era of theological travel-education with well-paid speakers, expense accounts, and popular themes, a panoply of workshops, lecture series, mini-courses, and symposia drawing not dozens but hundreds of listeners. The first speaker was Harvey Cox, Baptist professor at Harvard, whose book, *The Secular City,* had brought to many readers the welcome, if shortsighted, news that the cities dominating contemporary society were in a state of rapid improvement and that progressive urban life was linked to the Bible's reign of God. The speaker had just begun his address when the moderator of the event approached the podium and announced that Martin Luther King, Jr., had just been killed in Memphis, Tennessee. In outrage over the death of a black prophet by the gun of a white drifter, Boston and some other cities were already in a state of riot. Professor Cox's home in Roxbury was threatened by riots and he decided to fly home immediately. I remember nothing more about the symposium, nothing of the ideas or meetings on the campus except a sterile but well-attended memorial service for King held in the Methodist neomedieval church of the university. Within 24 hours Durham was under threat of riots, and police stood in the streets in combat gear. At a reception, I learned that the professors' maids were reluctant to move between white and black neighborhoods (to walk six blocks away from central streets was to find the neighborhoods of the poor where the streets were red mud). Each hour brought reports of fires in Detroit, Washington, Memphis. Returning to the Midwest, at the Chicago airport we were greeted with the sight of an army on patrol, jeeps with mounted automatic weapons, and thousands of soldiers guarding O'Hare.

Hardly had the shock of Martin Luther King's death been absorbed when in early June Robert Kennedy was shot while celebrating a victory in the California presidential primary. Americans watched for a second time the televised funeral of a Kennedy. At the offertory procession, Kennedy's young children brought the bread and wine to the altar of St. Patrick's Cathedral in New York as the New York Philharmonic, under the direction of Leonard Bernstein, played the slow movement from Mahler's Fifth Symphony. The music sang of struggle but also of resignation. Civil rights, the Asian war, the cities' poverty, rebellion against institutions might be more difficult than at first expected. Society did not leave easily its tight secularity fueled by a boundless capitalism and controlled by centers of power in Washington and elsewhere. The light of hope faded a little, overshadowed in that year by further deaths of the famous and of the unknown, deaths in America and Vietnam. Hard years of work for peace, social justice, and equality lay ahead, calling on more and more people. What began as the new, the sensational, and the romantic would eventually become ordinary, persevering labor for peace and justice.

In June 1968, I was in Washington for a theology conference, my first. The Catholic Theological Society of America
was holding its annual meeting under the leadership of its president, the Jesuit scholar Walter Burghardt. The scars of the fires
in the black ghettos could still be seen. But new issues had
quickly surfaced. The feeling against the war, tangible in Lyn-
don Johnson's leaving the presidency and in the opposition of
Eugene McCarthy and then of Robert Kennedy, was no longer
the only cause of protests. For more and more Americans,
racism and poverty were linked to the war in Vietnam. King's
successors orchestrated a great march to Washington focused
on racism rooted in poverty. The business meeting of the theology convention was filled with resolutions concerning the
issues out on the streets. Then, in an act that five years earlier
would would have seemed bizarre to the Society's gathering of
priest-seminary professors, the assembly moved to adjourn its
sessions for a few hours and join the poverty march at its cli-
mactic point in Washington.

The year 1968 continued on its course: students and workers marched in France, the Russians invaded Czechoslovakia,
the civil rights movement for Catholics in Northern Ireland
began, black power salutes from athletes marked the Olympics
in Mexico City, and in the United States protests against the
war multiplied.

I went from the convention in Washington to South Bend
where I was teaching summer school at the University of Notre
Dame. On the day after the Fourth of July, the dean of the
Dominican theology school in Iowa called me. He said in a worried voice that the archbishop of Dubuque had informed him
that the bishops of Iowa, the governors of the seminary section
of our school, had asked for two of the Dominican faculty to be
removed: a professor in moral theology and me. No reasons
were given. As the accused often do, despite the unreality of
their crimes, I felt guilty. Since the struggle was over church,
religion, the realm of the divine, whatever errors I had made

were not just mistakes but must be sins; I must be a bad person to bring bishops, even the church, to the point of taking action against me. My condemnation would be spread about, in Iowa and in the media, among relatives and friends and then widely through the press avid for church conflict. Ahead, I saw a life of disgrace. Hot and humid days in Indiana increased my feelings of oppression and isolation (I was not to exacerbate this situation by talking about it). As I walked through dark green groves on the campus to teach class, I felt already convicted. The days passed, and one reason for my dismissal surfaced: A few months earlier I had allowed the seminarians to receive communion in their hands at a class-Mass. I could understand why Catholics were rebelling against a system: seminarians against rectors, friars against provincials, bishops against the Vatican, priests against bishops, monks against politicians. For decades, societies of rulers and police never explained their disciplinary actions, but only pointed to rules to excuse punishment for the slightest deviation. That July, Notre Dame was sponsoring a meeting for bishops. Once or twice I passed on the campus the archbishop who had given the order for my removal. He did not recognize me, of course; he had never met me except to ordain me to the diaconate.

To question an episcopal decision was to question a bishop's grace of office. He was empowered; he was responsible; he knew best. There should be no questioning. Behind the scenes the Dominican dean, a determined and emotional man, worked to change the bishops' decision. While he saw clearly the injustice of the request, he did not welcome ecclesiastical conflict. Other superiors in the Order advised obedience to the bishops; my removal was a small price to pay for ecclesiastical tranquillity, and I had probably caused trouble anyway. The dean found out to his surprise that not all the other bishops of Iowa had approved or even had known about the demand: It was the work of the archbishop. The firing of the two Dominicans was intended to be a compensation. The seminarians' revolt the previous January had forced the bishops of Iowa to replace an outdated staff, and now the Dominicans should make a similar gesture and replace some of their faculty. Flying from one episcopal city in Iowa to another, the dean convinced the bishops that the firings were a grave mistake. Catholic University had been the scene of a large student protest in support of Fr. Charles Curran, and there were other cases of innocent Catholics being removed. They were all given extensive coverage by the press. In Iowa, too, authoritarian action would lead to protests drawing the media to yet another sensational illustration of "the Catholic Church in Conflict." The protagonists would appear in a positive light, while one group surely would not: the bishops.

The episcopal demand was withdrawn. The entire incident passed unrecorded and forgotten, but there was a price to be paid, for the bishops never forgave the Dominicans. Not only had we been rumored, incorrectly, to have instigated the seminarians' revolt, but subsequently we had been the object of episcopal frustration—even if that sentence had been imprudently and unjustly set in motion. Unquestioned episcopal authority issuing from a dark, carpeted office handed out decisions to be obeyed. This one had been blocked—but only for a while. Within a year the bishops closed the diocesan seminary, an action removing more than half of the students from the school. The Dominicans had established that seminary 20 years earlier at the bishops' request. They had been paid, for the entire faculty and all educational costs, a fixed yearly amount of $12,000; when the administration of Aquinas Institute asked for the contents of the card catalogues from their reference library in the seminary, they were told to submit a bid. The bishops sold the seminary buildings quickly to a congregation of teaching nuns.

A few weeks later Pope Paul VI issued an encyclical on birth control. He went against his chosen commissions and much of the theological and episcopal opinion in the world. The day the encyclical appeared, American theologians and lay people expressed views contrary to the pope on television's evening news. Instead of a papal letter in parchment sealed with red wax reaching Vienna or London after months of travel, in the age of media a papal decision found its hearers quickly. And its critics. Television brought rapid information and also wide dissemination of events and ideas. Why should the pope alone decide an issue about which he knew little and which has no mention in scripture or tradition? In an age of education and postconciliar freedom, informed Catholics no longer felt that their views on faith were something without value. Moreover, Catholics now had not only American social causes, governmental military issues, and local church renewal as agitating interests but also modern papal authority.

At the end of the summer of 1968—its weeks had been punctuated by the violence of assassinations and protests—a group of Dominicans from the Midwest, of various ages and ministries, met to discuss the state of our group, our Province. Examined were the increasing involvement of friars in social issues, the rights of communities and individuals to have some say in their own lives, an end to secrecy concerning the Province's finances and personnel decisions, and the right to further education.

This grass-roots political action flowed partly from the distinctiveness of midwestern Catholicism. Midwestern Catholics were quick to see that they were not imitations of WASPs or recent immigrants. We had grown up in expanding cities and rural spaces with flourishing economies. Our minds, like our states, had open horizons. If our families had sacrificed to support churches and schools, we had learned to get along with others and to rise in a society where a Catholic minority was slightly suspect. Midwestern Catholicism was the source of most of what was new and active in an American diocese, from CYO sports to liturgical renewal and the Catholic Family Movement. The possible was also the real, and life offered possibilities to be seized and realized. Why stay in the past? Why be ashamed of this time and this place? These differences resulted in an unexpressed dissonance between the superiors from the East and the younger Dominicans from the Midwest. The older priests, formed in the 1940s and now happy to be superiors, were little interested in theology, higher education, new ministries, or social liberation (they had known poverty and war), while the young priests and seminarians from Green Bay or Albuquerque were from an educated, even slightly affluent background. Their world was not one of Catholic ghettos, but of religiously and ethnically mixed cities and towns brought together in public schools and state universities.

What were the issues that so agitated most of the Province? Claiming to represent easily the will of God, provincials and priors had long treated individuals autocratically, although this approach was contrary to Dominican theology, spirituality, and government. Now, after the Council, they were not defending friars who stood up in public against racism, poverty, or the war. Priests working in the inner city or theologians writing books on church authority could find themselves exiled to some priory where they were simply told to keep quiet. Such moves had a demoralizing effect on everyone, and soon priests in their thirties were leaving the priesthood. At a time of great opportunity, as a hundred or more priests and brothers moved into new ministries or went off to graduate schools, the Province was too much adrift. Traditional church politics, with its condescending style of bestowing favors and positions in the manner of urban political machines, struggled to retain its control. This, however, was challenged by the postconciliar spirituality of individual dignity and the politics of protest. The consultative bodies of the Dominicans, an original gift of its democracy from the Middle Ages, had been packed with lifelong members or stripped of power, but in 1967 and 1968, international Dominican meetings restored the constitutions and brought back the original democratic forms, and provinces were encouraged to discuss openly and broadly their life and ministries.

That turbulent summer of 1968 a group of friars, young and middle-aged, met and wrote collectively a paper, "Towards a Theology of Dominican Life in the United States Today." What was called "the white paper" began with the theme of the Council: "God's Word was incarnate in a particular time and place, and Jesus could only preach to certain people alive then....We Dominicans have a mission to our fellow men alive now in this world." The paper singled out movements "of vital importance in American life" such as participation in government, education, the hopes of young people, changing ways of thinking, global unity, secularism, person and community, the future. After urging that the gospel be the basis and purpose for the laws of the church and the Order, and after advocating a critique of the ministerial purpose of church institutions, that manifesto developed a realism of grace and personality as the basis of religious life and its ministries. Decades later, in retrospect, that brief document seems commonplace as it talks about chastity not excluding love and about poverty relating to urban problems, but in 1968 those convictions were new.

After composing our position paper, we took a second step: We wrote to every member of the Province calling for a Province-wide assembly, a first such meeting. Those two acts, possibly brash and imprudent, were taken without any contact with the provincial office. The Province, despite threats of authority's censure, held its assembly in the days after Christmas, 1968, at one of our high schools, Fenwick, in a Chicago suburb. Most of the Province attended. Basically, the meeting was a rejection of an uninformed, self-righteous, divinely justified control of people who had out of high motivation become priests and brothers. The keynote speaker's slogan became famous: "Big Daddy Is Dead!" The members of the Province could be trusted; they should give some input about their Dominican lives and about the community to which they had given much. After that event, the still powerful roles of priors and provincials were exercised along with some consultative groups. Provincial chapters of superiors and a few delegates were preceded by an assembly of all the members; a newsletter was set up; a board admitted novices, and councils often assisted superiors in making major decisions. The Fenwick convention gave freedom for forms in religious life, in church and ministry, freedom from the past and freedom from aristocracy.

Much was being born, although some things were dying. Close friends left the brotherhood of religious life and the priesthood—some slowly and with pain; others rapidly and abruptly. When a young priest whom my family had known well left from my priory, my mother (my father had died three months before I went to Germany) wrote me a letter saying that I should feel free to leave if that was best for me. A few months later, at the end of December, she died suddenly of a viral influenza sweeping through the country.

Television reported on marches led by Father Groppi in Milwaukee on behalf of the freedom of African-Americans to choose better housing, the campaign of Senator Eugene McCarthy, and the sessions of the Democratic Convention in Chicago where the Dominican seminarians protested the war. In the streets, guitars, candles and songs protested politics as usual conducting a distant war that was ending the lives of young Americans. Chicago's Mayor Daley saw Christianity as a Sunday morning family routine, while the nuns and priests understood postconciliar Catholicism as a force critical of politics; he preferred a union of church and state behind the scenes, while the antiwar movement was proclaiming against the state a new incarnation of the gospel. Protest was a public liturgy, and it meant to young Catholics that faith and liturgy could have an impact on behalf of the teachings of Jesus out in society. All this turmoil and energy in the late 1960s marked the emergence of American Catholicism into public life, a setting aside of being an eccentric denomination marked by European customs and silent about justice in society. And so 1968 ended.

Wars, Riots, and Liturgies

That year, rocked with confrontation, had set in place some new dynamics in society and church. What was forecast as the easy implementation of the Council and the renewal of American society led the activism of 1969 and of 1970. Catholics worked to make their faith and church a voice and sign of Jesus' preaching of the kingdom amid the poverty and racism in the world. It was a question of first seeing injustice, arrogant control, excused lassitude and then of seeing grace present in politics; of seeing liturgy in places other than the dim sanctuary and Christianity as a force capable of incarnation outside of Europe.

We were entranced by emotion and hope, by service, camaraderie, and commitment. Drug use and communal amorality were the curiosities of some secular forms of the movement against war and racism, but I never entered that world or heard of it touching the growing number of Catholic activists; protest demanded time and courage, for the gospel might bring arrest and trial. Jesus, who had acted as a prophet for morality in past history, was alive again in streets and prisons. The church had hidden him away in tabernacles but now his Spirit had entered the pain of men and women calling for peace. The Jesus who stepped forward to lead had to be human and alive—and Catholicism believed in the risen redeemer present in people and Eucharist. Modern theories about religious texts or psychologies of self-improvement that dismissed divine supernatural presence lacked the power to summon up God's help and direction and did not prepare for work and sacrifice. Did an exegesis of the Bible showing that God had not been present in history or a secular theology proclaiming the death of God and the end of religion hold any power for confronting clubs and gas? While the official church proceeded slowly, Catholics organized more and more; often they went to jail, for, after all, they had never been fully part of the America of Jefferson and Emerson, and novitiates and seminaries had given some a foretaste of confinement.

American Catholicism began to appear on the front page. The media loved to trumpet change in a church that earlier had prided itself on stability and monoformity. Previously, the Catholic Church was mentioned only in short articles about Pope Pius XII being carried on a chair amid Egyptian fans, a devotional procession, or some medieval curiosity. To the Protestant or secular establishment, Roman Catholicism had been something marginal and eccentric, a warehouse of rituals and vestments Now, John XXIII was receiving Russian political leaders or speaking in a Roman prison of his own wayward relatives. *Time* and *Life* magazines could not produce enough stories on the "changing church." After the Council, in marches for civil rights, priests and nuns became visible in their clerical clothes (the new short-sleeved clerical shirt with inserted white collar was named after its first appearance, in the South: "the Selma shirt"). American activists drew the media to their efforts through liturgy and theater. A military base or a nominating convention could be blocked by impromptu performances in the streets. Catholic protesters could draw on reservoirs of the symbolic, on ancient rites, on an old-fashioned belief that symbols bore divine presence. The permission of the Council to bring the Eucharist out of church sanctuaries joined with the new theologies of grace immanent in society, a sacramentality of the world. Catholic activism, nourished by the informality of original songs, was composed of eucharistic prayers, emotional intercessory prayers, lit candles, banners, and people ready to be gassed or beaten or to go to prison. Leaders, when released from prison, said—this was not what the broader secular side of the "movement" wanted—

that their difficult experiences were possible only through grace and faith.

Often the Mass gathered Catholics together for protest. Against racism and war, the Eucharist regained its meaning as the sacrament of humanity listening to Jesus' teaching on justice and peace; it was the food needed to challenge society through suffering. Masses were a catalyst and symbol of freedom and humanity, of love. The liturgy emerged from the dim sanctuary and processed out into homes and parks, into the streets. There was a liturgy for peace, for weekly life, for children, a charismatic liturgy and a liturgy to begin a march for a just wage. Often a peace rally ended with Mass. Two to three thousand people attended one at the University of Notre Dame in the fall of 1969 during that day of the great "moratorium," a pause in the status quo of undeclared war that brought a million marchers to the streets protesting the continuance of the war in Vietnam. To begin the march of the Spring moratorium in 1970, Mass was celebrated before six or seven hundred in Harvard yard, the first ever in that Puritan enclave. Only a half-dozen years before, I had read Tillich's conclusion that few traditional symbols held any power to move people. He was wrong: Dozens of symbols led tens of thousands out into the streets. Those liturgies of processions and marches extended out into the neighborhoods of the poor or to assembly points for transporting recruits for the military forces. For young Catholics, whether they were nuns, priests, students, lawyers, or parents, the church was political not by endorsing a candidate but by advocating the human, becoming involved in causes such as civil rights, the war, and then the working conditions of the farm workers.

People were sacraments too. Catholics, along with others, began to burn their draft cards. At a dramatic liturgy in May 1968, nine Catholics, including Fathers Daniel and Philip Berrigan, removed 400 files from the draft board in Catonsville, Maryland, and burned them with homemade napalm. The Catonsville nine whose trial was made into a stage play and a movie argued that their action had secular and religious implications. They attacked material documents that were not just linguistic signs but true causes of the mortiferous, immoral control of young people. At the same time, their act pointed to the exploitation, racism, and violence within the value system of America, seemingly so pure and superior in its Enlightenment principles.

"Those draft files?" Berrigan wrote: "They were, of course, more than they purported to be. They had an aura. They were secular-sacred documents of the highest import."[2] While teaching the New Testament at LeMoyne College and writing poetry, he saw early on the issues of racism and war. A trip to Europe had expanded Berrigan's Jesuit education in the early 1950s: He came into contact with the writings of Henri de Lubac, Yves Congar, and Teilhard de Chardin. He had survived an exile to Latin America in 1965 imposed by Cardinal Spellman. In Berrigan's view, the peacemaking Jesus was now returning from an exile, and the Beatitudes, not solely the preoccupation of saints, were being proclaimed and lived. The new form of political liturgy, fire and blood, drew on French theories of the immanence of grace (prominent at Vatican II), the example of the priest-workers, and his own poetry. The Jesuit was arrested for the first time in 1967 at the Pentagon: He called prison denims "a clerical attire I highly recommend for a new church." The Catonsville burning with homemade napalm followed. After being sentenced to prison for antiwar actions, Berrigan suddenly disappeared: He was in flight from unjust government (Thomas Aquinas had boldly stated that an unjust law was not a law at all). Appearing confused and silly, the FBI could not arrest him because they could not find him. He entered into what he called a new kind of monastery, flight and hiding, whose brothers and sisters dared to hide him. Suddenly he would appear to speak out, to interpret his fugitive status as a journey into the Hades between war on earth and the eschaton.

Liturgy yielded to mysticism as he wrote a poetic paraphrase of John of the Cross, *The Dark Night of Resistance*. The Berrigans went to prison, were released, and then the government came up with its exaggerated and dishonest charges against them and others of planning massive disruption, and they went to prison again. But, by then, despite the delays of Kissinger and Nixon, the end to the war was inevitable.

A Catholic peace movement had existed already in the 1920s, and Dorothy Day and the Catholic Worker movement were the sources of the formation of peacemaking organizations. In 1952, I remember feeling shame when the newspapers reported that Dorothy Day and others refused to take part in air defense drills—an embarrassment to minority Catholicism in America. The documents of Vatican II were a big advance in presuming that peace rather than the illusive just war was normal, and Pope Paul VI's address to the United Nations while the Council was in progress criticized the atmosphere of the cold war. Around the ordinariness and televised violence of an unproclaimed war and the possibility of selective conscientious objection against the war in Vietnam, that moral and theological conflict would rage in the United States. The antiwar movement certainly did not begin with Catholics, but out of parochial schools came Mario Savio of the Berkeley Free Speech movement and Thomas Aquinas Hayden of Students for a Democratic Society. By 1964, a Catholic Peace Fellowship had been established with the Berrigans, Jim Forest, Tom Cornell, and Martin Corbin; Thomas Merton was struggling to get his writings on peace past Trappist censors. While challenging church passivity toward the growing war after 1968, Catholics wrote pamphlets, set up counseling centers at campuses, marched in the streets, went to jail. Close to 90 raids on draft boards followed. If liturgy could figure into protest, protest could be liturgy. Liberation, dignity, justice, life—weren't these the themes of the Bible? Flesh and blood, whether beaten by police or imprisoned for justice, bore some relationship to the bread and wine that became the body and blood of the One crucified for human justice and for a new creation. The marches for peace fulfilled the processions on Corpus Christ, Rosary Sunday, or Holy Thursday, while the protests over draftees taken off to camps recalled school stories of Roman martyrs.

The bishops (with a few exceptions), comfortable with the status quo and uncomfortable with something as dramatically new as a public morality of peacemaking, offered only a simple version of the just-war morality. "But who owned the tradition, anyway," Berrigan asked, "and who was worthy to speak on its behalf? Was it the cardinal of New York and his chauvinism? Was it the silent bishops and their uninstructed flocks, playing follow-the leader, paying up, sent off to war?"[3] In the autumns of 1968 and 1969, the American bishops finally issued documents supporting selective conscientious objection, a teaching not difficult to deduce from the ethical teachings of papal documents, seminary textbooks, and Aquinas. From my vantage points in Dubuque, Madison, and Boston, I watched the Catholic peace movement grow enormously from a few hesitant groups at the edge of other student groups to dozens and dozens of movements, institutions, and events. A Catholic theology of peace was inevitably one of grace active in society and thereby more than a rhetoric of total pacifism or a psychology of limitless personal freedom. The "Catholic Left" was not Marxist—Marxism was the great persecutor of the church in Eastern Europe—and the ideas behind activism were derived not from Lenin but from Vatican II.

In a few years, the antiwar movement had become filled with Catholics who five years earlier were timidly watching Kennedy's campaign. But was Catholic faith in the reality of God in history, in the sacramental power of the church's Eucharist, and in the holiness of being human strong enough to change a little institution?

●

The turbulent 1960s, the unexpected 1960s, the transformative 1960s. And yet, in light of the traditional theologies of church, liturgy, and social ethics, there was little that was radical; indeed, much of what was exciting and new was old. Protest was religious rediscovery. What was new was Catholics in the United States having something to do and something to say.

A journey had begun, a journey from the 1960s and through the 1970s to future decades. There was always more change, more implications, more needs for change, more awareness of the failures of church and society, more demands on the human spirit, and, perhaps, more projects, previously left neglected or unfulfilled, from the Holy Spirit.

---

1. Teilhard de Chardin, *The Divine Milieu* (New York: Harper and Row, 1960), p. 154.

2. Daniel Berrigan, *To Dwell in Peace* (San Francisco: Harper & Row, 1987), p. 221.

3. *Ibid.,* circa p. 227.

CHAPTER NINE

• • • • • • • • • •

The Force of Time

Are there patterns in the flow of time? Time is more than a succession of pulsing, similar, anonymous moments. There is not only time but times. In the 1960s, I was led into time as something real: I saw it alter quickly the lives of millions; I saw it question the inevitability of racism and war; I saw it end institutions; I saw it destroy people.

What brings change in science or architecture, in war or finance? What comes first, an era or its prophets and artists? What was the spark that energized so many in the 1950s to change the face of the church: in parish centers in Paris, on the docks of Marseilles, in Catholic worker houses in America? What brought protests against war, a sudden awareness of racism? What fired the debates of the Council and sustained the explosion of theological education and ministry in the last third of the twentieth century? Was it history? Was it some divine force?

In the Munich libraries, I saw the tomes of modern German theories written over the past two centuries confidently claiming to hold the laws of time. Theory after theory made time a mental framework, something predictable, a necessity; temporality and history lay not out there amid the trees and stars but were produced from within the human self. What all those philosophers and psychologists sketched, however, was too vague, too cerebral to be of use in forecasting the future; the more radical the theory the more abstract and irrelevant it was. Could politics and economics be charted? In fact, an age arrives unpredicted and, initially, even unnoticed. An era, however, does arrive and does exist; there has been something called Alexandrian Hellenism and Florentine Renaissance, new forms for the arts and religion, new poets and scientists bringing forth a world.

The 1960s were a time, and a world.

I had seen the interplay of art and philosophy of 1260 in Paris or of 1910 in Munich. When I returned to the United States in 1967 I experienced something similar, a synchronous upheaval altering society and bestowing a similar style to art and politics, sports and movies, church and university. The church did not escape the issues of change: Criticism and protests aimed at the amoral and stagnant university and military were also directed at the authoritarian church as the gospel of peace and justice confronted war and racial violence. The liturgy, the Mass celebrated outdoors with guitars and singing joined to signs and marches symbolized an active church, a church that had something to say to society, a liturgy that was again public.

Within so many upheavals, was not some spirit, some *Zeitgeist* at work? Was not a *kairos* taking place in America? I, the slow student of the Baroque and the hesitant witness to the modern, saw how American cultural upheavals were the displays of a new age; the placards and sit-ins, the meetings in churches and interruptions of the machinery of the draft affirmed that humanity is called to freedom and capable of justice and peace, and that history can bring something new. Just as the Enlightenment had in 1800 faded before Romanticism, now its solitary grandchild, existentialism, yielded to a new Romanticism with its own popular style in music and movies. Amid this Romantic restoration Catholicism, long marginalized by science and individualism, emerged in largely Protestant

American public life to general surprise to address poverty and peace. The religious dominance of Calvinist America began its decline, and Catholicism stepped out of the shadows of antique rituals to be a dominant religious voice in the American scene.

The Church Time Brought

Now I move my narrative rapidly forward, recalling not only years but decades. After its sessions were completed, Vatican II continued on: Conciliar documents brought forth postconciliar changes. The Council gave permission to think, to live, to act, and layers of moribund forms disintegrated. Amazingly, the church did not break apart and suffered almost no schismatic fractions after Vatican II, and yet unresolved questions and needs for renewal multiplied. Immediately, the Council brought many changes mainly in the liturgy, and soon there was an unexpected expansion in two areas: education and ministry.

After my return from Munich, I taught for a dozen years or more in seminaries that had become graduate theological schools; the students included future priests but also—something new—nuns and lay men and women preparing for ministries. From 1967 to 1980, most of my teaching took place back in northeastern Iowa at a Catholic seminary and graduate school situated next to Presbyterian and Lutheran seminaries. I also taught for several semesters at the Jesuit seminary in Cambridge, Massachusetts, and at the Dominican seminary in Ibadan, Nigeria. In 1977, I gave a month of classes in New Zealand, a trip that led me on to Australia and Japan. So with few exceptions, my theological journey continued amid the prosaic hills and valleys of the upper Midwest. After 1981, I joined the theology faculty at the University of Notre Dame, a department entrusted with required courses for 8,000 undergraduates, courses for theology majors, graduate programs for seminarians and laity entering the ministry, and for several

The author introducing Karl Rahner to an audience at Aquinas Institute of Theology in Dubuque in 1967

areas of doctoral studies. My only significant journey away from Notre Dame was to give lectures in Slovakia and the Czech Republic shortly after their freedom from Communism. After 1967, I taught every year in the same areas: the theology of the church, the theology of grace, the history of modern philosophy and theology, and the theology of Thomas Aquinas. During the years of the arrival of ecumenism and early conciliar renewal, I often gave classes in adult education, in Lutheran as well as Catholic parishes, on Sundays or weekday evenings in small towns and medium-sized cities. Each summer I taught priests, nuns, and lay people in M.A. programs.

The talks I gave in the late 1960s and 1970s usually had as their topics some variation on the theme of change in the church or of grace liberated to move through the world. Typical of my enthusiastic ideas in those first years was a booklet commissioned in 1969, *The Presence of the Spirit of*

God: I began with the blast of *Apollo 9* joined to Henri de Lubac's parole, "Every time man gives up a particular way of thinking, he fears he is losing God,"[1] and then Thomas Aquinas and Luther were summoned up as examples of religious thinkers who lived in a time when a new age was being born, while Paul Tillich and Karl Rahner were interpreters for today's new ideas of salvation-history and human existence. If the 1960s were bringing a reversal from religious isolation, a setting aside of controls over God, this absence was really a new presence. So the world and the world of grace seemed in the decades after Vatican II. During that cycle of teaching courses and giving workshops, what I had experienced and studied in Europe was silently instructing me, and the conciliar theologians remained my teachers. In the Midwest, under the pressure of farmers asking about the influence of original sin in the texts of the new baptismal liturgy, or bankers asking what was the difference between being a Presbyterian and being a Catholic, I drew on the theologies I had learned.

From my years in Europe, I had understood that change was normal, that religious ideas and prayers viewed as old were often recent, and that periods of culture and religion did not last forever. From Karl Rahner I had learned to begin with the human person, with an appreciation of the complexity of sin and grace in each individual, and to accept and ponder a diversity of people—parishioners, mystics, religious seekers, Buddhists—responding to a grace that was not a heavenly jolt but a perduring love from God. There was no more valuable insight than the difference between the things of religion and the underlying presence of the Spirit of God in the individual. The Risen Christ worked through the history of church forms whether in devotions or statues, through people, through the entire religious history of men and women. God did not disdain the human forms, but they did not control the divine and their value was to be judged by God.

The Catholic Church was characterized in the years after Vatican II by a surge in population and by a presumption that the church had much to learn and much to do. This vitality and growth led to education and ministry. After 1965, American Catholicism went to school.

Prior to 1965, only priests could receive graduate education in any area of theology or church life, and even their years of postgraduate theological education did not receive formal accreditation by the state; in short, for their four or more years of study the newly ordained received no degree. Teaching nuns had little religious education and often not even a bachelor's degree in any field. Themes and approaches that in Europe had formed the Council, ideas ranging from instructing parishioners about the sacraments their children were about to receive, to the themes of the gospel according to John were unknown in America outside the small readership of a few periodicals (diocesan papers reported swimming meets, while journals for priests discussed rubrical conundrums). Up to 1950, very few American Catholics lived in the realm of academia and research, nor could they imagine studying religion outside of parochial school. The expansion of religious education in university, seminary, and parish required courses and educators, while the issues of society and of the church required a biblical and theological preaching. Not surprisingly, after the Council the need and desire for education exploded.

Clergy, nuns, and lay people went to school: on Sunday mornings in parishes, at evening lectures given by theologians in proliferating academic programs, and in conferences and workshops. Many, including priests with eight years of seminary study behind them, now learned something more than a catechism's answers and studied for the first time a theology that let the New Testament and the great theologians and mystics inspire their lives and inform their ministry. As summer schools granting graduate degrees were founded at seminaries and universities, entire generations of priests and nuns went back to school to get a degree in theology. What were the origins of the eucharistic prayers? What were the major themes of the Gospel according to Mark? How was the church presented by St. Bonaventure or Hans Küng? Did psychology condition morality and influence spirituality? The schools' programs drew from the new books and journals of recently founded publishing houses, books by theologians such as Edward Schillebeeckx and Yves Congar, Otto Semmelroth and Josef Goldbrunner. Soon there were American theologians who could write their own books, and educators took the ideas of the institutes in religious education at Paris or Brussels into Catholic high schools.

Study can be dangerous. Should Catholics who a decade before knew only the lives of patron saints, a few phrases from a catechism, and a few axioms from Aristotle learn about the degrees of church authority or the differing approaches to moral theology? Immediately after the Council, it was clear that church life would be marked by a higher level of education as it was distinguished by a richer array of liturgies. It would not be possible to live in the postconciliar church without some understanding of how sacraments touch children or the sick, how the Risen Jesus is present now and in the future, how the church makes different kinds of decisions, and how the gospel addresses the political. Theological education emerged because people wanted to know about a faith made more interesting and because there were new questions. At the same time, the activities and ministries of the diocese and parish underwent an unprecedented change, one of the major alterations in the history of Christianity. The ministry of all baptized Christians was affirmed anew after centuries of neglect as the context for church life, and the number of ministries in the parish expanded.

On the eve of Vatican II, priests were the only ministers in the parish. They offered Masses, baptisms, and confessions; converts were quickly instructed, and marriages needed only an hour of preparation in church law. One characteristic of pre-conciliar parishes was how little they did, although in many parishes what they did was temporarily exhausting: a tiring string of Masses consumed all of Sunday morning and early afternoon. No one not ordained—the altar boys were more angelic than human—entered the sanctuary. Little ministry, that is, activities formally and publicly mandated by the New Testament and connected to the church's life, took place outside of the sanctuary. Nuns worked tirelessly but in schools and hospitals. Lay people had no direct ministry—collecting canned goods or coaching basketball teams are not what St. Paul had in mind with *diakonia*—although their lives were ministry to each other. Suddenly the goals and program of parish life opened up: Nuns and parishioners were organizing religious education for adults, liturgies for young people or for charismatics, and services for the sick and elderly. Where before there had been the pastor and one or more curates with nuns conducting a school, now there were married deacons, directors of religious education, music and liturgy ministers, and, if the parish could afford it, ministers for youth, for the sick, and for peace and justice, or for community improvement and assisting the poor. Thousands of nuns and brothers in religious orders moved from ministries that did not necessarily need the commitment of priest and nun (teaching typing, doing the laundry) to direct services to the gospel and grace. Beyond the parish, the diocesan chancery no longer housed just a court for dissolving marriages and a superintendent of schools, but also offices supporting parish ministries. This parish ministerial group found its liturgical symbolism in the various readers, acolytes, and communion ministers for Sunday Mass.

Society's needs and social ills had become public in the 1960s, and Catholics, no longer suspect in society, could enter further into American society with their faith and service. Apparently the Holy Spirit, at work for 1,400 years in the services of hundreds of religious orders, was now intent upon drawing more Christians into the ministry, the baptized as well as monks and nuns. In short, the churches after 1965 were rediscovering the biblical universality and diversity of service. What did Paul mean by saying that baptism brought charisms, inspirations for service, to all Christians. Was everyone to be a minister in the church? "Ministry" had not been used by Catholics, while "charism," too emotional and subjective, was always suspect. In the spontaneous life of the church after Vatican II, trajectories appeared and remained: the Pauline theology of the body of Christ with varied Christian services; the inadequacy of the distinction between clergy and laity as the sole description of the local church; the ministry of women; ministry as more than prayer, charity, good intentions; a picture of the local church composed of circles of ministry. Eventually, it would be clear that in theology and format a Catholic parish or a diocese was beginning to resemble a church in the second century more than one from 1860 to 1960. Later, in the 1990s, some said that there was now the greatest number of public ministers the church had ever known.

Nonetheless, the postconciliar expansion of the ministry through nuns and the laity was accompanied by a decline in vocations to the diocesan priesthood and religious orders. Was that disruption a decline in the number of priests and nuns, or was it an expansion in the number of ministers in the church? Life in the many religious orders for women, flourishing during years of unprecedented increase from 1860 to 1960, was approaching an end, as was a high number of vocations of healthy men to the priesthood. Those declines, however, began before Vatican II. A period of a little more than two decades, from 1935 to 1955, had witnessed the entrance (but not always the perseverance) of large numbers of people in the priesthood and religious life. Later research showed that decline in numbers had begun by 1958. The eastern and northeastern parts of the United States had each year produced large ordination classes in the decades before and after World War

II, while in many other parts of the United States there had never been many vocations. In my own Dominican Province, the time for many candidates lasted less than ten years, and no matter how many people had entered the novitiate in one year, after 1970 those classes of the 1950s had around ten members who remained priests. A large number of vocations in the past were tied partly to aspects of urban and rural Catholicism, to opportunities for humane work but also to opportunities for a professional life and education. By 1965, the immigrant world had passed, and there were fewer priests, and lay people were seeking education and ministry—changes indicating not exhaustion but expansion. The many nuns and priests had done well: They had fashioned the numerous institutions of the American church that inspired so many of the baptized to want to act as liturgical, social, and educational ministers. Why should there not occur at the end of the century further stages of expanding ministry?

A second, related upheaval appeared after the Council: priests and nuns left their vocation and ministry. This happened first and foremost because they were free to do so. For the first time in a thousand years or more, the church permitted them to be dispensed from their ecclesiastical office or vowed state, and the surrounding Catholic community no longer condemned them. Why did they leave in such numbers? Some left because they thought the church was not moving fast enough, not developing effective ecclesial forms; others left over the uncontrolled and arbitrary exercise of authority by bishops and religious superiors quick to censure new ideas and ministries. A few left because they could not face the demands of the new church: education and competency, much more work, and the fatigue of constant change. Certainly, the Council reintroduced the spirit or specter of work: one had to preach and teach, study and learn. Some had entered monastic and priestly ministry to avoid work and so, challenged to develop a pluriform parish and to preach well, they dismissed everything connected to change and renewal. Finally, some left because they had been attracted to monastic life and ministry in their youth but later found it too limiting for a lifetime. Others discovered that they were not suited to a rather solitary life of prayer and service.

I found myself, a young teacher, meeting a wide range of people: Lutherans and Presbyterians, social activists and charismatics, the young who thought the church was too timid and the middle-aged who found it too surprising and daring, lots of people who were religious but hostile to churches. The old dividing lines of Catholics and non-Catholics, Christians and non-Christians, Sunday communicants and the alienated were no longer ultimate. I had to try to understand the journey of individuals, to see how grace was working in their lives, to be a voice and minister but not a judge and security guard of the presence of grace.

The incarnation of Jesus continued in sacraments but also in the sacramentality of people's lives, even of political movements. Sacrament means not only liturgical sacraments such as confirmation and marriage, but also every interplay between the symbolic and the spiritual, the material and the presence of God in ever-wider circles of men and women. Catholics nourish and love sacramentality; they prize incarnations and colorful meditations of grace in the material and the human. The long history of salvation in which the Holy Spirit leads the people of God and the human race toward its destiny has many pasts and many futures. Grace in the church assumes through time different forms: The structure of the church of Cyprian in the third century was not exactly that of the church in Boston in the nineteenth century.

Yet the new church remained the old church: The monastic orders restored many of their medieval forms; the liturgy exchanged sixteenth century aspects for those of the fourth century; the expansion of ministry around the one order of priesthood originally called the presbyter was a rediscovery of the perspectives and life of the church of the New Testament churches. Time need not be feared. There the Spirit was at work.

A new but original sacramentality diffuses itself through the church to create new forms and to vitalize old rites and ecclesiastical structures. The Catholic mind longs for the harmonious and the synthetic: for the glow of the mosaics in Santa Prasede or the windows in Chartres. The theologians of Vatican II unfolded the wider world of grace like a sunset or a panorama of art. Karl Rahner pointed to a general underlying presence of the Holy Spirit in people above which, in the turmoil of history and church, grace became concrete in beliefs, prayers, devotions, and vestments. Edward Schillebeeckx traced the liturgical sacraments to the one sacrament of Jesus of Nazareth, the word of God, from which the church and all its incarnational rites and liturgies, sacral things and sacred places, flowed. Pierre Teilhard de Chardin went further, finding the pattern of evolution in the reign of God, affirming the holiness of matter and grace, seeing them both move forward to the second coming of Christ. The church was not a gallery of French and Italian paintings, but a rich universal sacrament of salvation continuing the incarnation of Christ in peoples, and Catholic variations and expansions suggested the development in Latin America of a theology of liberation and to North American parishes the expansion of ministry.

Circles of sacraments of God's presence caused in the postconciliar period a shift in models: A linear model dividing the haves from the have-nots yielded to a model of concentric circles where forms of liturgy and ministry, world-religions and spiritualities, flow from an incarnational center that might be Christ or the Spirit in the community. Christ is the paradigm, the power, the center, the interpretation of the interplay of the human and the divine—for that reason he is truly divine and truly human—and symbols and sacraments of grace are located in wider circles of life and religion. There are circles of grace around Christ's Spirit where God seeks to minister variously to free and educated people, and the theologian and minister needed to discern degrees of implicit grace amid billions of men and women. The person arriving in Istanbul or Paris by train or someone on a bus riding from the airports of Shanghai or New York into the city's center—how should they interpret the hundreds of thousands they see around them. Saved or damned? Christian or something else? Ultimately, there are only two theological perspectives: the dividing line or the circle of circles. Sectarians damn all that do not belong to a particular (small and recently founded) group; the other view, including medieval and modern Catholic initiatives, affirms degrees of grace, even grace potentially active in other religions and yet existing in implicit ways before and outside the possibility of knowledge of the Savior (although for the Christian centered in Christ). Only a theology of circles around a center, of degrees of a special presence, can make sense of the world. Still, how should I, drawing on both the teaching of Jesus and the problems of people, explain these elusive but powerful themes of the divine presence in the upheaval of American life?

In the School of Praxis

Liturgical renewal, parish expansion, a positive perspective on a world of religions, changes in parish life—none of this came from bishops or from concrete plans drawn up by chancery officials, nor from sociological surveys of churchgoers or from academic observations on American religion. Then where did these changes originate? From the religious quests and journeys of people—and it seems unavoidable to conclude that they came from a new encounter between the Spirit of the Risen Lord and the people of God, from a new emphasis upon baptism, from the dignity of being a people ready to serve society. The church was becoming what its deeper self wanted. I had learned in Germany that Catholic theologians at Tübingen viewed the church as a collective person active in different people through their graced activities. The church was a fullness, a pleroma, a communal world—in St. Paul's words, the body of the Risen Christ. German professors and French theologians after 1930 had restored that motif to influence in the discussions and texts of Vatican II. This collective person touched by the Spirit found itself in the 1960s in the midst of educational programs, publications, workshops, and countless meetings.

I remember some of these gatherings vividly. The Chicago priests had established in 1966 an independent association, a group that preceded and was more independent than the diocesan senate of priests mandated by Vatican II. They, the priests, could discuss openly their problems and plans and begin to escape from the clerical slavery in which priests in English-speaking countries had worked. This large association of priests sponsored a symposium in the autumn of 1967 to encourage a new maturity and identity for priests, some protection from church autocrats, some voice in their own ministry. Andrew Greeley spoke as did Edward Schillebeeckx. The conference offered priests from around the country fraternal encouragement and reasons for founding similar organizations.

Two other conferences remain in my memory: one on the popular selection of bishops, and a second on the possibility of a national pastoral council for the United States. I particularly recall, however, a third conference, conducted in May 1970, on the renewal of church structures, sponsored by a newly founded institute for sociological research in American Catholicism, The Center for Applied Research in the Apostolate (CARA), along with the Catholic Theological Society of America, and the "Urban Task Force of the United States Catholic Conference." The list of participants—Geno Baroni, Charles Curran, George Higgins, Richard McCormick, Jerome Theisen, Philip Murnion, Michael Groden, and Dorothy Dohen—and the issues discussed are striking if one recalls that five years earlier ministry consisted often in teaching rubrics or baseball to ten year olds. A sociologist described the changing urban scene, a pastor discussed new ministries in a modern metropolis, and an urban planner spoke on the relationship of the church to New England cities. What impressed me as I listened to them was the great reservoir of energy and ideas in men and women who on their own had gained a new theological vision. The American church had tens of thousands ready to work for a renewal of church and society: Priests, nuns, and lay people were facing the issues of shifting populations, racism, poverty, family needs, the format and plan for local churches, and war and peace.

Around 1971, the faculties for the three Dominican theological schools in the United States met at Notre Dame. The main speaker was Msgr. Jack Egan of Chicago, a pioneer of the 1940s who called attention to the existence of black Catholics in northern cities; an early associate and friend of Saul Alinsky, he was a first developer of community organizations. Egan was at the University of Notre Dame because the erratic and embattled John Cardinal Cody, archbishop of Chicago, had forbidden him access to ministry in the archdiocese to which the priest belonged. At the Dominican gathering, Egan generously asked me if I would like to attend the meetings, one or two a year, of an organization he was directing, the Catholic Committee on Urban Ministry (CCUM). For the next few years, I had the opportunity to listen to some of the leading activists of American Catholic life discuss their projects, ranging from housing developments to community awareness groups, all fairly new enterprises. CCUM brought together the leaders of the social side of the church, people working in ethnic parishes or civil rights. This was a time of movements and meetings, of coalitions, of groups being formed: the National Association of Women Religious, the National Office of Black Catholics, and, for Hispanics, *Padres* and *Hermanas.* Federations of priests' associations and the superiors of men and of women in religious orders set up national offices. In CCUM, theology and action came together, and CCUM people, unconcerned about livelihood or status, never wavered from working and thinking about pastoral renewal amid social change. Expectations were high, people were impatient, and opportunities and problems multiplied. I kept quiet and listened to the plans and programs from around the country that brought ecclesiology and city together. My notes from a meeting in 1974 sketched the new ecclesiology of an active laity and clergy whose social action was rooted in Jesus' preaching. Theology had for centuries been Platonic, that is, hierarchical, in that ideas and services came normally from the top down through a process by which lowly levels in the church meekly received some higher light; the world around was shadowy, shifty, and fallen.

From the Council of Trent in the sixteenth century until Vatican II, the church sailed on unmodified except for the addition of new congregations of men and women with their schools, hospitals, and orphanages. The movement of the pendulum to the monopolizing center in Rome had, in 1965, suddenly halted, and church life began to move in the opposite direction, away from the all-absorbing papal organization whose most controlling realization was Pius XII, the most powerful pope in history. Rome yielded a little to the diversity of local churches scattered around the globe. This was the meaning of phrases the Council made popular such as "collegiality" and "participation." Did Jesus want the church and its authority to be that of a monarch's court and a judge's courtroom? Or was the church a living collective personality with many centers of energy, with new ministries, and with hundreds of thousands of men and women who have faces, abilities, charisms, and divine destinies? This was the view of the New Testament. In the late 1960s and early 1970s, church activists were pursuing a different style, ministry for and from people, movements and vitalizations for the grass roots, and cultural translations of the message of Jesus. The countless pastoral plans, reports, books, pamphlets expressed a practical ecclesiology about national councils, the selection of bishops, the identity of the priest, the mission of nuns, the relationship of liturgy to social justice.

The Council returned identity and vitality to the local church, and yet at the same time the Spirit was leading the universal church to be a world-church. Christianity, passing through time, had been a Roman *societas,* a Germanic monastery, a medieval and Renaissance urban community, and a Baroque place of devotions. Could the church now flourish in a post-European mode, in a communal cluster of activities? Christians in Sri Lanka or the Cameroons, Catholic cultures in Latin America, new dioceses in the United States or in India wanted to be Catholic but also to be themselves, to retain in faith and church something of self and culture.

The 1970s moved into the 1980s, and changes brought by the Council were altering the face of Catholicism. The church faced growth and shifts in population. In North America over four decades, migrations, greater than anything witnessed at the end of the Roman Empire, moved from the inner city to the suburbs, from Latin America to North America, from the Northeast to the South and West, from working class to affluence, from the old ethnics to the new. The religious topography of America changed: new parishes in North Carolina and Arizona, huge dioceses in California but smaller ones in New England, the decline of Anglo-Saxon Protestantism, the rise of fundamentalisms of all sort.

Did the postconciliar era bring too much change too rapidly? Eventually, the postconciliar decade turned out to be exhausting; Catholics, by 1980, were tired because the parishioner could only absorb so much change from the church, and social and familial issues multiplied. I saw around me anxiety and loss of identity, fear of uncertainty, anger at the present and at the future, withdrawal from community and ministry by those who had been ordained to lead them. At the same time, priests, sisters, and lay ministers forged ahead, dealing with frustrations and conflicts, skittish church leadership, and difficult apostolates; building and rebuilding centers and ministries; intense in what would be decades of service. They were the postconciliar church: the renewers of theological education and of parochial schools, the martyrs of social protest and liberation theology, the advocates of the parishes of American minorities, the missionaries who saw missions turn into young churches, the theologians who, decade after decade, never tired of writing articles and giving conferences, all the teachers and pastors who saw that the very essence of Catholicism lay in the union of sacrament and social action.

Leaving the Baroque

Thomas Merton wrote at the end of the Council: "The present institutional structure of the Church is certainly too antiquated, too Baroque, and is so often in practice unjust, inhuman, arbitrary and even absurd in its functioning. It sometimes imposes useless and intolerable burdens on the human person and demands outrageous sacrifices, often with no better result than to maintain a rigid system in its rigidity and to keep the same abuses established, one might think, until kingdom come. There is everywhere a kind of hunger for the grace and light of the Spirit in forms that can be actually experienced....The idea that the Church does all your thinking, feeling, willing, and experiencing for you is, to my mind, carried too far. It leads to alienation. After all, the Church is made up of living and loving human beings."[2] The Council gave opportunities for the church to pass beyond the seventeenth and nineteenth centuries, to leave the Baroque.

The Baroque, as I had learned in Munich, was the past, albeit one extending its influence up to 1960 and beyond. The Baroque period of the church did not end in 1750, but went underground during the Enlightenment and then partly re-emerged after 1800 with the arrival of Romanticism. The restored Baroque of the nineteenth century, church life from 1830 to 1960, had presented again the saints of the sixteenth and seventeenth centuries to inspire the priest or nun helping people, had let the papacy become an even more centralized autocracy, and had offered past devotions in the vernacular as an alternative to the silent Latin Mass. Sadly, the original optimistic splendor of the Baroque was sometimes replaced by an ethos of suffering and guilt suited to a church increasingly marginalized from society. Thus, before Vatican II, to enter a Catholic church was to find a dim sacral precinct populated by saints in plaster and stained glass, men and women who were—too few knew this—the patrons of soldiers, teachers, or farmers. Sentimental stories about miracles and saints, however, were far removed from ordinary life in the United States. Catholics in the period before Vatican II were unclear about their history—immigrants have little time for the past. What came from the medieval or from the early church, and what came from the nineteenth century? What came from the Irish appropriation of French Jansenism and what came from Slovakian rococo? Few bishops, much less firemen and farmers, knew. Catholics and others believed that the church was displaying an antiquity drawn from Roman catacombs or Cistercian monasteries when, in fact, its liturgy and devotions came only from two decades or two centuries before. C. S. Lewis observed that in times of change the period people consider to be hallowed by antiquity is usually the one just before their own.

What did Vatican II end? What did it begin?

The conciliar years struggled over one issue: Could anything change? Was there only one way of being a Catholic, and was that one way an imitation of medieval France or Baroque Spain, both gone? Was the church of the New Testament and the first centuries to be repressed? Should church life simply reproduce forms and mottoes of Christianity pretending to antiquity but hardly a century old?

What will fade before the force of time? Most of the congregations of religious life founded since 1830? Liberal Protestantism along with some entire main-line Protestant churches? Prayer books and statues from the nineteenth century? A solitary papacy? Church administration and ritual monopolized by celibate clerics?

After the Council, Catholicism did not become modern or postmodern, although it assumed with its own modifications some valuable stances of modernity. There was no denial of the resurrection, eucharistic presence, or the Trinity. Through the 40 years since Vatican II the media have featured stories on the Catholic Church in conflict. Family life, activist nuns, Hispanic immigration, or the ordination of women are treated with little appreciation of how they are only some examples of change in an unchanging Western Catholic Christianity. Religion, revelation, and tradition are inevitably conservative, while for a faith seeing the human and the divine together in time, there is always a past and a future. Religions and churches move slowly, quite slowly, and yet in the recent 40 years Catholicism changed rapidly as the Council began a time of liberation and discovery. The publicized fears that Catholicism had plunged into modernism, into viewpoints where antisupernatural exegesis and historicism had weakened the churches of the Reform, have been, if one understands anything of a diocesan chancery or the Vatican, absurd. New issues lay in the ethics of family and science, in the structure of the parish and church, in liturgy, in the ordination of women or the preaching of laity, in issues such as divorce and gene research, war and peace, economics and poverty. To be liberal in the postconciliar church was to have an open attitude toward pastoral, ethical, and liturgical change and had nothing to do with dogmatic issues. Liberal Catholics were simply the billion people of the postconciliar church around the world.

Time never moves long in one direction. In the 1980s, a generally creative, expansive time was yielding to a more constraining one directed by Margaret Thatcher, Ronald Reagan, and Pope John Paul II. To all that I witnessed in Europe during Vatican II, to all that I learned then in lectures and books, to all that I experienced in the subsequent decades of renewal, the pontificate of John Paul II more and more became the opposite. The pope intended some genuine assistance to Eastern Europe and to Catholics around the world, but on his terms and with little knowledge of their societies and churches. He ended up as a solitary figure without others to balance the limitations of his education and pastoral experience, a leader without much interest in the bureaucracies actually directing the church, an isolated person caught between trips and illness. The pope lived not in history but in a theater with journeys as performance-pieces, brief events on a large scale expecting from the distant audience applause.

Opposition to Vatican II had assembled an odd group: devotees of Marian visions in the style of the nineteenth century, Protestant converts transferring their disappointments over liberal Protestantism to conciliar Catholicism, Catholic CEOs fearing the church's social teaching, bishops willing to weaken the pastoral health of parishes in exchange for ambition rewarded. Masses in Latin were sought out not only by the elderly, but also by a few young people for whom that unintelligible rite could only be a play, while youthful members of new quasi-religious orders with shallow spiritualities and dubious founders were seen in American airports wearing cassocks, or in churches resurrecting neglected devotional objects. The pope and his assistants at first permitted and then encouraged these directions. One began to hear of "Christians" (Protestant fundamentalists), of Catholics who were "orthodox" or "traditional" (doctrinally rigid and historically ignorant) or "conservative" (to be a Catholic is inevitably to be somewhat conservative), and of "restorationists" of the past from only 40 years earlier. Evidently some felt left out, irritated by how Vatican II had torn away their world of altar rails and seminary metaphysics; they waited for a chance to reenter the spotlight and after 1980 bring back the phrases and practices of 1950. Soon, it was clear that in the eyes of some the Council itself offended.

Catholic fundamentalists appeared, endowing a devotional phrase or cliché, a logic of syllogisms proving things about religion, and Baroque clothes with an exaggerated divine power. While Protestant fundamentalism finds easy authoritative answers in the Bible, the Catholic version finds it in holy objects or Roman pronouncements. The agents of reaction, knowing nothing of canon law or the hermeneutics of papal documents, were ignorant of the long history and inner diversity of Catholicism and could not distinguish one school of moral theology from another, one religious order from one founded four centuries later, one devotion from another. The church's life, when healthy, lives from time. Past figures and objects such as palms and ashes, Italian or Hispanic devotions, cultural avatars of Mary, colorful Christmas traditions remain but in new metamorphoses of liturgy or art.

In the late 1980s, driving toward St. John's Abbey north of Minneapolis and St. Paul, I seized the opportunity to visit my Dominican Province's former novitiate, the building and place where in 1955 and 1956 I had spent my first year in the Order described in Chapter One. The ownership of this property had passed from the Dominicans to various state clinical organizations, none of which succeeded. The last government owner sold the building to the Society of Pius X, an organization founded by Marcel Archbishop Lefebvre (once a bishop in French colonial Africa) that formally opposes Vatican II. The Archbishop's followers—deacons, priests, and bishops, and the baptized Catholics who worship with them—are in schism from the Roman Catholic Church. That day in February, I drove to the novitiate through dense fog and over dangerous patches of ice. The sandstone buildings in Minnesota Gothic, built in 1949, stood undisturbed among the spruce and birches grown older. Clean, new doors underneath the sculpture of St. Peter Martyr led into the chapel around which were windows of Dominican saints with their youthful and naive faces, the faces of novices and not of saints. I noticed at once the smell. As I remembered the novitiate chapel it had a fresh smell, a hint of the open air because it led out through a small vestibule onto the countryside. Now the chapel smelled like an old, musty European church. There were a few additions, a lacy altar cloth, a reliquary, additions in the bad taste that was a hallmark of much of American Catholicism from 1850 to 1950. There were no hymnals, missalettes, no liturgical books of any sort except for a blank loose-leaf collection of Latin texts and a few simple pieces of Gregorian chant. The absence of books was unsettling, an intimation of emptiness as if no one worshiped here.

The next morning I returned for an early Mass. With seven other people, all under 65, I waited for a Mass, which, in its psychological and social context was to be a liturgy unlike any other I had known. About 40 seminarians, roughly ages 22 to 36, were in the choir stalls dressed in cassocks with starched collars and surplices. The young celebrant in a bland vestment of the 1950s began the Mass; he spoke the Latin quietly, almost inaudibly but reverently, but it was clear that this dead language was being recited quickly. One could not or would not speak one's own language that rapidly. The celebrant followed the rubrics of the Tridentine rite, but unlike someone who had experienced that form of the Mass when it was alive, his gestures and words were learned, too stylized and perfect. The prayers after Mass were said in Latin, while before Vatican II they had involved an exceptional use of the vernacular. The seminarians were a pleasant-looking group, silent and sleepy. During the Mass, some followed its texts with bilingual missals, but some read from devotional books. In comparison to the old Dominican rite for which the chapel had been built, this quick and silent Mass was impoverished and vacuous, a ritual without much action or movement, a liturgy where little, human or divine, happened. A complexity of feasts with texts, music, and rituals had existed in the framework of the Dominican life with its proper rite, its medieval origins and context, its Dominican spirituality. My novitiate had a reality and a harmony to it, but this imitation was nothing like the past.

When I left the chapel after Mass, the sky was bright blue and the sun spread over the snowy hills with their birches and rocks. I felt a sadness and respect for my past, for this Dominican meeting place of transcendence and immanence. The novitiate had years before moved to Colorado and this building, my novitiate, was one of the casualties of the ruthlessness of time. The sun was lighting up the fields reaching out in all directions, and the snow mirrored the white and blue Minnesota sky. It was not 1260 or 1560, not even 1960, and this was the only day that existed. It was time to face again the great issue for which our novitiate had not prepared us in the least, but that was to dominate our lives, how the Holy Spirit is acting in history.

One cannot restore a culture or a church. A restoration cannot even offer the past: It gives weak imitations of the Baroque or the nineteenth century. People receive a mixture of phrases and practices whose relationship to the incarnation is thin, whose voice in society is eccentric, and whose spirituality borders on the childish.

The world I saw fading in Rome in 1963 cannot be restored. The recent pontificate eventually placed a pall of religious superficiality and repressed ministry over the American church. The enervating motifs of the preconciliar church—authoritarianism, the pursuit of ignorance or the trivial instead of the gospel and its history of interpretation, bad art and architecture, a cult of sacral priesthood, and the distraction of the miraculous—reappeared. The vast majority of Catholics in parishes, however, were interested only in the church of the Council, and not a few had to suffer under clerical directives hoping to drive the laity back to passivity. Most Catholics were caught up in the spirit of Vatican II, and the 1990s brought not at all a divided church but an uncertain and silent, waiting people of God whose priests, nuns, and lay ministers were concerned with enormous numbers of parishioners and with the amount of pastoral work.

What Vatican II began cannot ultimately be halted. What has arrived? Ministry instead of clerical clubs, theology instead of catechisms, dignity and activity instead of passivity, liturgies in different languages and in new and old forms, Catholic institutions in Eastern Europe, vast churches in Africa, new spiritualities of North America and social movements in Latin America, a broader church with belief in a wider grace. The years of the postconciliar period race on, urged forward by the struggles of society and by the longing of people for life and truth. Evidently the Holy Spirit wants to deepen and expand the gift of its loving self to people. But how long it takes the Spirit to accomplish anything.

Waiting for the Next Future

Pieces breaking off from icebergs and crashing hundreds of feet down into the green water of an Arctic July, a sudden blizzard in October, an avalanche in April—and yet, nature's forces are little in comparison with the changes of human time because then not a repeated season but an entire epoch is born. History is not a reproduction or a preservation of the past, not a scholarly study of past texts and monuments, but a shaft of light letting the present reveal itself in a sculpture or a play. If time slips quickly into the past, its present moment pushes into the future.

What a trickster time is. Stepping into the streets of Rome and Munich, I met the past and in the same mornings I met the future. The worlds I touched on the stones of basilicas and palaces, the time I met in books and teachers hover still, although they belong clearly to the past. Four decades have passed since my first European days in September 1963. Almost no time at all. More time occurred between Julius Caesar's campaigns and the death of Augustus, more time in the years between Fra Angelico and Raphael, more years between Haydn's birth and Beethoven's death. Temporality flows on.

This narrative is coming to an end. I have been visiting what St. Augustine called "the enormous aula of my memory."[3] Larger than the arches of the baths of Caracalla or the concourses of an international airport, memory retains so many impressions and emotions, selecting and holding, hiding and revealing images and feelings. I have written down these memories to be a witness to a time, to recall that I once stood on the edge of a change in history that still continues. A human life is like music: Through a few themes with their unexpected counterpoint, the individual, without fully grasping it, composes a life according to the laws of beauty and pain. And faith, religion, I had learned repeatedly, was not unlike art. Rilke wrote, "The artist is someone who moves through the centuries youthfully, who has no past behind him. If pious people say, 'God is,' and sad people say, 'He was,' the artist smiles: 'He will be.'"[4] The gestures of Bernini's statues, the horn cadenzas of Richard Strauss, the last lines of an essay by Teilhard de Chardin, the documents of Vatican II—they all point forward.

In the 1980s, when I would visit Munich to do research, I found most of the Dominicans I had met in 1963 when I arrived in Germany still at their posts. The rector of the church retained his post from age 35 to 85, and others had not moved on to ministries elsewhere in Bavaria or Austria. They were happy to see me and, as time passed, were more and more inclined to tell and embellish stories about the years we shared at St. Kajetan's. Eventually, illness caught up with Pater Magnus and Bruder Benedikt, and one May I had the sadness of visiting them in convalescent homes they never left. Younger members of the Austrian-Bavarian Province came to work in the priory's ministries, and eventually the remarkable perdurance of the 1970s and 1980s was gone.

At the end of a visit about ten years ago, when I realized that my Munich world was passing, I was awakened early one morning in the priory's second floor guest room by a phone ringing: first in the room nearby, then briefly in my room, and then somewhere downstairs. I opened the door to find Bruder Benno calling up the stairs to me: "Did Father Albrecht ask you to say the 6:30 morning Mass?" I said that he hadn't, but that I world be glad to do it. Benno was upset: At 6:23, he had no one in the spacious Baroque sacristy vesting for the liturgy, since the priests were all away. He was reluctant to give orders, and when I asked again if he wanted me to say the Mass, he said, "There's no one else to do it." So I threw on my clothes and rushed to the sacristy. As I vested, he briefed me on the liturgy for that day in May, but I was distracted, going over in my mind the basic texts of the Mass in the German I remembered from years earlier. We went out into the enormous church. The sunlight of a late spring morning spilled through the clear windows to fill the church, to present the white Baroque statues and reveal the colors of the huge paintings. People were coming in through the rear door opening onto Odeonsplatz. The books were marked, and I had no trouble remembering the liturgy in German. Turning to the opening prayer, I was surprised that the book was open to the feast of St. Lawrence, August 10. But the date and the feast were the least of my worries, and I presumed there was in May some special Bavarian feast for the deacon-martyr.

I stood behind the people's altar with its Baroque gilt edges and looked out upon the vast church, just as I had done on so many winter evenings in 1963 and 1967. Was this an accident, a priest forgetting to find a substitute? Was it a way for me to say good-bye? Ending up here this morning was so unexpected, so strange, so un-German. In a few minutes, I had been led down to the church where on many Sundays I had celebrated a Eucharist surrounded by the polyphony of Palestrina or Orlando di Lasso.

When I entered the sacristy, Benno's calm had partly returned. Far from congratulating me on the job of plunging into the liturgy in German (for him there was only German), he was baffled over my mistaken choice of the opening and concluding prayers. Hadn't I understood what he had told me in the sacristy before Mass? This was a minor feast of St. Dominic in May, and that was why the book was open to August where the prayers for the major feast of St. Dominic were given. But I had read the prayers from the opposite page, for the wrong feast day. After all, this was May, and, as he put it, "The whole world knows the feast of St. Lawrence comes in August!"

My few years here in the 1960s had lasted beyond their time. I had on this peaceful weekday morning been drawn into the church to take my leave.

●

Almost each summer or fall I go back to where this book began, walking along the hills edging the Mississippi, in southwestern Wisconsin or eastern Iowa, back where I went to college and where the Dominican school of theology was located in a little city of colleges and seminaries before it moved south to St. Louis. There the Platte (Wisconsin's not Nebraska's) is flowing into the Mississippi after having meandered for a hundred miles through rich dairy farms and having let fox and deer drink from its water. On old maps, the river bears a name brought by French traders, "the river of the Parisians." In a county courthouse about 50 miles over in Iowa, I found the records of the selling of Iowa land in 1847 to my great grandfather and his rejection of allegiance to Queen Victoria when he became an American citizen. Nearby is the center of the Dominican nuns (they taught me in high school), where my mother spent her first year of college before the school moved to the western suburbs of Chicago, and before she left to complete her education in the worldly halls of the universities of Iowa and Wisconsin. Here, too, my father's business trips passed between Wisconsin and Iowa. On this side of the Mississippi, to the northeast in Wisconsin, I lived during high school, and up the river 200 miles I entered the monastic novitiate of the Dominicans more than 40 years ago. No longer aunts and uncles but cousins and their children and grandchildren live in the states through which the Mississippi is flowing.

In September, nature parades its abundance although the year is beginning to die. How strange it is that autumn, the fall of leaves, the death of one year, seems to be a beginning. Autumn for many is their favorite season: new beginnings in the air, new feelings of energy and hope, a new school year, the work year holding new projects. Through countless Septembers similar leaves have turned red or yellow. Am I walking in a corner of a woods where no one has ever been? Who am I, the observer of stars and dragonflies? What are thousands of years in comparison to light from a star leaving its fiery source millions of years ago. How can I make sense out of this one planet in an exploding universe? At this moment, in various galaxies, stars are burning out, while elsewhere millions of suns are being born; we have just learned that a few of those suns have planets.

How sad that the message of Christianity becomes connected with narrow minds, rigid groups, condescending authorities. God gives in Jesus not judgment but love of people, information about life. The Christian incarnation does not argue against life on other planets, although they, free of sin, might not need a savior. Thomas Aquinas said that the word of God could be incarnate in many creatures. The incarnation on earth reveals not magic in one man but the generosity of God toward all men and women. In a universe of so many different worlds, is it not likely that there are countless gifts of grace and incarnations given by the Triune God?

Back where I began, I realize painfully that the church's leaders and workers will need to find a new beginning, will again have to accept people and their histories, and revere the reality of the gospel. Under new popes, the church will have to practice a little giving up of what my teacher in Munich, Fries, called "ecclesiastical narcissism" and let all the baptized develop their churches and ministries. The same issues that I read about in books during Vatican II in the 1960s are still central, repressed but clamoring for attention: freedom in the church, the right moral theology for family life and new bioethical issues, liturgical diversity, competence in preaching and teaching, the presence of the gospel in society's struggles and developments, women in ecclesial roles, the many religions of humanity within a salvation somehow drawn from the Christ. The Spirit has its own course and plans, wanting not so much to be celebrated by crowds or administered by rules as to be understood and received by each person and by all peoples.

Through all these turbulent decades, there were moments when in uncertainty and solitude it was not clear that history is more than a senseless, overpowering flood, times when it was hard to believe that Someone was ceaselessly and lovingly near. Now it is time to start anew and to continue the best of the past. The ceaseless business of technology, the reduction of religion into tricks and baubles, the final collapse of religious studies into opaque phrases, ecclesiastical and political display, greed corrupting even art, the neurotic quest to control God—even out of all of this will not grace emerge again and show its face?

The sky is clearing across the Mississippi. A farm several dozen miles over in the west is etched against a vast sky, an outpost on glacial rocks sitting at the beginning of the fertile prairie that stretches west; reds and oranges paint the moments of the sinking of the sun, and the pale blue sky is a sign of cold weather arriving. In the woods night comes quickly; a white moon is held by branches of trees above the road leading away from the river. Along with cosmic forces from suns and even from distant galaxies, God's nearby presence is moving through our world.

1.Henri de Lubac cited in J. B. Metz, "Gott vor uns," in *Ernst Bloch zu ehren* (Frankfurt: Suhrkamp, 1964), p. 233, and in O'Meara, *The Presence of the Spirit of God* (Washington: Corpus, 1970), p. 1.

2. Thomas Merton, *The Road to Joy: Letters to New and Old Friends* (New York: Farrar, Strauss and Giroux, 1989), pp. 95, 103.

3. Augustine, *Confessions,* X, 8.

4. Rilke, "Über Kunst," in *Samtliche Werke,* 5 (Frankfurt/Main: Insel, 1965), p. 427.